THE ELEPHANT MAN

Christine Sparks

The Elephant Man

Futura Publications Limited

A Futura Book

First published in Great Britain by
Futura Publications Limited in 1980

ISBN 0 7088 1942 7

Filmset, printed and bound in Great Britain
by Hazell Watson & Viney Ltd
Aylesbury, Bucks

Futura Publications Limited
110 Warner Road
Camberwell, London SE5

CHAPTER ONE

To Dr Frederick Treves' frustrated imagination the engines around him seemed to be those of Hell. They whooped, they bellowed, they belched out steam and stinking fumes. A hundred oil-lamps flickered inside and out of a dozen tents, fighting off the darkness that settled like a thick blanket over the fun-fair on Hampstead Heath.

That summer of 1888 was a good one for fun-fairs. The weather was kind, and show after show settled on the Heath for a week before moving on. Some of them, like this one, were circuses as well as fairs, and then his two young daughters clamoured louder than ever to be taken.

Almost always he said yes, and he and his wife, Anne, would set off together with the girls. But once they were there it would not be long until Treves slipped away alone. While Jenny and Kate enjoyed themselves, and their mother tried to keep them in some sort of decent order, Treves himself was to be found round the back of the sideshows talking to anyone who came his way, his eyes constantly flickering for the one thing that would catch and hold his attention. The only thing he knew for certain was that he would know it when he saw it.

Today he had wandered off alone at the beginning of the circus performance, and now that it was over he was waiting for his wife and daughters to rejoin him. He could see them in the distance, just emerging from the tent..

He fixed his eyes on his wife. At this distance she looked barely more than the girl of twenty he had married fourteen years before. The beauty that had taken his breath away then was settling now into domestic plumpness, but she was still an extraordinarily pretty woman.

He knew he had worn less well. Long hours and a fanatical absorption in his work had worn premature lines on his face and given his skin an unhealthy pallor. And the neatly trimmed beard that covered the lower part of his face only partly obscured the fact that he looked older than his thirty-eight years.

Treves combined the ardent soul of an adventurer with the settled ways of a man who liked neatness and order. Having once fallen in love with Anne he found it more convenient to continue loving her. To have ceased to do so would have caused disharmony, annoyance, inconvenience that might have interfered with the exciting part of his life, which was his work as a doctor. It was true that his love for her had also, in its turn, acquired a certain domestic plumpness but, as befitted a man of common sense, he kept it in prosperous condition.

She did not see him now. She was absorbed in the effort of staying calm in the shattering din. She was a small woman, and the waves of shrill music seemed to beat on her, but her face was resolutely set as she put a protective arm round each of her little girls.

Treves noted with amusement that neither child seemed to notice, or need, the gesture. They were enchanted by their surroundings, giving themselves up happily to the lights, the violent atmosphere. Their childish callousness contrasted sharply with their mother's flinching vulnerability.

He realized suddenly that he was standing outside the freak tent and wished Anne had caught up with him anywhere else. He would read the knowledge and faint accusation in her eyes, and answer it with a look of irritation born of guilt. He would make firm efforts to be rid of his family again before entering the tent in search of something he couldn't describe; something that would make his scientist's soul leap with excitement and anticipation. Anne knew this, only half understood it, and would hurry the girls away as quickly as she could.

It was Jenny, at ten years old the elder, who saw her father first and ran forward excitedly, calling him. It was too late to get away from the freak tent.

Treves looked down into his daughters' chocolate-covered faces and smiled. Anne, after one glance at the tent, became absorbed in cleaning the chocolate from Jenny's mouth. Six-year-old Kate bounced excitedly.

'Father, may we go in there?' she swept an arm towards the tent, and Anne's attention swerved sharply to her.

'All right, your turn,' she said, adroitly swivelling Kate so that she could no longer see the tent with its lurid signs. Treves abstractedly watched Anne at work, rubbing hard in her nervousness, so hard that the child's face was pulled and distorted into a hideous grimace. Kate drew away and at once her face settled back into its normal pretty lines.

Before she could repeat her request, the air was shattered by a sharp trumpeting, and the curtains of the circus tent were hauled aside. Through them came a line of five elephants, tails and trunks intertwined.

'Look, Mummy,' Kate pointed, 'the elephants we saw the clowns riding.'

'That's right, darling,' said Anne in a relieved tone. 'I expect they're being put to bed for the night. We'll go and take a last look at them.' She stood up and faced her husband. 'You won't be long?'

'I'll join you shortly,' he promised.

Jenny had not spoken so far. She was not a chatter-box, his elder child, but a girl who seldom opened her mouth unless she had something definite to say. It was a habit that had got her branded as sullen, except by her father who had been exactly the same. Now she stood doggedly by his side and pointed to the freak tent.

'I want to go in there with Father,' she said.

'Well, you can't,' retorted Anne in a sharper voice than Treves had ever heard her use before. 'Now come along.' She put out a hand but Jenny wriggled free from it and planted her feet more firmly than ever. Anne flung her husband a look that blamed him. In return he gave her his most innocent stare.

'Why can't I go with you?' Jenny demanded, looking up at him.

He smiled at her. She was his pet, to whom he could refuse almost nothing. But he would refuse her this.

7

'Because you'd be frightened,' he explained, talking to her seriously.

'Why?'

'Because the people in there are horribly ugly.' Treves knew as soon as he'd said this that it was a mistake. Jenny was not a little girl to be put off by the idea of horrors. On the contrary, she was as ghoulish a child as a medical father had ever produced, and she had inherited his own delight in the rare and strange. Not for the first time Treves wished she was a boy. Already she showed signs of the chilly, hard-bitten mind a scientist needed. What on earth would a woman do with such a mind?

He knew that the sensible course would be to exert his fatherly authority, tell Jenny to be silent and obey her parents. But as always, he yielded to a desire to know what her argumentative powers (which were already considerable) would throw up next.

'Are ugly people frightening?' she challenged him.

He bit back a desire to retort 'Of course they are, you cold-blooded little monster – that's why you want to go and see them' and settled instead for 'Most people find them so.'

'Then why do they go to see them?' Jenny's sharp eyes had flickered to the tent's entrance where a steady stream of people were passing through.

'Because they like being frightened, I suppose,' he said lamely.

'What about you, Father? Do you like being frightened?'

'They don't frighten me,' he replied, seeing too late where she was leading him.

'Then why do you want to go and see them?'

Before he could think of an answer, Anne intervened to put an end to what struck her as a totally improper conversation. The readiness of her elder daughter to take her father up on any point that came into her head horrified Anne almost as much as Treves' willingness to let his daughter lead him into these arguments. She flung him a look of reproach over her shoulder as she shepherded the

8

girls off towards the elephants. Treves watched them go with a grin that was partly relief. He would have found his daughter's last question hard to answer. Certainly he could never have replied in terms that she would have understood.

The sound of a nearby hurdy-gurdy filled his head as he paid his entrance money at a little booth in front of the freak tent.

His entry into the tent plunged him immediately into darkness. The walls and roof were made of black canvas, and there were no lamps. After a moment he realized he was standing in a place that had been designed as an 'ante-room'. The main part of the tent lay just beyond a faint chink of light that flickered uneasily beyond a slit between two flaps. He parted the flaps and found himself in the main area.

It was made up of canvas corridors, into which niches had been built. In every one of these niches stood some novelty for the delectation of customers. In the one closest to Treves was a very tall man in a long black cape. He was holding a conch shell aloft and blowing into it. Treves was surprised to find how well he could hear the resulting noise. The layers of canvas had muted the raucous fun-fair sounds till they might have been coming from a distant world instead of only a few feet away. The deep melancholy boom affected him unpleasantly.

He began to make his way down the corridor, blinking his eyes. The poor lighting consisted of oil lamps which smoked and stank and made his eyes sting. It was like ploughing through a thick fog, except that this one was warm and noxious. So too was the crowd that milled about, jostling him uncomfortably.

To his right hung a sign that read 'The Deadly Fruit of Original Sin', and beneath it the entrance to another small corridor could just be perceived. He vanished down it, hoping to find it less crowded. As a good doctor Treves passed for a humanitarian and a lover of his fellow-man. Nonetheless he found large quantities of his fellow-man in the noisy beery flesh hard to bear for long. This was strange

9

in one who was the least squeamish of men where a hideous injury to a patient was concerned. But had he been asked about it, he would have pointed to the indubitable advantage of the patient usually remaining quiet.

The corridor contained a series of flaps and turns designed to disorient the visitor. After negotiating them all he managed to push his way through the last flap and arrive at an inner chamber. There he confronted the Deadly Fruit of Original Sin and found it disappointing.

In a roped-off space stood a small stage set at eye-level, with curtains on three sides. On the stage was a bell-jar filled with greyish murky fluid lit from behind. The effect was to cast an eerie glow into the smoky chamber. Suspended in the fluid was the life-sized body of what at first appeared to be a baby until closer inspection revealed the rigidity of a china doll. A large snake grew out of its neck, the join being marked by a large blob of what might have been organic matter.

At the bottom of the jar lay an apple with two large bites out of it. Behind, raised so that the audience could see, hung a triple painting, with Adam on one side, Eve on the other, and the tree in the middle, immediately behind the jar.

Treves yawned. He'd seen fakes before but seldom one as clumsy as this. If the main exhibit was no better he'd have wasted his time.

The little crowd around this exhibit seemed not to share his scepticism. It oohed and aahed with fearsome delight. Treves looked back at the little show, trying to suspend his critical faculties for a moment, and had to admit that if you weren't too aware of the artifice the effect was disquieting. It had certainly upset an elderly man who had appeared out of the shadows and was standing near to Treves, his face ravaged.

'A wicked birth—' he whispered. 'Wicked . . .'

Treves wondered if he'd underestimated the effect of a few obvious tricks and a bit of dim lighting. The monster in the jar seemed to him merely unpleasant and absurd. But the man hurried away before he could speak to him, and Treves realized that he had been standing in front of another flap that led out of the chamber in a different direction. Perhaps down there lay better hunting. As he pushed his way through, he could hear a growing noise behind him, and without warning he was shoved aside by two policemen who swept down the corridor with a purposeful air. He shrugged and gave his attention to a niche on his left where a bearded lady was chewing tobacco and spitting into a spittoon.

Treves gave her the briefest of glances. Such a comparatively minor oddity was not likely to interest one who, as a small boy, had been taken to see the famous Julia Pastrana, 'The Ugliest Woman in the World', whose monkey face was covered in black hair. Treves wondered what would happen now if he reached over the rope that separated him from the 'bearded' lady and gave that beard a good tug. He was not sufficiently interested to find out.

He continued to ease his way through the crowds. Up ahead of him the policemen had apparently encountered some difficulty, for they were shouting, 'Make way! Make way!' an injunction to which nobody seemed to be paying heed.

Shouting voices reached him from another niche to his left, and a few more feet brought him face to face with it. A hugely fat woman was seated with two dwarves, both dressed as babies, in her lap, and yelling, 'Oh yes they are, they're yours all right!' to a man beside her who was so thin as to be almost a skeleton.

'I refuse to believe it,' the skeleton replied amid gales of laughter from the audience. 'I will not accept it! Those babies cannot be mine – they are *too ugly*!'

This produced an even louder shout of mirth, and he went on, bawling at the fat woman. 'I don't want them. Get rid of them! I don't want to see them.'

'Darling, don't be difficult,' the fat woman wheedled. 'Let's take our sweet lovely children on an outing.'

'We'll take these miserable whelps on an outing all right. We'll take them to the zoo – *where they will stay*.' The last words were delivered straight at the audience who roared with glee. But above and beyond these animal yelps Treves thought he heard something else – screams coming from further down the corridor. The fat woman paused for a fraction of a moment then shrugged and rushed on, as though bored with something she had heard many times before.

'Children, save yourselves,' she pleaded with the dwarves who were cowering against her. 'Prevail on your Papa!'

The dwarves slithered down from her knee and hurled themselves against the skeleton's legs, screeching, 'Papa, Papa, Papa – please!'

Treves turned away and almost collided with a man coming back down the corridor, holding a small boy in his arms. The child was clutching his father's neck in terror, while the man muttered to no-one in particular, 'This is too much. They should not allow it! They should not allow it!'

Thoroughly curious by now, Treves moved down the corridor as quickly as the throng would permit. He found himself unwillingly the leader of a little crowd all bent on the same ghoulish errand.

At the far end the corridor widened out to accommodate a stage which was sideways on, so that he could not see what it contained. A woman brushed past him pulling a small girl with a frightened face. Getting closer to the commotion Treves could see four policemen and a well-dressed official-looking man, whom he guessed was an alderman, arguing with a disreputable individual wearing shabby clothes, four days' growth of beard and a stove-pipe hat that looked as if someone might once have taken a punch at it. He was paying little heed to the alderman's attempts to remonstrate with him, as his attention was taken up by a hysterical woman who was pummelling him about the head and shoulders, crying, 'Beast, beast . . .'

Apart from his presumed occupation as freak-exhibitor, there seemed nothing particularly beastly about the man. The horror therefore lay on the stage. But as Treves moved sideways to see if he could get a view, he found his way blocked by one of the policemen.

'No, that's right out. Sorry, sir, no more viewing.' He turned and yelled over his shoulder. 'Drop that curtain!'

As the curtain fell, Treves' darting eyes managed to catch a glimpse of baggy trouser cuffs out of which projected two horribly deformed feet – so knotted with veins and lumps, and so covered with scaly skin, that he at first took them to be roots. He felt a sense of shock, for even that quick sight had been enough to convince him that this exhibit bore no relation to the frauds he had seen that afternoon. Whatever was behind that curtain was genuinely monstrous.

For an irritated moment he contemplated arguing with the policeman who was barring his way, then he abandoned the idea. There would be no getting past that implacably solid face.

The woman who had been attacking the owner had now been pulled away and was sobbing on the shoulder of an embarrassed policeman. The owner was brushing himself down and yelling at the alderman. Though husky, his voice had an oddly cultivated accent at variance with his appearance and method of earning a living.

'You can't do that!' he was protesting. 'I've got my rights.'

'I have the authority to close you down,' the alderman said firmly, 'and I'm doing just that.'

Treves edged away from the policeman to where he could get a good view of the front of the stage, now covered by the curtain. His sharp eyes had spotted a boy of about ten staring at the curtain with the same ghoulish glee most people reserved for the actual exhibits. When he got closer Treves could see why.

The creature depicted on that curtain could only have been possible in a nightmare. It was a crudely painted, life-size portrait of a man turning into an elephant. Palm trees in the background suggested the jungle habitat in which this perverted creature might once have roamed. To Treves, the most horrible aspect, as he suspected it was intended to be, was that the transformation was less than half complete. There was still more man than elephant. Through the crude garish strokes the artist had somehow managed to depict the agony of a man undergoing a hideous transformation that he had no power to stop.

The crowd was vanishing now and there was no-one to stop Treves edging his way quietly towards the curtain. The alderman and the exhibitor continued to rage at each other.

'This exhibit degrades all who see it, as well as the poor creature himself,' insisted the alderman.

'He's a freak,' the other bellowed. 'How else is he to live?'

'Freaks are one thing. No-one objects to freaks, but this is entirely different. This is monstrous and ought not to be allowed. These officers will see to it that you are on your way as soon as possible. Good day!'

He turned sharply and left the tent, leaving the other man to shake his head in disgust, and mutter, 'Moving again, treasure.'

Treves had reached the canvas by now. His hand stretched out. Another moment and he would lift the edge of that curtain and see . . .

'Have a care, my friend.'

Treves jumped as a large meaty hand came down on his own. Beer fumes were blown into his face, and he found himself looking directly into the piggy eyes of the exhibitor.

'Forgive me . . . ,' he murmured, and moved away.

He wasted no more time, for there was obviously nothing further to be learned today. Up ahead of him, he could just see the urchin who had been staring at the painted canvas moving towards the exit. Treves quickened his step, anxious not to lose the boy in the crowd, and caught up with him at the exit. A short conversation ensued, businesslike on both sides. A shilling changed hands. By the time Treves went off to find his wife and children, he was sure he and the boy understood each other perfectly.

CHAPTER TWO

The London Hospital stood at the eastern end of the White-chapel Road, bordering on the slum and light industrial premises from which it drew many of its patients. It was a massive, ugly, relatively modern building, governed by a committee that was justifiably proud of the hospital's up-to-date equipment and high quality of medicine.

As a surgeon at the London, Treves was more exposed than most to the ravages of industry. It fell to him to operate on the huge sweaty men who were brought in with their bodies gashed open by heedless machines. He hated this part of the business. It was at these moments that his boyhood in Dorset, much of it spent on his grandfather's farm, came back most strongly. There was something human and comprehensible about a kick from a horse, even if it broke your neck. Ironwork he regarded as the invention of the Devil.

Being no more consistent than any other man, he saw no irony in this attitude and his own reliance on the latest medical hardware provided for him by the hospital, which he used freely. When an operation was in progress, the theatre closely resembled the fires of Hell. A furnace roared within the cast-iron stove, kept at fever pitch by a pair of bellows constantly pumping air into the open great beneath it. From the mouth of the stove protruded the handles of several cauterizing irons, their heads embedded in the coals.

Close by stood the operating table where Treves worked, the stove casting a ruddy glow over him, the glistening of his face lit up by the oil lantern held up for him by a nurse whose sole function this was.

The theatre was well-furnished with a large sink and a cupboard stocked with dressings and other things a surgeon might need. Always included among these were several sets of manacles. Chloroform was commonly in use for operations, but the exact administering of the right dose was still a rough and ready business. All too frequently patients came round at the wrong moment (that is, if they had not died under an excessive amount), and then the manacles were useful.

Treves did not expect to have to use manacles in the operation he was performing today, with the assistance of two fellow doctors, Mr Fox and Mr Hill. He had ordered the administering of a large dose to his huge patient, a bull-like labourer who had received a set of gear-wheels in his chest that very morning. Fox had protested. Fox was an able doctor and Treves' closest friend among his colleagues. As such he was one of the few of his peers who ventured to criticize him, and Treves did not take kindly to criticism.

'I say, Freddie,' Fox had said in his languid voice. 'Don't you think that's a bit – I mean it's enough to kill him—'

'He can stand it,' said Treves briskly as he tied on the black leather apron he wore for operations. 'It's coming round that would kill him with a wound like that.'

Hill placed a cotton mask over the man's nose and mouth, and applied the chloroform. The patient struggled for a moment, but soon his moans of agony subsided and he slipped into unconsciousness.

Treves examined the wound, which was fearful. The marks of the gear-wheels grew progressively deeper as they neared a great open gash in the centre of the chest.

'How long has this man been here?' he demanded.

'Three-quarters of an hour,' Fox told him.

At the far end of the table two students held onto a rope which was tied to the patient's leg. They were pulling on it with constant pressure.

'Hodges, Pierce, come closer.' Treves ordered them. 'Mr Hill, take hold of the rope, please.' He waited till the exchange was complete before addressing the students again. 'It's a machine accident. I expect you'll be seeing a good deal of this.'

16

The two youngsters stared uneasily at the gaping wound, which bubbled bloodily every time the patient took a breath. Together Treves and Fox were doing an expert job of repairing the ripped chest. Treves chatted off-handedly as he worked.

'Abominable things these machines,' he muttered. 'One can't reason with them.'

'What a mess.' Fox made a face of disgust. There was some part of his stomach that still rose up in outrage at a sight like this. He felt ashamed of his weakness. A doctor should learn callousness. Look at Treves, a cold-blooded devil if ever there was one.

Treves glanced up at that moment and noticed the students' faces, which were ashen.

'Irons, please, Mr Hodges,' he said curtly. There was nothing like forcing a queasy student to take a practical part in an operation to make him forget his own feelings.

As the operation progressed, Fox had to admit that Treves had been right about the chloroform. The man's massive frame had borne it well. If anything, he was not sufficiently asleep, and as the work drew to a close the occasional groan was wrenched from him. But even Treves was not prepared to risk a larger dose. As he cauterized the wound, the other men were all holding the patient down.

The steam from the cauterizing dispersed, leaving Treves' face sweaty and satisfied. The work was good. He could see this even now. He stood back and threw the iron down, just as the theatre door opened to admit a boy of about ten with a scruffy appearance.

'Excuse me, Mr Treves, sir.'

'Yes?' Treves looked up, and a sudden tension in his manner caught Fox's eye.

'I found it.'

Treves studied the boy carefully. 'Did you see it?'

The urchin shook his head slowly.

'I'll be with you in a moment.'

The head vanished back behind the door.

'I say, Freddie,' said Fox in a low voice. 'What are you about?'

'Oh, nothing – nothing of any importance.' Treves had begun to roll down his sleeves and remove his apron. 'Nothing of any great importance. All right, you can take this man away.'

He departed quickly before he could be asked any more questions. He found the boy waiting for him in the passage.

'Where?' he said briefly.

'Turners Road. There's a line of empty shops. One of them is called Collys. It used to be a greengrocer's, but it's not used now.'

'I know the place. Are you sure it's there?'

'Camping out in the cellar. Don't s'pose they pay no rent. Mr Bytes ain't a great man for payin' rent.'

'Mr Bytes would be – ?'

'The owner.'

'*Owner*?'

'That's what he calls 'imself. Says it's 'is. 'E bought it from the last owner for a good price. 'E complains somethin' chronic. Says the p'lice keeps movin' 'im on and 'e ent made a profit yet.'

'Mr Bytes has been taking you into his confidence, has he?'

'What?'

'Mr Bytes has been telling you all this?'

' 'E tells anyone in the boozer 'o'll listen. 'E's known for it.'

'How do you know where he lives?'

'Followed 'im 'ome, didn't I?'

Treves gave the boy a coin, checked his destination again and almost ran out of the hospital. An excitement was growing within him, similar to the excitement he'd felt when he first read his final medical exam paper and realized that it was going to give him no problems.

Two days he had waited since he'd been forced to leave the fun-fair empty-handed; two days while the urchin had searched London for the mysterious monster – only to

18

track him down now barely half a mile from the hospital. From the little he'd seen before the curtain fell, from the uproar the creature's presence had created, Treves had no doubt that he was on the track of something rare – something that would cause a sensation when he presented it as the subject of a lecture.

It was a hard business to make a name for yourself when London was thronged with young doctors all trying to do the same. It was not enough to be a good doctor – you also had to be something of a showman, and your show had to be stranger and more startling than anyone else's.

The staff at the London Hospital were constantly alert for the new intake of patients that might prove to contain 'the one' – the one who might have that rare disease that they alone could diagnose and cure, that unknown condition with which they could cast new light on a hitherto obscure area. Members of the governing committee – Ebenezer Broadneck for one – had been known to remark that it was a scandal the way wretched patients were descended on by throngs of ambitious surgeons and physicians, to be pulled and pummelled and examined hopefully, and then discarded when their conditions revealed nothing that was not already common knowledge.

Other doctors, equally scandalous in Broadneck's oft-voiced opinion, did not wait for Mohammet to come to the mountain. They went out searching for him like the man in the Bible who scoured the highways and by-ways to provide guests for the feast. Treves was one of the latter kind.

He knew the arguments against what he was doing, and he could counter every one of them with an argument in favour.

'How does Broadneck expect medical science to progress if we're only ever to investigate what has been investigated before?' he had demanded one evening of Fox, whom he had taken to his own home for dinner. Fox had made no answer, rightly divining that his role in this instance was to listen while Treves got it off his chest. But he had glanced at Anne and received an understanding smile. Anne too knew her role as a sounding board.

'Anatomy has always progressed in the teeth of orthodox opinion,' Treves went on. 'And if it hadn't continually flouted that opinion, we'd still be living in the days of Hippocrates. Leonardo da Vinci used to descend into crypts at dead of night to dissect cadavers.'

'Good Lord, Freddie,' said Fox, revolted. 'I believe you'd have bought bodies from Burke and Hare.'

Treves' eyes flashed humourously. 'The name of the doctor who did that was Fox, wasn't it?' he enquired innocently.

Fox scowled. 'It was Knox and you know it, Freddie.'

Fortunately Anne had intervened at that moment and restored the atmosphere by serving Fox a large glass of brandy.

The afternoon was cold and wet. The streets glistened blackly with the recent rain and brought a chill to Treves, so recently emerged from the sweltering heat of the operating theatre. He looked for a cab but was unable to find one. He shrugged. For half a mile he could manage to walk.

The streets got dirtier the further south he went. Horse manure and filth of all kinds mingled with the rain, and the air was smoky from peat fires. Once he had to pass through a large butcher's yard and was nearly sent flying by a carcass being heaved up onto a shoulder almost as beefy as the meat itself. He had to stop once and ask the way from a man working a machine that belched out steam at an alarming rate without (as far as Treves could see) serving any useful purpose.

He came at last to Turners Road and found the shop he was looking for without any trouble. Heedless of danger from the authorities, Mr Bytes had grown daring and displayed his poster outside for all the world to see. The canvas covered the whole of the front of the shop, except for the door which was padlocked. It announced that the Elephant Man could be seen for twopence.

Treves made a futile effort to pull the canvas aside, but all he could see were windows opaque with dirt. He became aware of a small boy on his left, who was watching him intently.

'Do you know where the proprietor is?' he asked, holding out a coin.

The boy nodded, snatched the coin and vanished round a corner. It took him only a moment to find his quarry. He was in luck at the first pub. When informed of the boy's errand Mr Bytes hustled his coat back on, grabbed up the riding crop that he never liked to be without, swallowed the remains of his gin and crammed the last of a sandwich in his mouth. Then he was ready to go.

The boy, whose name was Tony, kept up with him only with difficulty until they reached the corner of Turners Road. There Bytes stopped so suddenly that his companion cannoned into him and received a cuff. The two of them peered round the building to where Treves could be seen studying the poster.

'He's not a peeler . . . ?' said Bytes after a moment.

'No, I don't think so . . . ,' Tony agreed.

'No . . . I don't think so . . .'

Together, and cautiously, they began to advance till their footsteps caused Treves to turn and face them. At once he recognized the man in the twisted stove-pipe hat that he had seen quarrelling with the alderman in the tent.

'Are you the proprietor?' he demanded.

Bytes stood back and regarded him with suspicion but no recognition. 'And who might you be, sir?'

'Just one of the curious,' said Treves, who had no intention of disclosing his true motives. He had discovered that it had the unfortunate effect of putting the price up. 'I'd like to see it.'

Bytes shook his head with every appearance of sadness. 'I don't think so, sir. No, sir, we're closed.'

Treves wasted no words. He pulled a purse from his coat, extracted a shilling and held it out.

'I'd pay handsomely for a private showing. Are you the proprietor?'

'Handsomely?' Bytes' eyes gleamed on the shilling, and into his face came the first hint of recognition. He stared at Treves, who was beginning to fall into place as the nosey-parker in the tent. 'Who sent you?'

'Pardon me?' said Treves.

Bytes threw caution to the wind and snatched the shilling.

'Never mind. I'm the owner.'

From a capacious pocket on the inside of his coat he produced a key and fumbled at the padlock on the door. It took him some time to unlock it, as drink had seriously impaired his aim. Treves tried not to show his impatience.

At last the padlock clicked open and the three of them entered the shop. It was almost totally dark inside due to the huge canvas poster that obscured all the windows. Bytes scrambled around in the darkness and managed to light an oil lamp, which cast little light owing to the poor state of the wick and the fact that the glass was thick with dust. When Tony shut the outer door, Treves had to peer hard to make out anything in the gloom.

The shop was empty and grey with dust. Some old tins and a few shrivelled potatoes occupied a shelf and some vague vegetable refuse was piled up against one of the windows. The stench of the place was appalling, and its cold, dank atmosphere added to the general air of gloom.

'This way,' said Bytes, leading him to a door at the back of the shop.

By keeping the oil lamp in view Treves managed to follow Bytes down a flight of rickety steps to a lower floor that he took to be the cellar. From what he could see of it, it looked as if it might have been used as a coal-hole. His eyes were now growing more used to the gloom and he could make out the way the end of the cellar was blocked off by a curtain suspended from a cord by a few rings. As he approached it, Treves became convinced that this was

22

the true source of the smell that had been growing stronger as he descended, and which was now almost overpowering.

Bytes led the way to the curtain.

'Here we are, sir. My treasure.' He began to recite as though sleep-walking. 'Life is full of surprises. Ladies and gentlemen, consider the fate of this creature's poor mother. In the fourth month of her maternal condition she was struck down by a wild elephant.' Bytes leered. 'Struck down, if you take my meaning, on an uncharted African isle. The result is plain to see, ladies and gentlemen – the terrible Elephant Man!'

With a flourish, he rattled back the curtain to reveal a bent figure crouching on a stool, its body almost entirely covered by a dirty brown blanket. It seemed to be trying to draw warmth from a large brick that stood on a tripod in front of it, heated from below by a bunsen burner. The head was turned away towards the far wall so that, beyond a general impression of massiveness, Treves could form no clear idea of it. The only part of the creature that he could see well was its left arm which protruded from the blanket to warm itself over the brick. The arm was perfectly normal.

The thing gave no sign of having heard Bytes' voice or the rattling of the curtain rings. It remained silent and immobile, with the settled look of one who had been so for many weary hours. To Treves the hunched figure, locked eternally in the freezing solitude of this cellar, seemed the embodiment of loneliness. He did not normally consider himself an imaginative man, but there was about the terrible despairing silence of this creature something that made him think of a captive in a cavern, or a wizard, waiting thousands of years for some unholy manifestation. In the street above, the air was cool and fresh. Treves could hear a tune whistled by an errand boy, the companionable hum of traffic in the road and the footsteps of a world going about its business, unconscious of this dank, smelly cellar and the figure that waited in dreadful isolation.

He stepped closer, unpleasantly aware that Bytes was

watching his every move and leering at him in a disgusting, conspiratorial manner. Suddenly Bytes banged his riding whip against the wall and yelled at the crouched thing as if speaking to a dog.

'*Stand up!*'

'*Stand up!*' shrieked Tony in nervous imitation, dancing about just behind Bytes.

Like a dog the creature obeyed the tone of command, rising to its feet and letting the blanket fall to the ground as it turned to face Treves.

Accustomed as he was to all kinds of deformities from both disease and mutilation, Treves could not repress an appalled gasp. Nor, for the life of him, could he have prevented himself from stepping backwards in an instinctive movement of self-preservation. Never in all his days had he seen anything so hideous, so monstrous, so piteous.

The Elephant Man was naked to the waist, below which he wore a pair of shabby trousers which had been cut from the dress suit of a very fat man. His root-like, knobby feet were bare. From the picture outside Treves had imagined him to be of gigantic size, but this was a smallish man, of below average height, made to seem more so by the bowing of his back.

His head was enormous and mis-shapen, its circumference as big as a man's waist. From the brow there projected a huge bony mass, almost obscuring the right eye, and the nose was a lump of flesh, recognizable only from its position.

From the upper jaw projected another mass of bone, that protruded from the mouth like a stump, turning the upper lip inside out, making the mouth little but a slobbering aperture. It was this that had been exaggerated in the painting to make it appear to be a rudimentary trunk.

The head was almost bald, except for a handful of lank, black hair at the top. At the back of the head hung a bag of spongy skin, resembling cauliflower.

His right arm was enormous and shapeless, the hand like a knot of tuberous roots. Indeed it could barely be called a hand; it was more like a fin or a paddle, with the back and palm being exactly alike. The left arm was not only normal, but delicately shaped, with fine skin. It was a hand a woman might have envied.

From the chest hung another bag of flesh, like a dewlap of a lizard, and the whole body gave off a stench that made Treves gag.

Bytes had made some effort to trick his exhibit out. Behind it were two crudely constructed palm trees. As Treves stood there, speechless with horror and disbelief, Bytes rapped the wall again and yelled. 'Turn around!'

'Turn around, turn around!' Tony echoed in malicious glee.

Slowly the Elephant Man began to turn, revealing other loathsome cauliflower growths on his back, some of which hung down to the middle of his thighs. He completed his turn and came to rest in his original position. His head was turned towards Treves who found himself unwillingly searching the eyes for the accusation that should have been there. All was blank. The face was devoid of expression, and incapable of it. But as Treves gazed on him, the Elephant Man closed his eyes.

The words of the man in the tent came back to Treves. 'A monstrous birth.' More monstrous than the most nightmarish brain could conceive of. But even as pity and disgust warred in him, ambition rose up and joined them. This was it, the thing he had been looking for, the spectacular specimen that would turn all heads his way.

'I've seen all I can – down here,' he said to Bytes.

The rings rattled, the curtain fell back into place. Doubtless behind it the Elephant Man had reseated himself to wait for the next gawping visitor. Bytes began to lead the way out.

'Down here?' he queried.

'I'm a doctor, Mr Bytes. I work at the London Hospital, where I also lecture in anatomy. A man like that could be – very interesting to medical science.'

'He's not for sale,' said Bytes at once.

'I don't want to buy him from you. Just – hire?'

They had reached the shop. Bytes held the lamp closer to Treves' face. 'For how long?'

'A few hours. I just want to examine him and make some notes. Later I might want him back again.'

'At a good price?'

'Of course,' said Treves in disgust.

They settled on a shilling for every visit, and Bytes agreed to have the Elephant Man ready when a cab called the next day.

'Now what can you tell me about him?' said Treves.

Bytes shrugged. 'Only what his last owner told me. He's English and his name's John Merrick.'

It came as a small shock to discover that the creature had a human name like any other man.

'Any idea how old he is?'

'About twenty-one, I think,' said Bytes. 'But how could anyone tell?'

'Is anything known about his parentage? Where in England was he born?'

Bytes shrugged again. 'The last bloke said he was born in Leicester, but I don't know how he knew that. He didn't seem to know anything else.'

'But his mother and father – were they deformed in any way?'

'Search me. No idea.'

'Well, if so little is known about his parents,' said Treves impatiently, 'why are you so sure his mother was knocked down by an elephant "on an African island"?'

Bytes gave a ginny chuckle and nudged Treves knowingly. 'Come, my friend, I don't have to pretend with you. The public likes a little drama – a little showmanship – with its exhibits.'

'Then I can assume that this elephant story is a total invention?'

'It's as good a story as any,' said Bytes. 'Look at that bit of bone coming out of his mouth, like a trunk. He *looks* like an elephant.'

Treves grunted, satisfied. He had never placed any reliance on the too-convenient story of an elephant charge, and it was useful to know that Bytes had no evidence for it. The trunk-like protruberance of bone on the face was sufficient explanation of how the story had started.

They had reached the street by now, and as soon as they stepped outside Treves began to drink in the fresh air. It was like wine after the atmosphere of the cellar. He tried frantically clear his brain. As soon as he produced his purse, Bytes thrust out his hand for the coins Treves dropped into them.

'There's the shilling in advance for tomorrow. I'll send a cab at 10 a.m.'

'He'll be ready.'

'Here is my card.'

Bytes pocketed the card, then seized Treves' hand in a greasy shake.

'Now we've got a deal. We understand each other, my friend. We understand each other completely.'

He gave him the look of a conspirator that made Treves long to wrench himself away. Instead he bid a polite goodbye and turned off down the street.

CHAPTER THREE

Mrs Mothershead *was* the London Hospital. An inflexible woman in her early fifties with a hard, powerful face, she had been the hospital's head matron for fifteen years, which was longer in a position of authority than could be claimed by anyone else— including Mr Carr-Gomm, the head of the Hospital Administrative Committee. As such she commanded respect. Carr-Gomm himself addressed her with careful courtesy. Young doctors avoided her. Established doctors said 'please'.

Mr Mothershead had always been a shadowy figure. One doctor, who had been a medical student fifteen years ago and remained on the staff ever since, maintained stoutly that the husband had no existence, and that Miss Mothershead had slipped gradually into Mrs about the time of her elevation to the highest nursing post. This was widely accepted as accurate and natural. Somehow authority sat more easily on a married woman, even if the title was only one of courtesy.

Of her background only one thing was known for certain, and that was that she was one of the new breed of nurses that had emerged in the '60s under the influence of Miss Nightingale. Prior to that, nurses had been drunks, prostitutes, women of whom so little moral standing was expected that it was actually preferred for them to have had an illegitimate child. Above all they received no training. To be female and squalid was considered enough.

Miss Nightingale altered all that. Returned from her great work in the Crimea, she had set up the first English Training School for Nurses, attached to St Thomas's Hospital. In July 1860 it took in its first batch of students, one of whom was Mrs (or Miss) Mothershead.

The school was designed to do two things – to provide future nurses with a whole year's training, and to establish nursing as a profession for decent women. No student was taken in without a certificate of good conduct, and if her standard of personal behaviour did not remain impeccably high she was thrown out. The students lived in a Nurses Home, their outings were scrutinized, and reports about their characters and actions flew back and forth at speed.

It was a revolution, and like all revolutions it produced its fanatics – like Mrs Mothershead, who had been told so often in her student days that the whole future of nursing depended on her and women like her that she had never been able to forget it; a woman who still made daily entries in her diary, just as she had done in those long ago days at St Thomas's, knowing that at the end of the month what she had written would be studied by Miss Nightingale herself in a frantic attempt to get into her students' minds and prise out any thoughts that might threaten the success of the experiment.

Mrs Mothershead watched her own students with the same suspicious eyes that had once been cast on her. She demanded that they live like nuns and nurse like saints; she froze them with her contempt when they displeased her, but warmed them with her generous praise when she felt they deserved it. She was capable of huge kindness, but she was even more capable of ignoring human emotions in the service of 'her' profession.

These days ordinary nursing duties took up less and less of her time. Mostly her life was spent teaching or sitting at the long desk at the end of the Receiving Room. From her position of advantage in this bare grey-painted hall she made entries, issued certificates, checked details. The hardest part of this job was shutting out the disturbing noise of frightened people as they entered the hospital and crowded onto the long rows of benches in the hall. Children wailed, men with injuries moaned, and amid it all Mrs Mothershead tried to get her paperwork right and wished the noise would go away.

On this particular morning she had succeeded in reducing the racket to the background so successfully that its sudden cessation affected her like a thunderclap. She looked up to see what had caused the silence and saw two figures walking down the length of the room to her desk.

One was a man of middle age dressed in outdoor clothes and heavily muffled against the chilly day. Mrs Mothershead recognized him as a cabman who had several times brought patients to the hospital. It was what was walking behind him that drew her astonished eyes.

She could not tell whether it was male or female, as the left hand was only part visible. This and the fact that it was walking upright were all that identified it as human. The figure was enveloped in a black cloak so long that it swept the floor. In the left side a slit had been cut, and the hand that protruded from this clutched a crude walking stick, with which the creature helped itself to make slow painful progress.

On its head was a very large black hat with a wide brim, and sewn round the edge of this brim was a grey flannel curtain that dropped down into the collar of the cloak. A small hole had been cut into this about where the left eye would be. As the creature approached, it carried with it the most appalling smell. All Mrs Mothershead's years of training had to rise up and do battle to prevent her retreating.

The cabman reached her first and handed her a card which bore the name of Treves.

'I'm looking for Mr Frederick Treves, please, ma'am.'

Mrs Mothershead stared at the approaching swathed figure, then towards the cabman, her eyebrows raised in a demand for an explanation. But he only shrugged.

'Very well,' she said. 'If you'll wait here, I'll send for him.'

From further down the room a young male voice called, 'Cor, what a stink!' and other voices were immediately raised in agreement and protest. The figure in the black cloak gave no sign of having heard.

To Mrs Mothershead's relief, Treves himself appeared at that moment. He looked a little startled, though whether it was his visitor or his visitor's weird clothes that surprised him she couldn't tell.

'Mr Treves,' said Mrs Mothershead quickly, 'I was just going to send for you, sir. This man wants to see you.' She handed him the card the cabman had given her.

'Thank you, Mrs Mothershead. I was expecting him.' Treves looked at the cabman. 'Is there no-one else with you?'

'No, sir. Just this – er – gentleman.' The man waved a vague, anxious hand in the direction of the creature, who stood silent and immobile. Only one eye could be seen through the slit on the left side of his face, and that was so deep in shadow that the effect was of a blind statue. To Treves this was momentarily more disconcerting than the reality that he knew to be hidden underneath. He pulled himself together and thrust some money into the cabman's hand.

'Very well. Thank you for your trouble.'

'Not at all, sir. My – pleasure.' The cabman's voice was filled with relief as he departed.

Still the creature made no move, no sound, gave no sign that he was aware of anything happening around him. Remembering how it had obeyed Bytes' shouted orders the day before, Treves thought that something, no matter how little, *must* be getting through. But perhaps it was like giving orders to an animal. Only the tone of voice was understood.

He became aware of Mrs Mothershead staring at him.

'I'll be in my rooms, Mothershead,' he told her. 'I'm not to be disturbed.'

She nodded silently and shifted her stare to the silent figure between them. Treves forced himself to address it.

'Come with me, please.' He turned on his heel and made to leave. At the door he looked back and found that the creature had not moved. The head was turned in his direction, and from a short distance away the impression of blind incomprehension was even more marked. A silence lay over the entire room. Everyone in it was now watching

31

the little scene. At last Mrs Mothershead said, 'You heard the doctor. Go on.'

Her voice held a firm note of command, and after a moment the creature began to shuffle very slowly to the door. His feet, which he could not lift properly, were encased in old bits of canvas sacking, clumsily sewn together in the rough shape of shoes, and as he walked they made a horrible, scratchy dragging sound. Treves stood back to allow him to pass through the door and then closed it behind him. Even through the thick oak he could hear the excited babble that broke out immediately.

It took an age for them to climb the two flights of stairs and go down the three long corridors that were necessary before they reached his office. Treves ground his teeth in frustration. At every point they were stared at by nurses, doctors, even other patients who happened to be out in the corridors. The man shambling painfully along seemed oblivious to this harsh curiosity, but Treves had an uncomfortable sense of being stabbed by knives. He was used to being stared at – with respect by students who attended his anatomy lectures, with awe by patients he was treating, with open hostility by other doctors when he had hot-headedly overstepped the bounds of professional etiquette. He quite enjoyed the respect and awe, and hostility held no terrors for him.

But these stares were different. They held the jeering curiosity that the normal offer to the different. They were primarily for the clumsily grotesque creature, but they also took in the man with him. Treves got his first experience of being treated as a spectacle, and he did not like it. He felt a twinge of discomfort, remembering that his own first gaze at the Elephant Man had contained something of the same character.

They reached his room at last and he opened the door to lead the way in. The creature paused on the threshold and turned his head uneasily. Treves gave him what he hoped was an encouraging smile and beckoned for him to come in. As the silent figure passed him he tried to get a furtive glimpse at the eye-slit, but whatever was inside was in shadow.

As he closed the door he tried not to gag. In the small room the smell of the Elephant Man was overwhelming. It was an effort to force himself to go close and help the creature to sit down, and when he had done so he went to the window and opened it as far as it would go. When he turned back, it seemed to him that the shrouded figure drooped, as if in shame. He told himself not to be fanciful. He could not remember being so nervous before.

'My name is Frederick Treves,' he informed the bent head. 'I am a surgeon here at the London Hospital, and I lecture in anatomy at the Medical College.' There was no response of any kind. He went on hurriedly. 'I would very much like to examine you. Would that be all right?'

Just how much, if anything, could the thing understand? It sat quite still, staring at the floor, seemingly oblivious to its surroundings. Treves' sense of discomfort was growing. His own voice had begun to sound ridiculous in his head. He looked at the floor for a moment, then locked his gaze on the figure's left arm, the one part of it that looked normal.

'Ah – yes. Um – first I would like to ask you a few questions. Would that be all right?'

All the formal words and expressions that had served in other, similar situations now clattered uselessly to the floor between them. Treves made the awkward discovery that when the familiar lines proved inappropriate he had no others at his command. He must go on, reciting the useless part.

'Good.' He sat down at the desk and picked up a pencil. 'Now let's see, your owner . . .' – the word slipped out before he could stop it, and he could have bitten off his tongue. But the Elephant Man seemed to notice nothing. He sat there, immovable in the silent agony of his own world. 'Um – the man who – who looks after you – tells me that you are English and your name is John Merrick. Is that correct?'

He had not really expected to receive a reply, nor was there one.

'Do you know where you were born?' he persisted. 'Where you come from?'

Still the silence, but the Elephant Man lifted his head very slowly and stared blindly at Treves.

'I tell you what,' said Treves desperately, 'I'll ask you a question, and you shake your head like this for "no", and nod like this for "yes". All right?' Silence. 'Do you understand?'

After a long interminable moment the ponderous head waved uncertainly up and down, once, and a wheezing sound came from the chest as though the effort had been great. Treves gave a sigh of relief, and his voice became businesslike.

'Have you always been—' he fought for a description that the thing could comprehend, 'the way you are now?' he said at last.

Again there was no response, and Treves wondered if he had taken too much for granted. Perhaps it was beyond whatever existed in that huge head to discern the difference between himself and other people, in which case a phrase like 'the way you are now' had no meaning for him.

'Are you in any pain?' he asked.

This time there was a reaction, violent and startling. The creature began to babble in a series of staccato gulps, punctuated by wheezes. Through the tiny slit in the face mask a stream of desperation and distress seemed to flow.

Alarmed, Treves interrupted, 'No – just nod your head like this for "yes" and shake it like this for "no".' He demonstrated slowly. 'Now, are you in any pain?'

This time there was no babble, just a slow shake of the head.

'Are your parents still alive?'

Immobile silence. The thing before him might have been a block of wood. It was exasperating when he had thought he was beginning to get through.

'Do you understand? Are they dead? Your father . . .' he waited a long time. 'Your mother.'

At once a desolate moan filled the room and the Elephant Man began to rock back and forth as if in agony. From behind the mask came sounds that might have been someone trying to weep, but unable to.

Treves stared at him, feeling desperately uncomfortable. But he was saved from having to offer some response by two sharp raps on the door. The Elephant Man flinched perceptibly.

Fox's head appeared round the door.

'Freddie, what are you doing for—' he wrinkled his nose in disgust. 'I say, do open a window in here or . . .' for the first time he noticed the Elephant Man. 'Oh, I'm dreadfully sorry. I had no idea that . . . I say!' his voice died away in embarrassment.

Treves crossed the room in two strides, seized Fox by the arm and bundled him forcibly into the corridor, closing the door behind them. Fox blew out, hard.

'Good Lord, Freddie, what have you got in there?'

'You'll know presently. At the meeting of the society. But until then, I beg of you, Fox, keep it to yourself.'

'Certainly, if you insist. You must have quite a find there.'

'I don't know what I've got.'

Fox gave him a cynical glance. 'Nothing of any import-ance, eh?' he repeated.

Treves turned to re-enter his office, but looked back at the last minute.

'Keep it to yourself, Fox. Please.' He went in and shut the door firmly behind him, turning the key in the lock. Then his eye swept the room in dismay. The Elephant Man had gone.

It was impossible. There was no way out except by the door – unless the wretched creature had contrived to throw himself out of the window. For a terrible moment he half believed it, then a faint movement caught his attention and he breathed again.

In a far corner stood a glass display case filled with specimens, each one neatly labelled. There was just enough space between the end of the case and the wall for a man to stand, and there he was. Even through the enveloping cloak Treves could see that he was shaking.

'Come and sit down,' he said gently.

The Elephant Man's only reply was to press himself further back against the wall as though he would vanish into it. To the stench of his body was added that of his terror.

For a moment Treves wondered if it was all worth it. Wouldn't it be better if he simply packed this thing up into a cab and returned him to where he came from? But the meeting of the Pathological Society of London was only two weeks away and he had nothing better than this to introduce. Nor would anyone else have.

He went to stand in front of the man, taking the left hand firmly in his own. Slowly, without wrenching him, he drew him away from the wall until they had reached the chair.

'Sit down,' he said, keeping his voice quiet and friendly. He had seen enough the night before to be certain that whatever the original state of Merrick's mind he must now be half-crazed with terror and ill-treatment. Overcoming that would be half the battle. As if in confirmation the man resisted no further and sat down.

Treves found himself at a loss. There was plainly no point in asking further questions of someone who seemed unable to understand or reply. With relief he decided to put that part of it off.

'I think I'll examine you now,' he said. 'I'll save the questions for later. Will you take off your hat now, please?' The Elephant Man did nothing, and Treves tried to make his voice re-assuring. 'Don't be frightened, I simply want to look at you. Do you understand?'

As he reached out his hand the man leaned his head back at what seemed a dangerous angle, considering its weight. He seemed to be looking at Treves, but as Treves could not make out the eye he had an odd sensation of being spied on. He put one hand on each side of the grey flannel curtain and began to lift it out of the cloak, all the while muttering words of reassurance, just as he had done long ago to the horses he had ridden on his grandfather's farm.

'That's right, don't be frightened . . . don't be frightened.'

He had thought himself partly prepared for the shock of that head, but he was wrong. He wondered if any familiarity could subdue the initial impression of horror the face gave, or would it be ghastly all over again with each new viewing?

In the light thrown by the window he saw every piteous deformity with a clarity denied him in the cellar the afternoon before. The protrusions of bone seemed bigger now, the distortion of the mouth more marked, the cauliflower growths more loathsome. How could any human being be born imprisoned in this monster's shape? If there was a merciful God in Heaven, how could he permit it?

He managed to undress the Elephant Man without further trouble. The smell was appalling, the growths revolting to the touch, but he persevered and began to make notes as he saw more clearly the extent of the deformity.

When the creature stood naked before him he could see that one hip was noticeably higher than the other – the explanation of the limp. But what drew Treves' horrified attention was the fact that the Elephant Man's sexual organs were normal. It was as though Nature had tossed a cynical jeer at her distorted creation.

Treves worked for an hour before sending the man home. As he saw him into the cab, he thrust a letter into his left hand. It was a note to Bytes telling him that the cab would call again for him in two days.

Promptly at 10 a.m. two mornings later, the Elephant Man re-appeared in the Receiving Room. This time Tony was with him.

'For the shilling,' he said, extending a grubby hand.

This same performance was repeated seven times over the next fortnight. As the meeting of the Pathological Society neared, Treves' excitement grew. He was well prepared. He had had a series of photographs taken showing the Elephant Man's deformity from several different angles, and his notebook was now full.

It was hard to form theories with a patient who could tell you nothing of his past history, but within those limits Treves was confident of his diagnosis. The elephant charge theory he discounted completely. He was convinced the man's condition could be accounted for by spontaneous mutation. The growths that covered him were the result of fibrous tumours that had developed under his skin and round his nerves. To Treves' eyes, they had the appearance of things that had grown with the years, meaning that the Elephant Man had become worse as he grew older, not that he could ever have been anything but hideous.

Everything Treves required of him he performed docilely and without response. Occasionally he made noises that were gibberish, but mostly he sat in silence broken only by the wheezing of his chest.

The meeting of the Society was to take place in the lecture hall of the College of Anatomy that was immediately next door to the London Hospital, and attached to it. That morning Tony brought the Elephant Man as usual, and found Treves waiting for him by the Hospital entrance. He stared as Treves dropped two shillings into his hand.

'That's because I shall need him for a lot longer today,' Treves told him. 'I'll send him back when I've finished with him.'

'When d'you want 'im again?'

'I don't know. Not for a week or so.'

'*How* long?' Tony was dismayed. 'But you 'ave 'im most days.'

'I know. But I shan't be needing him nearly so much in the future. I'll let you know.'

He steered the Elephant Man into the College and gave

him into the hands of the two assistants who were to display him to the audience. When he was sure they understood their instructions, he left them and went to his room to take a last look at his notes. When he had read them through completely, he took a deep breath. He would no longer need notes to help him. He had every inch of the Elephant Man's body imprinted on his memory. He had done all he could this last two weeks with the chance that had been offered him. He wouldn't fail now.

He advanced on the Lecture Hall with a feeling of tension that had nothing in it of fear. Rather it was an anxiety to begin, a straining at the leash.

It was early yet but the hall was already filling up, and he was pleased to see that several names of considerable eminence had placed themselves prominently along the front rows. No doubt some rumours had got around. The comings and goings of a shrouded figure for the last fortnight must have attracted attention. Good. Treves smiled inwardly. This was his moment at last, the moment that always came to you if you were sufficiently determined that it should, if you spent your life watching for it. He had worked for it, he had a right to it, and he was going to take it.

He made a last check with his assistants, who had brought the Elephant Man to sit behind a curtained stall from where he could be produced quickly. The man, wearing nothing except a loose loin cloth, sat silent and motionless as he always did. The smell from his body was overpowering.

When the hall was full, Treves took up his pointer stick, advanced to the front of the podium on which he was standing, and tapped the stick against the small raised desk to indicate that he was ready to begin. The noise of many male voices died down, but a murmuring hum still came from several parts of the hall. Treves ignored it. He would soon have their attention.

He began by a brief introduction of himself, and a

carefully censored version of how he had happened to run across the Elephant Man.

'He is English, he is twenty-one years of age, and his name is John Merrick,' he told them. 'Gentlemen, in the course of my profession I have come upon lamentable deformities of the face, due to injury or disease, as well as mutilations and contortions of the body, depending on like causes; but at no time have I met with such a degraded or perverted version of a human being as this man.'

The moment had come. Treves signalled to his assistants who opened the front doors of the stall. The low mutter in the Lecture Hall became a startled roar, then died away completely. Treves could hear his own footsteps as he went to the stall ready to indicate various parts of his specimen with the stick. He felt excited and gratified. He had them now.

'I wish to draw your attention to the insidious conditions affecting this patient. Note, if you will, the extreme enlargement of the skull . . .' he pointed with the stick, 'and upper limb, which is totally useless. The alarming curvature of the spine . . . turn him, please,' – it took several moments to get Merrick positioned to his satisfaction – '. . . the looseness of the skin, and the varying fibrous tumours that cover 90 per cent of the body.'

A faint air of discomfiture that he had first sensed in his audience had vanished. The attention of each man was riveted.

'And there is every indication that these afflictions have been in existence, and have progressed rapidly, since birth. The patient also suffers from chronic bronchitis. As an interesting side note, in spite of the aforementioned anomalies, the patient's genitals remain entirely intact and unaffected.'

The assistants untied the knot of the loin-cloth, which dropped to the floor. The Elephant Man stared straight ahead. Nothing that was happening seemed to penetrate his consciousness, for which Treves felt a twinge of guilty relief. He moved the stick up and down the patient's body, talking all the while.

The lecture lasted nearly an hour. By the end of it his audience were leaning forward, anxious not to miss a word, and Treves was experiencing the rising sense of exhilaration that success always brought him.

'So then, gentlemen, owing to this series of deformities – the congenital exostoses of the skull; the extensive papillomatous growths and large pendulous masses in connection with the skin; the great enlargement of the right upper limb, involving all the bones; and the massive distortion of the head – the patient has been called "The Elephant Man".'

At a signal the curtains closed round the stall. Treves laid down his stick with an air of finality. The applause was thunderous. At the last minute Treves had to restrain himself from yielding to an instinct to bow. That would have been a crass touch of theatricality.

He wondered if the entire talk had been a mite too theatrical. He knew his lectures to students at the hospital were popular because of their witty, racy style, so different from the dry assertions of fact favoured by other lecturers. He'd tried to keep that aspect of things muted this afternoon. The men of the Pathological Society were distinguished doctors who would have marked him down at once as a mountebank had they detected any whiff of the footlights. Treves was glad of the hour of questions and discussion which followed his talk. It served to calm the atmosphere down.

Afterwards he could hardly get through the corridors which seemed to be packed with men wishing to congratulate him. But he escaped from them at last and made his way back to his office, where he'd given instructions that the Elephant Man was to be waiting for him.

He found him there, shrouded in his all enveloping disguise. Merrick made no sound or movement of recognition as he came in and Treves realized for the first time that this blankness was something he was coming to rely on. It made it possible to maintain the necessary attitude of scientific detachment if you had a patient who displayed no more awareness than a stone or a tree. Some of the terms he had used that afternoon – 'perverted' and 'degraded', for instance – would have been impossible in the hearing of a man who understood what was being said about him.

He took out his notebook on the Elephant Man (he was now on his second) and began to enter into it points that had arisen out of the discussion. He had enough now, he decided, to start writing the paper that would consolidate this afternoon's work. He wrote on and on as things came back to him, hastening to get it all down while it was still fresh in his mind.

'Hmm?' Treves looked up, recalled to the present by a vaguely heard noise. He was alone except for the statue-like creature in the chair before him.

'What?' he said enquiringly, wondering if the noise had really come from that quarter, and if it would be repeated.

But there was silence. What he had heard – if anything – had been no more than a sigh. Of weariness possibly.

'It's been a long day for everyone,' Treves agreed.

He closed his notebook and rose. 'You'll need a cab. Stay here.'

As soon as he was alone, a change seemed to come over the Elephant Man. With his left arm he grasped the arm of the chair and levered himself upright. When he was on his feet, indecision shook him and he looked round, first in one direction then the other. At last he began to shuffle tentatively round the room. He lingered a long time by the wall where hung the various certificates that proclaimed Treves to be a member of various learned societies, and reached up a hand to touch them. The cold feel of the glass seemed to puzzle and repel him.

He moved on to the desk and began touching things. He ran his hand slowly over the calipers. Then he paused as though something had struck him. He was staring at the blotter. Tucked into one corner was the calling card that

Treves had given to Bytes. He recognized the little square. He had seen it first in Bytes' hand then in the cabman's as he studied it to find his destination. The Elephant Man's hand flickered out for a moment, then the card disappeared into the folds of his cloak.

The sound of footsteps approaching down the corridor made him shiver. When Treves re-entered he was crouched back in the corner behind the glass case. This time the doctor knew where to look for him without hesitation.

'Come with me,' he enjoined.

He took the Elephant Man down to the front door and pointed out the cab waiting for him at the gate across the square. The creature had just begun his slow painful movement over to the cab as Treves turned back into the hospital. He wondered if perhaps he should escort him to the cab, but there seemed no need by now. He had done so the first couple of times, but since then the man seemed to understand what was required of him. And Treves was tired. He began slowly to climb the stairs.

At a small landing on the first floor he stopped and looked out at the square. He could see the Elephant Man, who had almost reached the waiting cab. He became aware of Fox standing behind him.

'Congratulations, Freddie. You were very impressive.'

'Since when were you a member of the Pathological Society?' Treves demanded with a grin.

'I slipped in at the back. I wasn't going to miss your moment of glory. Besides, I had to find out just what "nothing of any importance" was.'

Dusk was falling. Lights gleamed from the windows of the hospital. Still Treves stood there, watching.

'You never mentioned his mental state,' said Fox.

'He's imbecile, no doubt from birth. He speaks but – it's all gibberish. No, the man's a hopeless idiot.' Treves spoke almost to himself. 'I pray God he's an idiot.'

Footsteps sounded in the hall behind them. Hill had arrived with two older colleagues from the hospital, both of them members of the Society.

'Quite a coup, Freddie,' said one. 'You'll look splendid in the journal.'

'Wherever did you find that creature?' The other was slapping Treves on the back and the three other men followed suit. Treves hardly noticed. His eyes were fixed on the Elephant Man who had reached the cab and was about to climb in.

And then the man did something that spoiled everything. He turned and looked back at the hospital, his head lifted, the black hole in his mask seeming to scan the facade of the building as if he were searching for something. It was nonsense, Treves told himself, to be so fanciful, but he could almost have sworn that the man's eye had come to rest on the sight of himself standing there in the window, surrounded by colleagues, all cheerfully congratulating him. Mr Frederick Treves' finest moment.

He tried to shake the fantasy off. It was too far and the light was failing. The Elephant Man could never have picked him out so clearly. But why did he stand like that, immobile beside the impatient cabman, his head turned remorselessly in this direction? Treves froze inside, for he had a feeling as if the man had screamed at him across a great distance.

Then the feeling died, the shadows cleared from his brain. The man had turned and was climbing clumsily into the cab. In another moment the door had slammed, the wheels were turning, and the square was empty.

He got away quickly from the hospital. He wanted no more congratulations that night. He wanted his home, his wife and his comfortable untroubled atmosphere.

Anne came to meet him as soon as she heard the door.

'Did it go well, darling?' She kissed him and helped him off with his overcoat.

'Yes, very well, I think.' They were standing in front of the hall mirror. He turned her suddenly so that their faces were reflected side-by-side, his own worn out, Anne's fresh and smiling, but both blessedly normal.

'What is it, Freddie?'

'Nothing. I was just thinking how pretty you are.' He kissed her. He had a sudden longing to see his children, to re-assure himself. 'Are the girls in bed?'

'Yes, and they send their kisses.'

'I'll go and say "goodnight" to them anyway.'

'Freddie, they should be asleep by now.'

He had already started up the stairs. 'Well, it won't hurt them to wake up to see their father.'

'I'll have your sherry ready when you come down.'

'No, I think I'd prefer a whisky.'

He could feel her surprise, for he seldom drank spirits, keeping them mainly for guests. But he couldn't bring himself to tell her that what he wanted wasn't really a whisky. It was a bath. He felt unclean.

CHAPTER FOUR

Bytes knocked back a mouthful of gin from a mug and wiped his mouth with his sleeve. The light from the bunsen burner cast a flickering glow over his sweaty face.

'Are you sure you got it right?' he demanded.

Tony sighed. They had been over this so many times and Bytes couldn't take it in because he didn't want to.

'I told you, Bytes—' A cuff from the back of a hairy hand knocked him flying before he could say more.

'*Mr Bytes* to you.'

Tony picked himself up from where he had fallen against the cellar wall and went to sit exactly where he had been before. He and Bytes were in the 'desert' alcove that had been set up for the Elephant Man, cooking breakfast over the hot brick. Bytes had taken the little stool for himself, leaving Tony to sit on the floor. The Elephant Man was nowhere to be seen, but snuffling sounds from the darkness enveloping the main body of the cellar announced that he too was partaking of his daily nourishment.

Bytes examined a sausage he was attempting to cook. 'Tell me again,' he ordered. 'And try and get it right.'

'I took '*im*—' Tony cocked his head towards the darkness 'in the cab, to get the shilling from that doctor feller. Only this time he gave me two shillings and said it was 'cos 'e'd be sending 'im back later than usual. I said when did 'e want 'im next, and '*e* said 'e didn't know, but it wouldn't be for a bit.'

'That's the first time he hadn't asked for him back,' said Bytes grimly. 'You know what that means?'

'No more shillin's,' Tony confirmed at once. 'Not unless you can find somethin' else just as good.'

'Where am I going to find anything else like that?' Bytes demanded bitterly. 'This last two weeks he's been like a gold mine – shillings every other day. And now, suddenly, just like that – finish. Don't send him any more, thank you very much, Mr Bytes. I'll let you know when I have further use for you.' Bytes' voice had become a whining caricature of cultured speech. 'This year, next year, sometime – *bloody never!* And who cares if I starve. That creature doesn't. Listen to him.' He cocked a head towards the slurping noises coming out of the darkness. 'Eating. Never stops. He'll eat me into my grave.'

'Not on potatoes and water,' said Tony cheekily.

'Hold your lip. Potatoes and water is all he needs. He stays alive on it, doesn't he? What more do you want?' He studied the sausage and decided it needed a little more doing. 'Listen to him?' he said again. 'Why can't he eat without making that noise?'

''E can't close 'is mouth,' said Tony.

The gusty animal sounds became noticeably worse, indicating that the Elephant Man was now trying to drink. Bytes threw him a venomous look that contained all his disappointment over the sudden loss of business. When the slurping came again, his temper snapped. Snatching up his riding crop, he jabbed it in the rough direction of the noise and poked about till he found his target.

'Belt up, you misbegotten garbage,' his voice sank to a self-pitying mumble. 'How can I eat with that?'

He took a mouthful of gin and mockingly slurped it in imitation of the Elephant Man.

'How can I eat with that?'

He went back to the sausage, which now seemed to be done to his satisfaction. When Bytes' whole attention was given over to eating, the Elephant Man tried another drink. But fear constricted his throat and he began to spit and cough the water out onto the floor, gasping and wheezing for breath. Instantly Bytes was on his feet, smashing him across the shoulders with his riding crop.

'Out of my sight!'

The creature's ponderous feet seemed to catch in each other as he struggled to move. With his good hand he grabbed the plate of potatoes but this left him nothing with which to lever himself up off the ground. All the time Bytes stood over him, panting with fury at his slowness.

'*Now!*' Bytes jabbed his victim with the end of the whip, spilling the potatoes and water over the floor.

'You clumsy sod!' Bytes said viciously.

His temper was feeding on itself. He jabbed the poor creature again and enjoyed doing it, releasing his sour resentment that the easy living of the past fortnight was over. Then again, harder, lurching forwards to get a better aim. Without warning, his foot, which had trod on a potato, slithered from under him. He came down hard, crying out with shock as he hit the stone floor. He stared for a moment at the Elephant Man who had staggered to his feet and was backing away, whimpering with fear.

'*You . . .*' he breathed.

He did not remember rising and crossing the floor. It just seemed that the next thing he was doing was lashing at the thing savagely with the riding crop. Drink and venom drove each blow forward ever harder. The man backed, fruitlessly attempting to shield himself with his arms. Choking whimpers came from him as the whip rose and fell.

It was beyond the Elephant Man's power to stand upright under this barrage. His clumsy feet struck an unevenness on the floor and he fell backwards. The great weight of his monstrous head seemed to be pulling him further and further down, forcing his neck to bend, constricting his windpipe. He began to gasp for air, his wheezing becoming more panic-stricken as he felt himself choking. He had not the strength to lift his head, and anyway Bytes was slashing his face in a frenzy.

'Bytes – don't . . .'

Tony had watched the mounting scene as though paralyzed. At first he had cared little. Bytes was always beating the creature. But now it dawned on him that if the man didn't stop there'd be a murder charge in the end – for them both.

48

'*Bytes! Bytes*—' he screamed, his hands uselessly pulling at the big man.

But Bytes was beyond hearing. His frenzy of hate and disgust had blotted out all else. Through drawn-back teeth he was muttering mindlessly.

'This won't do, my lad. This just won't do.'

At last his fury spent itself and the rhythm of his flailing arms slowed. The blows became mechanical, the winding down of a machine that has gone on too long. He gave one final slash and stepped backwards. He was breathing heavily and his face streamed with sweat. Tony stared, wide-eyed. Ugly, shuddering gasps shook the Elephant Man as he lay on the floor, unable to help himself up.

'We better get 'im up, Bytes.'

'Who cares about him? Let him lie there.'

'S'pose 'e dies. You'll 'ave to buy somethin' else.'

Bytes swore and threw the riding whip away. Together they raised the Elephant Man till he was sitting upright, and propped him against the wall, where his head immediately dropped forward against his knees. The agonized gasps continued unabated.

'Get that doctor,' said Bytes curtly.

''E'll charge yer.'

'Oh, no he won't.' Bytes' piggy eyes gleamed. 'How can he, when he sent my property back to me in this condition? I've a right to protect my investment. Get on with you.'

Tony turned and fled the cellar. It took him six minutes to cover the half mile between Turners Road and the London Hospital, and when he arrived he hurled himself straight into the Receiving Room without stopping to speak to anyone. He knew who he had come for, and by good fortune he found him at once.

'Our man is sick,' he told Treves without preamble. 'Come right away.'

'What is it?' Treves demanded.

'Like this,' Tony made painful heaving movements in imitation of the Elephant Man.

'I'll get my bag.'

49

'I've gotta get back.' Tony was out of the door before Treves could tell him to wait. He didn't want to face any awkward questions on the journey. Let Bytes do the explaining.

Treves arrived about ten minutes after the boy, and to Tony's admiration Bytes went immediately into the attack, pointing at his property and demanding furiously:

'What did you do to him? He's been like this all night?'

Treves hoped he didn't show the sinking of his heart as he looked over to the figure covered with a blanket and gurgling wretchedly against the wall. Was it possible that he had compounded the creature's misfortune by overtiring him the day before and bringing on some kind of attack?

'What do you mean?' he said mechanically.

'He was fine when he left here, and now look at him!' Bytes yelled.

'I intend to.'

He knelt down beside the man and pulled the blanket away. Then he froze. This was no hysterical attack brought on by strain. The Elephant Man's body was covered with bruises and bleeding cuts that looked as if they had been inflicted only a few minutes before. He gave a sharp look up at Bytes.

'What happened?' he said quietly.

'He fell.' Bytes' tone became guarded. Something had gone wrong. 'He – falls.'

Treves' eyes found, as if drawn by a magnet, the riding whip laying where it had landed on the floor, then at the clearly marked welts across the man's back.

'He must have taken quite a fall,' he said, still in the same quiet, grim tone.

Bytes began to bluster uneasily. 'He's a clumsy sod. Never watches where he's going.'

'Why is he sitting up like this? He needs rest.'

'That's the way he sleeps. If he lays down, he'll die.' Bytes dropped his own head back to a neck-breaking angle and brought it upright again. 'Head's too heavy.'

Treves returned to the figure who still sat hunched and

50

trembling. Gently he took the massive head in his hands and drew it backwards. It came easily, as if it had no will of its own, and Treves was forced to hold it steady while he examined his eyes. He saw the shock of recognition in them. For a moment the Elephant Man's eyes were all he saw. They were human eyes, agonized, appealing to him, and suddenly Merrick's good left hand was clutching timidly at his arm.

Regarding his own motives, Treves did not feel he could take any great credit for his dealings with the Elephant Man. But he had always spoken to him gently, and touched him only in kindness. And now he realized, with an awful clarity that was like the shifting of a thick fog, that he was almost certainly the first person in years to show him this much consideration. He had studied him, made his notes and then packed him off back to Bytes with a shilling to pay for his use. He had not speculated too closely on just what he was returning the man to. He had had too many other things on his mind.

Now those eyes were begging him and the feverish clasp on his arm was becoming frantic.

'This man belongs in hospital,' he said abruptly.

'Can't you fix him up here?' Bytes protested. 'Listen – he's my livelihood.'

Treves bit back the retort 'Not any longer'. He didn't want to have a fight getting the man out of there. Time enough for Bytes to learn the truth when the Elephant Man had passed safely into Treves' 'possession'. Possession was supposed to be nine points of the law, wasn't it? So he tried to make his tone reasonable.

'You're not going to have much of a livelihood if this man dies. He's very weak, and I don't know how much damage has been done by this "fall". Now stop wasting time and fetch a cab.'

It seemed that Bytes saw the force of this argument, for he snapped his fingers to Tony, who scurried out. A horrible ingratiating grin covered his face like slime.

'I truly appreciate this, my friend. You know, there's

many things that I can do for you. I move in the proper circles for this type of thing' – he made a gesture towards the crouching figure. 'In fact, anything at all, if you take my meaning.'

Treves took his meaning perfectly and despised himself for the sudden leap of interest and hope inside him. The memory of the previous day's triumph was still glowing. But a man could not live for ever on one success. He'd need other specimens. He was fixed in his determination not to return the Elephant Man to Bytes, but perhaps Bytes could be squared about that. There was always money. Something could be sorted out . . .'

He stood there, tongue-tied, unable either to reject such a golden offer or to utter the despicable words that would seal the bargain, while all the while Bytes squeezed his arm in a man-to-man manner that made him want to punch him on the chin.

'I like doing business with you.' Bytes leaned forward and favoured him with a ginny grin. 'You and I understand each other completely. I know I can trust you. Can't I?'

Now was the moment to say, 'I'll see you in Hell before I enter such a monstrous agreement with you.' Instead he said stiffly, 'Everything will be seen to.'

CHAPTER FIVE

Nurse Nora Ireland hurried as she pushed the cart full of empty breakfast trays down the hall and past the open door of the women's surgical ward. From inside she could hear Mrs Mothershead's voice, and she was unwilling to attract the head matron's attention. Not that she had done anything wrong, but Mrs Mothershead, who delighted, it seemed, in finding fault with the younger nurses, had a specially hawk-like eye for Nora.

Nora often thought this strange, as she knew, without conceit, that she had been the best student in Mrs Mothershead's class during her probationer year. It was usually Nora who produced the right answer first, Nora who grasped a difficult concept the most easily, and Nora's hands which were most quick and deft in demonstrating how to change a dressing or staunch a flow of blood. Then there had been the curious words uttered by Mr Carr-Gomm when she received her certificate.

'Congratulations on becoming fully qualified, Nurse Ireland,' he had said, giving her his most delightful smile. 'Mrs Mothershead thinks very highly of you – er – very highly indeed. We're glad you're going to remain on the staff of the London Hospital.'

If Mrs Mothershead thought so highly of her, Nora thought resentfully, as she clattered along with the cart and tried to control the yearning of her stomach for breakfast, it was a wonder that she always seemed to be ready to pick on her. She would have been amazed had she heard Mrs Mothershead's comments only the night before the certificates were given out.

'Too pretty,' the head matron had said crossly, 'too pretty by far to be a nurse. She'll not last.'

'But we have to give her the certificate.' Carr-Gomm had protested. 'You've said yourself she is the best.'

53

'Oh, give her the certificate by all means. She's earned it. But she'll not last. If I had my way, girls who looked like that would be weeded out at the selection stage.'

'That would be very hard on the patients, Mrs Mothershead,' Carr-Gomm ventured. But his smile faltered and died under Mrs Mothershead's virtuous stare.

It was not that Nora was a great beauty; rather that she had soft brown eyes, a neat well-sculpted face and a perfect complexion. True, her features were rather on the blunt side. She had yearned for delicate features ever since she had been a small child, and planned how she would go on the stage and sweep the world with her beauty. But she had had to settle for being merely pretty and becoming a nurse, which was the job pressed on her by her father, a Methodist lay preacher, who had dreaded the thought of his daughter becoming 'an actress and a wanton' as he used to put it.

Safely past the ward door now, Nora decided she could relax a little. At the top of the stairs she stopped to rub her back. The cart was built at just the level that meant you had to lean uncomfortably to push it. Just as she was about to go on, something caught her eye. From here she had a perfect view down the stairs and into the hall to the entrance. Two figures were coming through it. One she recognized at once as Mr Treves, but the other one held her riveted.

She couldn't see what was underneath the enveloping cloak and grey-flannel mask that hid the whole face and head. But whatever it was seemed to be having a lot of trouble. It was moving slowly and wheezing desperately with every step. The two moved towards the bottom of the stairs and began to climb them laboriously, Treves' strong right arm supporting the other figure. Nora shrugged and passed on into the kitchen.

She gasped at the heat as soon as the door closed behind her. The kitchen nurses were absorbed with a grey mush that they were ladelling into bowls. Nora remembered the rich creamy porridge her mother used to make and felt

54

faint. She yearned for breakfast, but when it came it would be this stuff.

A nurse pulled the cart of empty trays away from her and signalled her to wait. Gasping from the heat, Nora thrust her head out of the door into the corridor. After the steam and cacophony of the kitchen it seemed a haven of peace. She could just see Treves and the shrouded figure at the far end of the corridor, about to climb a staircase. On the wall by the stair a notice pointed upwards, stating 'Isolation Ward'.

The new cart, piled high with fresh full trays, was ready for her now, and she wheeled it out and down the corridor to Women's Surgical. With any luck Mrs Mothershead should have gone.

Her luck was out. The head matron was still in the ward, but down the far end, absorbed in a conversation with a patient. Nora edged the cart in slowly and steadied it while other nurses came forward to lift trays off and begin gliding swiftly down the wards to serve breakfast. Many of the patients looked as though the sight of the grey sludge made them want to gag. Nora wondered if it was cooked on the assumption that sick people didn't know what they were eating. Just how sick did you have to be not to notice this stuff?

She remembered the strange hooded figure in the corridor. What sort of illness made someone want to cover himself completely? A skin disease perhaps that covered him with ugly patches? That would fit in with the patient being taken to the Isolation Ward.

She wished she knew more about skin diseases. In fact she wished she knew more about everything. Nurses, it seemed to her, weren't taught anything much except how to be medical maids of all work. Half of it was scrubbing and cleaning and cooking, like you did at home. It wasn't really interesting work like doctors did. Now if only . . .

'*Nora!*'

She came out of her reverie to find Mrs Mothershead's stern face confronting her. 'Nora, mind your duties. If you

55

don't concentrate, you'll only make more work for the rest of us. Now get about your business.' She frowned. 'And *do* get your collar straight, dear.'

The last word was not an endearment, but it took some of the brusque edge off the words. Nora fumbled hastily with her collar.

'I'm so sorry, Mrs Mothershead.'

'Do get on with it, Nora.'

She walked on without waiting to see the results. Nora finished her repair work and picked up a tray to begin serving. When next she looked, the matron had gone. She wondered when she'd get her breakfast.

It took Treves nearly twenty minutes to get the Elephant Man to the top floor of the hospital because of the lengthy stops at the start and finish of each staircase and the slow dragging progress down the corridors. At first he was aware of the odd stares from people they passed but, absorbed in his patient, he soon became oblivious of them. He did not even notice when the door of Mr Carr-Gomm's office opened, and the chairman of the Administrative Committee looked out for an explanation of the strange noises in the corridor. After a moment Carr-Gomm returned to his office and closed the door.

The Isolation Ward was a small attic under the roof, well away from the rest of the hospital and containing only one bed. High up on one wall was a small window, tightly barred. All too often contagion meant typhoid, and typhoid meant delirium. Not too many years ago a typhoid patient had hurled himself from an upper window to his death.

Apart from the one bed the room was furnished with two hard chairs and a table. Treves dumped his bag on this and used both arms to help the man lower himself slowly to the bed. He loosened the cloak and pulled it away, letting it fall round the man on the bed. The hat and mask he tossed onto a peg on the wall. The Elephant Man neither helped nor protested. He seemed ten times weaker than when they had left Turners Road. The journey had exhausted him and his breathing was more agonized than ever.

Treves went to his bag and took from it two bottles, one of dark fluid, one of light. He took out a glass and in it mixed a small quantity of each fluid. Then he looked critically at what he had mixed. It was what might roughly be described as a 'pick-me-up', of little medical value, but useful in the short term.

He pressed it gently on the Elephant Man, who spluttered and gagged, but finally managed to get it all down. Treves' mind went back to the potatoes and water he'd seen spilled on the cellar floor. Doubtless that was what the Elephant Man lived on. Here at least was something that could be remedied quickly. The kitchen would be just serving up breakfast now; though whether the hospital's breakfast would do him much more good than Bytes' potatoes and water was something Treves wryly doubted. He wondered what would happen if he abandoned all medical etiquette and gave the man good strong whisky. Probably perk him up like nothing else.

At the door he stopped and looked back. There was something he had to say.

'I don't know if you will understand this,' he said slowly and clearly, 'but you will never go back to that man again. You're safe now. No-one will ever harm you. Do you understand?'

He had his answer in the blank eyes that met his unseeingly. He sighed as he closed the door behind him. It was hopeless, hopeless. But he felt better for having said it, as though somehow he had safeguarded himself against temptation.

His arrival in the kitchen caused a pleasurable stir. He was a favourite with the nurses both for his personable looks and pleasant manners. He always said 'Please' and 'Thank you' to nurses whom other doctors, especially the older ones, often treated like skivvies. Nor did he mind cracking the odd joke with them. There were smiles when he picked up a bowl and advanced towards the nurse ladelling porridge out of the huge urn.

'Breakfasting with the patients this morning, Mr Treves?' she said archly, allowing a big dollop of the unappetizing stuff to flop into his bowl.

'It's for a patient,' he told her.

He felt self-conscious making his way down the corridors clutching a bowl of porridge, and when he saw Carr-Gomm approaching him he tried to be inconspicuous. But without success.

'Mr Treves, come over here a moment, won't you?' Carr-Gomm's voice was as genial and courteous as it ever was, but Treves did not make the mistake of failing to recognize an order for what it was. He had seen other men underestimate Carr-Gomm, who positively invited underestimation by hiding a shrewd and often ruthless mind behind a smile as bland and ingenuous as a baby's. Those men had always regretted their blindness. Carr-Gomm was fifty-four, a tough medical administrator who made sure he knew everything that was going on in the little world under his rule.

Treves intended to approach the chairman about the Elephant Man himself, but later, when he'd had some time to improve the man's condition and do some thinking. In the meantime he wanted to keep his presence in the hospital a secret. He knew it would be difficult to hide anything from those deceptively guileless eyes, and impossible if he gave himself away by creeping round the hospital corridors clutching bowls of porridge. He silently cursed his luck and made foolish, clumsy efforts to hide the bowl, which were abandoned when he realized Carr-Gomm was regarding him satirically. There was nothing to do but brazen it out.

'Good morning, Treves.'

'Good morning, sir.'

Carr-Gomm pointed at the bowl. 'You've acquired a taste for this?'

'It's quite nutritious, sir,' Treves hedged.

'Don't be mad. This muck can kill you,' Carr-Gomm

declared robustly. He signalled to Nurse Nora Ireland, who had just come into view further down the corridor, relieved Treves of the bowl, and gave it into her hands, requesting in a smooth voice, 'Take this up to the man in the Isolation Ward when you have a moment, won't you?' He cast a humorously malicious look at Treves' stunned face.

'Yes, sir.' Nora looked nervously between the two of them.

'Don't be frightened,' Treves told her. 'He won't hurt you.'

'Indeed.' Carr-Gomm's eyebrows were raised a fraction and he made a gesture towards his office door.

Nora watched the two men enter the office, then she set off for the Isolation Ward. Apprehension stirred like quicksands inside her. She was as much frightened by Treves' last words as by the prospect of confronting the mysterious figure she had seen smuggled in. Why should he hurt her? Was he delirious from fever or – she gulped – a madman?

She stopped, drew a deep breath and tried to stiffen her resolve. Her father had always told his children to advance with courage in the Lord.

After a few moments spent talking sternly to herself, Nora advanced with courage up the stairs to the Isolation Ward.

Francis Culling Carr was a man in whom the strain of hereditary pride had increased in direct proportion to his distance from its source. The family glory was rooted in a faint connection with Field Marshall Sir William Gomm, the distinguished soldier who had begun a great career as aide to the Duke of Wellington in the Peninsular War and at Waterloo.

Francis, younger son of an obscure Kent clergyman, had faced life with two weapons – his Gomm connection and his brilliant facility for the law. Together they had been enough to win him a major's daughter for a wife. The marriage, a happy one, had lasted ten years, during which

Jeanie had given him two living sons and one dead, and died in childbirth when her husband was thirty-five.

The next five years of his life had been spent in India as a district judge in the Madras Civil Service, until at last a desire to see how his two surviving sons had fared in his sister's care had made him return. He had arrived in England to find Sir William Gomm on the point of death.

Grief and loneliness had toughened Francis Carr's heart, as the Indian sun had toughened his skin. He made a swift decision. Sir William had no children or any close male relatives. His nearest kin was his spinster niece Emily Carr, who was plain, thirty-two and on her last prayers. Carr used their distant relationship to effect an introduction, and they were married within four months.

When Sir William Gomm died, the Carrs applied for, and received, the Royal Licence to assume the surname and arms of Gomm, although, to do Francis justice, he thought more of his sons (who now numbered three, thanks to Emily's efforts) than of himself. Now they were Mr and Mrs Carr-Gomm, and Emily played the lady of the manor to perfection.

For the last five years, Carr-Gomm had been chairman of the London Hospital. He brought to the job the characteristics of the trained lawyer and also a mind that had learned deviousness in India. His nature was precise, proud and subtle. He could be deeply generous, but his generosity was a considered response. There were numerous stories of his kindness, but kindness was seldom his *first* instinct. As a clergyman's son he practised compassion from Christian duty. As a lawyer he practised rectitude from a sense of good order.

His office was a large, high-ceilinged room, dominated by two huge windows that ran side by side all the way up one wall. In front of this stood the chairman's desk; and whether by accident or design, Carr-Gomm had placed his chair exactly in the centre of the space between the windows. The effect was to throw an almost blinding light on his visitors, making Carr-Gomm himself hard to see.

'I had better confess now that there is no sorcery in my knowledge,' he said when Treves had seated himself. 'I saw you helping the patient down the corridor outside this office barely half an hour ago. I presume it is the same man? Or is it woman? It was rather hard to see.'

'It was a man.'

'He has been through the Receiving Room presumably, and all details given at the desk?'

'No, sir. I admitted him myself. You see—'

'In other words, if I had not happened to look out of my office door at just that moment, this man's presence in the Isolation Ward would have remained known only to yourself?' Carr-Gomm's sense of fitness and order was deeply offended.

'Sir, if you'll just let me explain . . .'

'I do wish you would,' said the chairman plaintively. 'A hospital is no place for secrecy, Mr Treves. Doctors spiriting hooded figures about are liable to cause comment. Why wasn't this patient properly admitted? Is he contagious?'

'No, sir. He's got bronchitis and he's been badly beaten.'

'Why isn't he in the General Ward then?'

'Well, sir,' Treves hesitated between saying too much and too little – 'he's quite seriously deformed and I fear the other patients would find him – rather shocking.'

'Deformed? Is that it? Then I am to assume that he is ultimately incurable?'

'Yes, sir.'

'What are your plans then, Treves? You are aware that the London does not accept incurables? The rules are quite clear on that point.'

'Yes, I'm well aware of that. But this case is quite exceptional.'

'Oh?' Carr-Gomm's eyebrows lifted coolly. 'Is he a friend of yours?'

'No, more of an acquaintance. I've – examined him a good deal over the last fortnight and – the fact is I feel rather responsible for him.'

'Am I to assume that this is the Elephant Man with

whom you caused such a stir with the Pathological Society yesterday, Treves? I was regrettably unable to attend myself but the reports – glowing reports, I may add – of your success reached me almost at once.'

'It *is* the same man—'

'And naturally you take an interest in his general health even though your need for him as a specimen is now a good deal less. That is very proper and humane, and what I should have expected from you. But, my dear fellow, let us not lose our sense of proportion. You naturally feel an obligation – even perhaps gratitude to a man who has been of so much benefit to you. But you cannot be responsible for him for the rest of his life. Presumably he has a home?'

'Not a home I should ever send him back to. He is kept by a man called Bytes, who describes himself as his "owner" – as if he was an animal. He exhibits him wherever he can – for twopence. I first encountered him at a fun-fair side-show, which the police were in the process of closing down as an affront to decency.'

'Good grief!' said Carr-Gomm, genuinely appalled.

'When he is not on display he is abused and beaten and fed just enough to keep him alive. And the next time Bytes is not permitted to display him for profit I'm afraid he will be abandoned to starve altogether. In the circumstances I didn't feel I could leave him where he was, and this hospital is the only place I knew of to bring him.'

'I certainly sympathize with your problem, Treves. Why don't you try the British Home or the Royal Hospital for Incurables? Perhaps they would have a place for him.'

'Yes, sir, I'll look into that.' Treves hesitated. 'Would you like to meet him, sir?'

Before Carr-Gomm could answer, the peace of the hospital was shattered by a shrill, terrified scream that echoed down through two floors. Treves leapt to his feet. He didn't have to ask where it had come from or what had caused it.

'Excuse me!' he said tersely, and was out of the door, running fast down the corridor past the shocked faces of nurses and doctors. He took the stairs like a madman until he reached the small landing outside the Isolation Ward, where he found the sight he'd most dreaded. Through the open ward door he could see the Elephant Man, his hideousness nakedly apparent, crouched on the bed, trying to squeeze himself out of sight in the corner. On the floor lay the shattered ruins of his breakfast where Nora had dropped them. Nora herself was on the landing, one hand clutching the railings, the other covering her face as she fought to control her hysterical sobs.

Hurriedly Treves closed the door and put one arm round Nora, holding her in a strong steadying hug.

'I'm sorry, my dear. I should have warned you. I'm so terribly sorry. Please forgive me,' he said gently.

With a valiant effort she forced herself to seem calm and wiped her face with her apron. When she looked up at him, she was biting her lips to stop them trembling but she had herself under control again. Treves kept his voice to a soothing monotone.

'There, you're all right now?'

She nodded, still not able to speak.

'Go downstairs and please ask Mrs Mothershead to come up. Tell her to knock on the door and wait for me. All right?'

'Yes, sir. I'm sorry, sir.' Drying her eyes, Nora went down the stairs and made a thankful escape.

Treves stood on the landing and cursed the ill-fortune that had intervened in his plans this early. In his mind he could reconstruct the scene only too easily. Nora's approach, the man's growing nervous awareness of her footsteps, the opening of the door, her first unprepared sight of that shocking body and even more shocking head, her scream that had driven him cowering into the corner. And now what did the Elephant Man think? That he had been rescued from one jeering hell only to be plunged into another?

Treves stepped into the Isolation Ward and closed the door behind him. The Elephant Man was still crouched in the corner of the bed, but he had stopped cowering and was looking directly at Treves.

'I'm very sorry about that,' Treves said quietly. 'Are you resting well?'

He regretted the idiot question as soon as it had escaped his lips. It was one of the standard questions you asked patients, but for this man none of the standard questions were applicable. Treves felt uncomfortable as he edged his feet forward onto uncharted territory. The Elephant Man garbled a noise that could have meant anything, and Treves seized on it.

'Ah, good. Well then . . . oh yes, we'll have to get you some more food. I'm sure you must be simply famished, hm?'

The Elephant Man stared at him. He did not seem reassured by the hearty tone that was normally such a success with patients.

'Of course you are. Now then, I think you'll be quite comfortable up here for a while. I'll see to it you have everything you need, and – uh yes . . . .'

It was a relief to come to the end of the meaningless words. There was only one thing for it, Treves thought, and that was to do as he would do with an animal. He stretched out his hand and laid it gently on the Elephant Man. He could feel the instant flinch backwards, but the man made no other move, and for a moment his eyes were as they had been in the cellar, human, pleading. Treves sighed.

The knock on the door came as a relief. He opened it and went out onto the landing where Mrs Mothershead was standing with an iron face. He closed the door behind her, taking care to keep himself between her and the creature inside the room.

'Ah, Mothershead. How are you feeling today?'

The heartiness succeeded no better with her than it had with Merrick. But where the Elephant Man's rejection of it had been caused by incomprehension, Mrs Mothershead's had an ironic tinge.

'Perfectly well, thank you, doctor.' Her eyes met Treves, filled with suspicion.

'Good, excellent. Now then, Mrs Mothershead, I want

you to come into this room with me. Inside there is a man with a rather – unfortunate appearance.'

'I've heard,' Mothershead said drily.

'Yes – well, I want you to clear up a little mess. A breakfast tray was spilt. And bring up another breakfast.' He hurried on as he saw her eyebrows raise. 'I would not normally ask someone in your position to undertake this kind of duty, but this is rather special. In view of the circumstances I don't feel I can entrust this man into the care of a less experienced nurse.'

'Since they appear unable to stop themselves screaming the place down, I imagine you're right,' the matron said crossly. 'Will there be anything else, doctor?'

'Yes. When you've done that, you and I shall give the man a bath.' He moved towards the door, then stopped. 'Mothershead, I'm counting on your many years of experience to get you through this. Above all, do not scream, do not cry out, or in any way show this man that you are frightened of him . . .'

'Sir, you don't have to worry about me. I'm not the sort to cry out. Shall we go in?'

'Yes – yes, let's go in.' He opened the door and stood back hastily as she swept past him, going right up to Merrick and standing in front of him as though he were nothing out of the ordinary. Treves had to hurry to close the door and catch up with her. He found her regarding Merrick with an impassive face.

'I would like you to meet Mrs Mothershead,' he said to Merrick. 'Mrs Mothershead, Mr John Merrick.'

Merrick had averted his eyes from the tall woman standing over him, but now he looked up at her and realized that she was gazing at him steadily. She plainly had no difficulty being in his presence, or looking at him.

'How do you do?' she said coolly.

When he made only a garbled sound in response, she turned briskly away and stared at the mess on the floor. It took her only a few minutes to clear it up, but when she had lifted the tray and was turning to leave they were all pulled up short by a knock on the door. Mrs Mothershead answered it, making sure her body filled the gap, just as Treves had done earlier. But she need not have bothered. It was Nora who stood there, holding another tray on which stood a fresh breakfast.

'I thought I'd better bring another one up, Mrs Mothershead.'

'I'm glad to see you do think sometimes, Nurse Ireland.' Despite the hard words, Mothershead's tone was kind enough. 'Give it to me, and take this one back.' She held out the tray containing the debris.

'Wouldn't you like me to take this one in Mrs Mothershead?' Nora's face was pale but determined.

'There's no need for that girl. I'll take it in. You get this one down to the kitchen, and tell them I want some buckets of hot water up here, quickly. And then tell the Supply Department I want a large wooden tub sent up, and some soap and towels. But make it clear to them that they're to knock on the door and wait. Nobody is to come in.'

'Yes, Mrs Mothershead.' Nora turned back down the stairs, but halted as Mothershead called her.

'Nora?'

'Yes, Mrs Mothershead?'

'You're not such a fool as I thought you were. All right girl, get on. Don't stand there staring.'

Mothershead retreated back into the Isolation Ward with the fresh breakfast.

'Come along,' she said, placing the tray on the table. 'This has all got to be eaten, so let's have no nonsense.'

Treves, who felt that the tone of command might just as easily be addressed to himself as Merrick, aided the man in getting to the edge of the bed, and sliding his legs over the side.

'I think he'd better stay here to eat it,' he said apologetically. 'He hasn't the strength to move much.'

'Very well, sir.' Mothershead pulled the chair up close to the bed, and dipped the spoon into the porridge.

She handled the revolting business of feeding Merrick

66

in a way that won Treves' admiration. Nothing seemed to put her off, from the slobbering sounds that the Elephant Man made, to the frequency with which he spilled the porridge over himself. The smell she did not seem even to notice.

The meal took a long time, and before it was over there was a knock on the door. Mothershead shoved the spoon unceremoniously into Treves' hand and went to answer.

Treves found that Merrick seemed less nervous in his hands than he had been in Mothershead's, and wondered if the sense of exasperated duty that lay behind Mothershead's brisk efficiency had communicated itself. He wondered how the disgusting porridge tasted to one who had been fed largely on water and potatoes.

'I'll have them send you a good strong cup of tea later,' he muttered, barely knowing that he spoke. 'You'll enjoy it.'

From the door he could just hear Mothershead in conversation with a male voice that he recognized as belonging to Nettleton, the youngest of the porters.

'It's heavy, ma'am,' said the voice respectfully. 'Sure I can't carry it in for you?'

'Be off with you, my lad,' Mothershead told him firmly. 'I'll take it in myself. I know very well what you want, and you're not getting your nose in here.'

She backed in, pulling a large wooden bath tub behind her.

'I'm afraid there's going to be more of that, sir,' she said when she had shut the door.

'More of what, Mothershead?'

'Sight-seers. If only that silly girl hadn't screamed. It'll be all over the hospital by now . . .'

Another knock interrupted her. This time it was water, borne by a different porter, and roughly the same conversation took place. Treves listened to it, worried. He felt he could have avoided much of this by planning Merrick's admittance into the hospital more carefully. But then how could he have known in advance what would be needed, he argued with himself.

While Mothershead filled the tub with water, he finished feeding Merrick and began to remove his clothes. Merrick made feeble protesting movements, as though he would resist, but eventually gave up and sat, acquiescent while Treves knelt and unwrapped the sacking arrangement round his feet. He whimpered, however, when Treves began to unfasten the trousers, and seemed distressed as they were removed.

Without them he was perfectly naked, a fact which plainly bothered him. Treves wondered if Mothershead was the cause of this, and was sure of it when Merrick bent forward slightly, trying to cover his genitals with his left hand. Treves remembered with a sense of shame how casually he had used a stick to direct his audience's attention to those genitals, how clinically he had remarked on their perfect formation, so strange in the midst of so much hideous deformity; how confident he had been that Merrick understood nothing of what he was saying. He felt suddenly shaken. Why even Bytes had not done so much.

Was it only yesterday all this had happened? It felt as though it was a hundred years ago.

He persuaded Merrick into the tub at last and gently urged him to sit down. At once the water turned black. Mothershead took up a full bucket standing nearby and tipped the contents over Merrick's back. The water was the colour of sludge before it was half-way down. Making a face of distaste Mothershead took up a scrubbing brush and began to wash him. Whatever her feelings, it was plain that nothing was going to get in the way of the job in hand.

Merrick's body was slowly changing colour under the impact of Mothershead's scrubbing brush. Treves wondered if the loathesome smell might be no more than the natural effusion of a man who never had a chance to wash. He seemed to be covered with months of filth and accumulated excrescence.

68

When another knock came on the door, Mothershead called: 'Wait', and promptly dipped the two empty buckets into the water. She took them to the door and there exchanged them for a clean pair, in the process becoming involved in another crisp conversation with Nettleton, which the words 'Clear off at once!' seemed to terminate satisfactorily.

Returning, she tipped the clean water into the tub and went on scrubbing. This happened three times more, and each time Merrick became a little lighter. He had given up resistance and was leaning forward in the tub, with his eyes closed. He seemed to have protected himself from the outside world by escaping from it. Treves had taken up a seat by the tub and was leaning forward, examining his patient's back intently. The strange cauliflower growths on it could be more easily made out.

'Shocking,' Treves murmured.

He was almost unaware of having spoken aloud, but the sound of his voice made Merrick flinch and swivel his eyes towards him. Treves did not notice. He was too fully absorbed in his own speculation.

'I wonder how far it can go before it . . .'

Merrick jerked suddenly and tried to pull away from Mothershead's hand.

'Sit still,' she told him firmly. 'Don't wiggle about like a pup. I won't stand for any foolishness.'

Treves leaned forward until he could meet Merrick's eyes.

'Where are your parents?' he said slowly.

Merrick made no reply, but he grew still. His eyes closed, and he seemed to slip back into the reverie that had held him a moment before. Treves went on talking, half to Mothershead, half to himself.

'It's pretty certain that if he had the disease as a child he was abandoned. But what sort of parents, what sort of *mother* would turn her child away? She must have been a cruel, heartless woman.'

Mothershead gave him a cynical look. The mysterious

sentimentality of men about mothers was something she came across often as a nurse. Merrick's desertion by his mother did not surprise her in the slightest. She had seen the same sort of behaviour too often to remark it. She had seen women who bore deformed children deserted by their husbands, or the men they lived with, and left to endure the consequences alone. And a woman alone with a child was not treated kindly by the world. So she laid down the intolerable burden when it grew too much for her, and the world called her cruel and heartless. Mrs Mothershead's sense of duty was too strong for her to approve of such a woman, but her sense of justice did not allow her to condemn as glibly as Treves.

'But in any case,' Treves was continuing, 'he'd have had to have care. The very fact that he's alive bears that out. But where?'

'The workhouse,' said Mrs Mothershead.

His head went up, alert. 'Yes. The workhouse.'

In another instant he had jerked back, startled by Merrick's violent reaction and the splash of water it sent over the floor. Merrick had begun to babble wildly and thrash about the tub in terror. Treves' efforts to calm him were useless. It was the first time he had ever been unable to get through to him. The Elephant Man seemed oblivious to everything but his own panic. His moans rose into a high desperate wailing as he tried to get to his feet and escape from the tub.

It was Mothershead who subdued him with a hand clamped firmly onto his left arm. He yielded at once and sank back into the tub. His head fell forward onto his knees and his whole body was shaken with despairing sobs. Treves was appalled. He had assumed, without knowing why, that that blank face was incapable of expressing grief.

'The workhouse,' he said softly, as understanding dawned.

CHAPTER SIX

Renshaw stared fretfully into his beer tankard, the bottom of which was coming into view too quickly for his comfort. Somehow it didn't seem as if he could have drunk a whole pint, but there was the last mouthful sliding down now. He felt dreary, and dreariness was a feeling Jim Renshaw couldn't bear. He liked life to be bright and lively.

'I'm a man who likes a little of what he fancies,' he'd say to any audience who'd listen. If the audience happened to include a pretty girl or two (and it usually did) he'd give them a nudge and a wink and add, 'and a *lot* of what he fancies.' There'd be much giggling and flaunting, and usually he'd pick the prettiest, lean down in her ear and whisper, 'I do like a bit of fun.'

That was Jim Renshaw. A man who liked a bit of fun. No harm in that, though you'd think there was if you listened to the do-gooders always trying to get between a man and his booze, his betting or his bed-mate. Mostly Renshaw contrived to ignore such intrusions into his privacy and have his fun anyway. But things didn't always work out.

Take now, for instance. There was Mattie, a real little bundle of mischief when he'd first met her and he'd had no trouble getting her to move in with him. Renshaw never had any trouble in that department. He was a big well-made fellow in his middle thirties with a burly geniality that made him attractive to women who had not looked closely into his eyes and spotted the gleam of cruelty that lurked there – and even to some that had.

Mattie, like many before her, had fallen into his waiting hands like a ripe peach. Her predecessor had made a bit of trouble, but after Renshaw had twisted her arm a little (only a little, because knocking about the girls he'd lived with spoilt his memories of them and Renshaw was

71

sentimental about his memories), she'd seen sense. Mattie had moved in and he'd had the best six months of his life. Mattie willingly fitted her hours to his, sleeping in the day when he slept and rising in the early evening to cook his 'breakfast' before he went off to his job as night porter at the London Hospital. She was a good cook, never nagged about his boots, and was ready and willing at all hours. Renshaw had told himself his luck was really in this time.

And then the silly cow had spoiled it all by getting pregnant.

He groaned when he thought of it and banged his tankard on the bar to attract some attention.

'Fill it quick, Betty,' he told the girl who hastened to him. 'I've got to get to work.'

'Shouldn't you 'ave been there long ago, Mr Renshaw?' She smiled archly at him as she drew the beer.

He told her to watch her lip, but grinned as he said it. It was nice to be sauced a bit by a pretty maid whose face wasn't blotched with tears or twisted with screaming. Mattie had been like that in the beginning. Why did they have to change?

Marriage she wanted, if you please! What the hell had got into her? Their kind didn't marry and well she knew it. Renshaw's parents hadn't been married, neither had Mattie's, and now he applied his mind powerfully to the subject he couldn't think of any couple he knew who were married – and some of them had a dozen kids. You set up home, you had kids (not that he wanted kids). Tying it up all legal-like was for toffs with money to spend on that kind of thing.

He examined his behaviour to Mattie, and couldn't think of anything he'd done wrong. When she'd first started snapping about 'not wanting a little bastard', he'd agreed wholeheartedly and offered to find her some really experienced woman who'd do the job all right and tight and no trouble. He had a sister who'd used the woman three times. But that wasn't good enough for Mattie. Oh no. She wanted marriage.

He'd started spending less and less time at home during the day, wandering out in the streets to escape from Mattie's nagging, her sickness and her general evil temper. He felt hard done by. If only she'd agree to get rid of it, she'd be her old self again and they could go on enjoying themselves as they had before. But if she was going to be unreasonable, he'd have to give her the shove. There were other women who could cook and look after a man. He took a long look at Betty, who was serving at the other end of the bar. She caught his eyes and came tripping towards him, her breasts swivelling against each other in a blouse she was rapidly outgrowing.

'Give me a bottle of gin, Betty. I've got a long night ahead of me.'

When she produced it, he snatched it from her, ripped the top off and took a large swig. Then he thrust it at her.

'Have one.'

She giggled and tipped the bottle up to her mouth, taking a swallow almost as large as his own. He regarded her in dismay. Never mind. He'd get his repayment later. He leaned over to her and spoke softly.

'I'm a bit short of cash till I get paid Betty. Could you—?'

Her eyes wavered. Having drunk from the bottle herself, she was cornered. Then she gave him an arch smile.

'Your credit's always good, Mr Renshaw. I'll put it on the slate.'

'That's my girl. I'll be back tomorrow. We'll 'ave a good time together.'

He wandered out feeling justifiably pleased with himself. He knew that bottle would never appear on the slate. Betty would 'forget' about it. He took another swig.

Somewhere a clock struck ten-thirty. He was late for work but he refused to hurry. It was beneath him. Besides, there was something he wanted to think about, something that had happened earlier that day, something very funny . . .

It had been about noon. He'd fled Mattie and headed for

his favourite pub, using a short cut that had taken him past the rear of the London Hospital. He had stopped in a small alley that gave him a good view of the back entrance, and stood for a moment considering the sight of Nettleton staggering clumsily through the big iron door, bearing two buckets that seemed to be very heavy. Renshaw had nothing against Nettleton. He was a harmless young bloke who'd be all right when he'd learned a bit of respect for his elders and betters. Renshaw's enjoyment of Nettleton's difficulties was quite devoid of personal malice.

But the smile dropped off his face a bit sharpish when Nettleton tipped the contents of one of the buckets onto the stones. Renshaw jumped as some of the thick sludgy material splashed in his direction. He took a step out into the alley so that the young man could see what he'd done. He was pleased to note that Nettleton seemed nervous in his presence.

'What's all this then?' he snapped, indicating his boots.

Nettleton lacked the nerve to point out that, splashed or not splashed, Renshaw's boots were pretty much the same.

'Mr Treves is scrubbing his Elephant Man,' he said placatingly.

'Elephant Man?'

'Yeah – I hear it's a real horror. Even made Mothershead scream.'

Renshaw's brows contracted. He hated Mothershead who had frequently threatened him with the loss of a job that was the cushiest number he'd ever had.

'Fiend of the night, eh?' he grinned. 'I think I'll 'ave me a look at that.' He turned as if to go, but wheeled at the last moment and shot out his foot. His brass-heeled boot caught the other bucket, which Nettleton had stood on the ground, sending its contents soaking over the young porter.

'Now *you* need scrubbing, ducks,' Renshaw told him genially.

He waited to see if there would be any back-chat. When he was satisfied that there wouldn't, he turned on his heel and wandered back down the alley at a leisurely pace. He turned at the corner, to see Nettleton frantically shaking his wet trousers. He was grinning as he walked on.

The titbit of news had stayed with him all day, not as a matter of importance but as a morsel that might provide a little innocent diversion for a bored man in the long watches of the night. It rose again in his mind now, as he came within sight of the hospital.

He could see that the process of settling down for the night was well under way. Windows that he knew belonged to wards were already black. Other windows that led onto corridors showed a faint glimmer of light, indicating that half the gas-lamps had been left burning, as they would be throughout the night. Renshaw turned longing eyes to a large building at the side which he knew was the Nurses Quarters. Pale gleams came from it, but soon it too would be all in darkness.

As soon as he slipped into the front hall, Renshaw saw that the place was deserted except for Nettleton who still occupied the porter's cubby-hole.

'Anyone been down?' Renshaw demanded.

'Not recently—' Nettleton said uneasily.

'So no-one knows I'm late?'

'No—'

'Good. And you're not going to tell them, are you?'

The young man shook his head, dumb with nerves.

'All right, cut along.'

Nettleton didn't stop to argue. He'd given up arguing long ago about the times he had to cover up for Renshaw, who never paid the favour back.

It was two in the morning before Renshaw moved. That was the safest time. The emergencies that always followed the closing of the pubs were over by then. The hospital would have settled down again, and with luck many of the night nurses would be asleep at their desks. Now was the safest time for a little prowl.

He took another swig at his gin bottle, and settled it comfortably in the pocket of his coat. His brass-heeled boots echoed as he crossed the hall to the stairs. He often regretted wearing them on these expeditions, and constantly resolved to get something quieter. But he never did. He could not have borne to part with the feeling of power and manliness that the sensation of metal beneath his feet gave him. The brutal sound it made in these echoing corridors pleased him even while it made him glance over his shoulder.

On the second floor he stopped and paused outside the door to one of the women's wards. He knew Nurse Waters was on tonight, and Waters had an unfortunate weakness that made it hard for her to stay awake after midnight. A little visit would be perfectly safe. Tentatively Renshaw pushed at the door.

Every lamp in the ward was in darkness, but the moonlight slanting through the tall window showed Renshaw all he needed to know. Nurse Waters was at the far end, bent heavily over her desk, representing no danger. Renshaw began his slow, curious progress down the centre aisle. About him he could hear the night-time noises of many sick women, trapped together. Some were coughing fitfully, others moaning in their sleep. Many were very old, some had obviously been sent here to die. These Renshaw ignored. His eyes were flickering down the aisle in search of something, something that should have been there and didn't seem to be . . .

At last he found what he was looking for and a quick sigh of relief escaped him. A young and beautiful woman, engulfed in a fearsome-looking piece of traction apparatus, had never taken her eyes off him from the moment he appeared. Fear lay on her face like a suffocating blanket, fear that deepened as he caught sight of her and approached.

She looked wildly from side to side, but her nearest companions were elderly women, both snoring heavily. When Renshaw was standing at the end of her bed she began to struggle, but her arms were tied firmly into the traction machine. It rattled but did not give way. She was as trapped as an animal in a snare. A few feet away Nurse Waters snored.

Renshaw moved towards the bed and laid a hand on the rattling traction machine, stilling its noise. One finger was over his lips as he spoke softly, smiling at her.

'Hush, love, I told you before – one word from me, they'll toss you back on the street, and then those pretty little arms of yours will never grow straight.' He ran his hand down from the machine, stroking her arm all the way down to the shoulders, his eyes gleaming as he felt the shudder she was unable to repress. His hand delved lower, slithering beneath her hospital bed-gown, groping about to find the small perfect breasts. Her eyes grew wild, but she made no further noise.

'Now close your eyes,' he whispered. 'Close your eyes . . .'

She did so, turning her head away as if she would shut him out from her consciousness, but instantly he wrenched her back.

'I only said to close your eyes,' he reproved her. 'I haven't finished with you yet.'

He rammed his mouth savagely on hers, hearing and enjoying her gasp of fear and pain as the machine yanked at her. This was how he enjoyed it best. It occurred to him that something had been missing during the months with Mattie. She had been too willing. He thrust one hand down into the bed and began to draw up her bed-gown, using the other hand to pull down the bed clothes. The girl began to writhe frantically, making the machine above jangle. He knew it was no longer safe, but he was beyond turning back now. He pulled away and glared at her.

'*Shut up!*' he said in a savage whisper. 'If anyone hears I'll break every bone in your body.'

With almost one movement he ripped open his trousers and dropped onto her. She lay like a stone, motionless beneath him, and when he drew back he saw why. She had fainted in terror. He gave a grunt of satisfaction and did himself up. It took just a moment to pull up the bedclothes and make everything look ordinary again. Nurse Waters was still snoring as he slipped out of the door.

He made his way up to the top of the building without further delay. He'd used up a lot of time. On the last little landing before the Isolation Ward, he hauled out the gin bottle and took a mighty swig. If the object up there really was fearsome enough to make even Mothershead scream, then a man needed a little fortification.

He stopped again outside the door to the Isolation Ward and knocked back another gulp. From inside he could hear a strange rasping breathing. He took a deep breath and flung himself into the room.

At first he could make out nothing beyond the bed in the far corner and the shapeless thing sitting on the edge of it. He peered closer but the thing didn't move.

'Here he is,' Renshaw announced tipsily. 'The old fiend of the night, the terror of the London. Let's 'ave a look at you. Let's see what makes 'em scream . . .'

As he spoke he swivelled round to the gas-lamp and turned it up. The light fell directly onto the Elephant Man's head, illuminating every monstrous lump, deepening every hollow. Renshaw took an involuntary step backwards.

'Cor Blimey!' he uttered in deep awe.

For a moment he was shaken by a genuine horror at a sight that should have been human yet was so far removed from anything human. Then he noticed that the thing on the bed was trembling, and he had the sensation that something had clicked in his brain. Whatever that creature was, it was capable of understanding that Jim Renshaw was to be feared, and that was a situation Renshaw was used to.

He moved cautiously towards the bed, noting how the Elephant Man drew back from him and flinched from his hand. Renshaw's nervousness was gone now. He was in control, the only way he liked to be.

'So this is the Elephant Man,' he said with a grin. 'I ain't never seen nothing like you before. What the bleedin' 'ell 'appened to you?'

The creature's silent cowering into the farthest corner increased Renshaw's confidence yet more.

'Oh – dumb, eh?' He took a long swig of the gin and smiled. 'Good, I like people what can keep quiet.'

He moved quickly, offering the bottle to the Elephant Man in a movement that was almost a jab, grinning in a satisfied way as the thing tried to press himself into the far wall. 'Like a drink? Go on – go *on*, have some. No? You should try being more sociable, mate. You'll get yourself disliked.'

His eyes fixed onto the hanging growths on the Elephant Man's chest. Tentatively he pressed the cold bottle up against one of them. When nothing happened, he began to feel the misshapen body with his fingers. The man made small whimpering sounds and put up a protesting hand, but did not dare to try to push Renshaw away.

'You and I are going to be good friends, we are,' Renshaw told him softly. 'I've got lots of friends who I know would like to meet you. And they will, mate – they will.'

He pulled back abruptly and went to the door. He paused and looked back at his victim, raising the gin bottle to him in salute.

'Welcome to the London.'

He closed the door softly behind him and made his way down the stairs. He could hear his brass-heeled boots clicking triumphantly as he went. The sound cheered him. Life was fun again.

CHAPTER SEVEN

'Good morning, Mr Treves. If you don't mind my saying so, sir, with your early habits you'd 'a made a fine milkman.'

'Good morning, Charley. I'll keep that in mind.'

Treves dodged the milkman's horse, who would also have greeted him in its own fashion, and went into the front entrance of the hospital. It was the kind of cheerful encounter he had a dozen times a day while his mind was on something else. And people smiled and said how ready Mr Treves always was to exchange a friendly word, never knowing that he had barely seen or heard them.

Fast as he had travelled, his mind had raced ahead of him. He had been forced to leave the hospital early the previous day, and spend a boring afternoon in his consulting rooms at 6, Wimpole Street, dealing with the routine ailments he encountered in his increasingly prosperous private practice. He disliked these afternoons but forced himself to go on with them, partly through his ambition, which told him that no doctor ever made a name through hospital practice alone, and partly in fulfilment of the promise he had made to Alfred and Elizabeth Mason thirteen years ago, when his one thought had been to convince them that he was fit to marry their daughter Anne. A solid private practice with which to keep their daughter, he had promised them, and he had been as good as his word. The Masons, had they still been alive, could have had no quarrel with the consulting rooms or the home in Wimpole Street. As for Treves, he bent his head to the necessary yoke, but his mind lived at the hospital.

He had been forced to leave the Elephant Man in Mothershead's care. He knew she would be competent, even kindly in an impersonal way. But she could not be everywhere, and the minor uproar that Merrick's arrival had created convinced Treves that his patient needed constant protection. There was no-one to provide it.

He had left the strictest instructions that no-one but Mothershead herself was to approach the Isolation Ward, and he counted on the ripple of fear he had detected in the hospital to ensure that those instructions were obeyed. But he could not be easy in his mind, and on the day following Merrick's admission he made his best speed to the hospital, and headed straight upstairs, pausing only at the kitchens to collect Merrick's breakfast.

His first thought on opening the door of the Isolation Ward was that his worst fears had been realized and that Merrick had either been kidnapped or managed to escape. The Elephant Man was nowhere to be seen. A horrible thought struck Treves. Suppose his patient had died in the night? Suppose the blame were his own for failing to care for him properly—?

Then his eye was caught by a slight movement in the corner by the bed, and he breathed again. Merrick was crouched down, half hidden under the bed, his eyes still full of the terror that had filled them when he first heard the approaching footsteps. That much Treves could reconstruct for himself. He supposed it was only natural that approaching sounds should still frighten Merrick until he grew to know who was likely to be coming. What puzzled Treves somewhat was the gas-lamp overhead, which was still burning brightly. He supposed Mothershead must have left it on when she paid her final visit the night before, although it seemed strangely unlike her economical soul. Perhaps Merrick had been groping around and had accidentally put it on.

Treves made his voice as kind and gentle as he could manage, hoping that the Elephant Man would understand his tone.

'Good morning, John. I've brought your breakfast.'

This did not have the desired effect. Merrick began to babble miserably, making no effort to emerge from his hiding place. Treves placed the bowl of porridge on the table and went closer.

'What are you doing down there?' he said, still speaking quietly. 'Come up, John, come up on the bed. The cold floor is bad for you. I won't hurt you. Come on now . . .'

He put out his hand and grasped Merrick's left, pulling as he did so. The Elephant Man slid out unresisting and allowed himself to be helped up onto the edge of the bed where he sat shivering. Treves continued talking as he turned away for the bowl, giving the frightened creature a chance to absorb the soothing murmur of his voice.

'You must eat. We must keep your strength—'

He stopped, baffled. He had looked back to the bed, to find it empty again. Merrick had slipped back to the floor and was determinedly trying to crawl into the corner again.

'What on earth is the matter with you?' Treves demanded, trying to keep a faint note of irritation out of his voice. He replaced the bowl on the table and knelt down to look into Merrick's face. He felt exceedingly foolish.

'Now please, John, you must do as I say. Come up from there.'

Again he clasped Merrick's left hand and tried to draw him forward, but this time Merrick resisted, pulling himself away further into the corner and babbling frantically.

The sound of two sharp raps took him to the door. There he found Mothershead wearing her briskest, most efficient air.

'Good morning, Mr Treves. It'll be his bath-time soon. Has he eaten?'

'Not quite yet, Mrs Mothershead. There seems to be some difficulty this morning.'

He stood back from the door to give her a view into the room and they both looked at the bed. Merrick was disappearing under it as fast as his clumsy limbs would allow.

Mothershead's face set in no-nonsense lines. 'Won't come out, eh?'

'No, he's very upset about something.'

'Just being obstinate, sir. I'll handle it.' She strode across to Merrick and took hold of his left wrist. 'All right, my son, none of this fuss. Come up from there, this instant.' Her grip tightened as she tried to yank him out from under the bed, her lips pursed with concentration. At once his muffled sounds became deep moans. He struggled ineffectually to escape and hide himself further.

'No! Don't pull at him like that.' Treves urged her. 'We don't want to frighten him more than he already is.'

But she continued to struggle until she had got Merrick seated unhappily on the side of the bed. She stood back and regarded him dispassionately.

'Honestly, sir, you must be very firm with this sort. Otherwise they'd lay about on the floor gibbering all day long. All he understands is a good smack.'

He joined her in helping to settle the creature back against the mountain of pillows. His touch was gentler than hers.

'He's had his share of "smacks", Mothershead,' he said as they worked. 'I expect that's what drives him under the bed. We must use patience and understanding with this man.'

Finished now, she stood back and confronted him. 'Perhaps you've got the time for that, Mr Treves, I certainly don't. I've got an entire hospital to look after, and you have your real patients. Don't waste your time with him, sir, it's like talking to a wall. I don't mean to be harsh, but he doesn't belong here. Truthfully, sir, what can you do for him? I'll be back later for his bath. And Mr Carr-Gomm would like to see you when you have a moment. Good day, sir.'

She walked straight out of the room without waiting for him to reply or bothering to close the door behind her. Treves closed it himself. When he lifted his head he found himself looking straight at Merrick. The man (if that was what he was) was staring at him, petrified. He seemed incapable of moving himself.

'What good *am* I to you . . . ?' Treves asked, half to himself.

The creature on the bed gave no sign of having understood. Still that awful silent stare that managed to be terrified and vacant together. Treves was swept by sudden anger at his own helplessness. He was not used to being helpless. He was used to being the man who would act for good, while others stood uselessly by. He suddenly discovered that he was ill-equipped to cope with this new feeling of frustration. Still that stare. He controlled himself and came to sit on the bed.

'I can't help you unless you help me, unless I know what you are feeling,' he said gently. 'I believe there's something back there, there's something you *want* to say, but I've got to understand you. Do you understand me?'

After a moment's hesitation Merrick began to babble again.

'No!' Treves interrupted him firmly. 'You are going to talk to me! We are going to show them! We're going to show them that you're not a wall. We are going to talk! Do you understand? Nod your head if you understand me!'

He wondered for a fearful moment if that ponderous head could nod without snapping off . . . but it could, it did . . . Treves breathed slowly.

'You do understand me!' he spoke slowly. 'You understand. Now you're going to say it. I've got to hear how you say things. Now, very slowly, say "yes".'

At first he thought he was getting no response and felt a stab of disappointment. Then he became aware that the monstrous lips were fighting to make a shape.

'Yes,' he encouraged.

The eyes that stared back at him were still full of a fearful suspicion. Merrick had learned distrust by long hard lessons over many years. He would not unlearn it all in a moment now. But as Treves gazed steadily at his patient he thought he detected the first hint of something else in those depths – something that might even be an excitement. The distorted lips came together, parted, and a husky sound issued from the back of the throat. Then, finally, it came; a noise that was little more than a gasp, but with the beginnings of a word buried deep in it.

'Yyyy . . . yyyye . . .' Merrick stopped and forced himself to start again. 'Yyyyyeeess.'

'*Yes, John!*' Treves found he was grasping Merrick's left arm. In his eagerness he had reached out automatically. '*Yes,*' he repeated.

'Yyyyee . . .ess.'

'Yyyesss . . . ,' Treves mouthed slowly and distinctly.

'Yyyess.' This time the word was almost clear.

'That's much better,' said Treves emphatically. 'I could understand that "yes".'

He thought he saw a hint of pleasure steal across the face, but it was hard to be sure. How could those features ever register emotion, fixed as they were in their horrible lumps? But the eyes were gleaming, Treves would swear to that. Was it possible this thing was actually intelligent?

He thrust the thought away from him violently, for if the creature was actually clear-headed enough to be aware of his own predicament, then there was no merciful God in the heavens.

'Yes,' Merrick repeated, even more distinctly. His lips were moving more easily now, as though he was beginning to get the hang of what they were for.

'Very good, oh yes,' Treves told him heartily. 'Now listen. I'm going to say some things to you and I want you to repeat them – um—' he pulled himself up on the word repeat. He must remember to keep it very simple. 'I want you to say them back to me. Do you understand? I'm going to say some things to you and I want you to say them back to me. Do you understand?'

'Yes,' said Merrick at once, but there was no way of knowing from his face whether he knew what he was saying, or was merely reciting mindlessly the word he had learned.

'Excellent! Now, say . . .' Treves leaned forward and mouthed the word emphatically, 'Hello.'

Again there was the gusty choke from the back of Merrick's throat as he fought to form his mouth into the right shape. But eventually he managed near enough.

'Hello,' said Treves again.

'Hello.' This time the word was quite discernible.

'My – name – is—' recited Treves slowly.

This one took longer, as it was impossible for Merrick to close his lips as the letter 'm' demanded.

'My – name is—' he got it out at last.

'John Merrick.'

'John – Merrick.' The Elephant Man repeated the words almost as soon as they were out of Treves' mouth. His eyes were eager for more.

'Say "Merrick",' Treves instructed him.

Again the Elephant Man fought with the 'm' and it came out more like 'n'.

'Say "Mmmmmerrick".' Treves drew out the 'm' as long as possible to see if the creature would grasp the principle.

The twisted lips came together, parted, came together again.

'Mmmmmerrick,' the Elephant Man got out at last.

'Well, that's all right. I understand you. Now say the whole thing again. Hello . . .'

He would have repeated the whole sentence, but Merrick broke in on him.

'Hello – my name is – John Mmmmerrick.'

Treves looked at him with pride. There was a quickness in that head – not an intelligence – he couldn't allow himself to think that for a moment. But a quickness such as he had found years ago in a pet dog who had learned to do tricks for him.

They worked for an hour. Merrick seemed like a sponge ready to sop up anything that was offered him. Sounds he could make in the back of his throat came to him easily. Those that required the use of his deformed lips took longer and were blurred. But he had ceased to babble incoherently, and the eyes that looked back into Treves' were bright with willingness. More and more frequently he interrupted Treves in his anxiety to show how quickly he had grasped something. Once the doctor found himself remembering an incident from his days as a medical student when in his eagerness to show himself a superior student he had rushed to reply to a question from his professor before the words were fully out of the man's mouth.

'Not so fast, Treves,' the professor had reproved him. 'We cannot all be favoured of the gods. I dare say some of your fellow students would actually *prefer* to hear me finish?'

There had been a few titters of unfriendly laughter, for the young Frederick Treves' headlong rush to be first in excellence at everything had not won him popularity among the mediocre. Even then the criticism levelled at him had been 'too ambitious – too heedless of others'.

He marvelled that he, 'favoured of the gods', should have discovered something in common with this pitiable, unfavoured creature. But Merrick's hurry to demonstrate that he had understood was developing a faint but perceptible 'show-off' element that made Treves grin in sympathetic memory.

He was in a thoroughly good mood when a knock on his door disturbed him.

'Come in.' He swivelled his chair round to find himself confronting Mothershead and bounded up to speak to her, full of a joviality that made her eye him warily. 'Why, my dear Mrs Mothershead, how good of you to join us. Mr Merrick,' Treves wheeled back to face Merrick, 'will you please introduce yourself?'

Hesitantly but with clear emphasis, Merrick looked Mothershead directly in the eyes and said, 'Hello, my name is John Merrick.'

Mothershead gaped. 'Good Lord, Mr Treves.'

'We've made tremendous strides today, Mothershead,' he told her exuberantly. 'He listens and repeats with great attention, and this certainly isn't easy for him.'

She had recovered her composure and confronted him severely.

'Parrots can do as much, Mr Treves. It's all very nice,

but I don't see the point. You know they won't let him stay here.'

Treves lowered his voice and edged her firmly to the door.

'I'm sure that if Mr Merrick made a good impression on the Hospital Committee they'd see that he's the exception to their rule,' he said. He rushed on as she opened her mouth. 'Now I'm not expecting miracles. I'm not saying he'll be able to read or write, but I do think I can get him to think for himself. I'm going to arrange things with Carr-Gomm right now.'

He looked back at Merrick and raised his voice. 'That was very good, John, very good. That's all for today. We shall do some more tomorrow. Mothershead?' he stood back to allow her to put the tray down by the Elephant Man. 'I'll see you soon, John.'

It was easy enough, he thought as he descended the stairs, to say he was going to 'arrange things with Carr-Gomm'. He knew, and doubtless by now Mothershead also knew, that the chairman was not really on his side. He had been given time, but only time to get Merrick out of the building. As for the Hospital Committee, Treves had for them the contempt that a medical man feels for those who are not medically qualified, but who yet have the power to over-rule him. The Committee was formed of 'administrators', businessmen with a talent for the affairs of the world, or, as Treves would have put it, ignoramuses. The only one he had the slightest respect for was Carr-Gomm himself, and he knew how hard it was to make an impression on that wily brain.

The chairman's first words when Treves had seated himself confirmed his fears.

'Have you contacted the British Home and the Royal Hospital?'

'Ah – no sir. I had planned to see them later today.'

'Good. How is the patient?'

'He's doing very well. In fact that's why I came to see you. I think that if I were to present Mr Merrick to the

88

Hospital Committee, then they would have a chance to see for themselves not only the extraordinary nature of the disease, but of the man as well. If the committee had a chance to speak with him, hear him say a few words for himself, I'm sure they would see him as a patient, rather than as a violation of the rules.'

'A few words?' Carr-Gomm looked at him sharply. 'I thought he was imbecile?'

'Well, sir, perhaps I should explain . . .'

'I really don't think that's necessary, Treves. I'm quite sure the Committee will be able to make an equitable decision on the merits of the case, such as they are.' He gave a faint dismissive accent to the last four words.

'I don't agree,' Treves persisted. 'No one can make a reasonable decision about this man's future without at least meeting him. No doctor would presume to diagnose a patient he had never met.'

'No, Treves. It's out of the question.' Carr-Gomm's voice took on the deadly geniality that meant his mind had closed. 'Now if it was up to me, I'd say "Certainly, let's meet the fellow, by all means." I'm sorry, I simply can't speak for the other members of the Committee.'

'Then will *you* meet him, as a representative of the Committee?'

Carr-Gomm gave him a tired look. 'Mr Treves, it's out of the question. I want to hear as soon as possible what the other hospitals can do. I'm sorry.'

There was no arguing with that face with its careful look of bland kindliness. Carr-Gomm's tone was final, his attitude of leaning back in his chair was filled with expectation of Treves' immediate departure. Treves got out of the room as civilly as he could, but it was hard when his temper was beginning to flicker.

He didn't know what he'd expected to hear from Carr-Gomm. Certainly not sympathetic partisanship. Gomm had lived too long for that and seen too much. It was not in his nature to come down firmly on anybody's side. But reason, justice, a willingness to listen, these he had secretly hoped for; and he had been met with the dead stone wall of officialdom.

Treves walked down the corridor towards the stairwell and started down the steps, barely seeing where he was going until his eye focused sharply on the next landing below him and disclosed the unwelcome presence of Bytes. At the same moment Bytes spotted him and halted on the landing, yelling upwards like a fox that has sighted the prey.

'I want my man back,' he bawled.

Treves hastened down the stairs. The last thing he wanted was Carr-Gomm to hear this unsavoury creature and emerge from his office. He met Bytes half-way down and was immediately enveloped in a cloud of gin fumes.

'Just a moment,' he snapped. 'How did you get in here?'

Bytes glowered, refusing to be diverted. 'Never mind that. I want my man.'

'He's still very sick. Please come downstairs with me. I'll explain the situation.' He attempted to take Bytes by the arm and edge him back down the stairs. He made it as far as the first landing before Bytes wriggled free and bawled into Treves' face.

'DON'T . . . Don't muck about with me! You've had plenty of time to fix him up, and he's leaving with me, NOW. Do you understand me? Now, Mr Treves. We had a bargain!'

'You misunderstood,' said Treves flatly. 'This man suffered a severe fall, if you take my meaning.' He stared back at Bytes, feeling the hopelessness of trying to frighten a man made belligerent by drink and desperation. Some distant part of his mind prayed that no-one in the hospital would hear Bytes yelling about their bargain. 'He's my patient now and I must do what . . .'

'Pull the other one, why don't you! We made a deal!'

'I know what you've done to him and he's never going back to that.'

'He's a freak! That's how they live. We're partners, he and I, business partners. You're wilfully depriving me of my livelihood!' The legal sounding phrases came out with a dreadful practised ease. Treves wondered how many police interventions Bytes had fought off in the past.

'All you do is profit from another man's misery!' he said.

Bytes thrust his face closer. A terrible knowingness shadowed his eyes. Treves had to fight to prevent himself from flinching.

'You think you're better than me?' Bytes whispered at him. '*YOU* wanted to show the freak to all your doctor chums and make a name for youself. *You*, my friend. So I gave him to you. On trust, in the name of science! And now I want him back.'

'You don't own this man!' Treves said, tight-lipped with fury.

'*I want him back!*'

'So you can beat him? So you can starve him? A dog in the street would fare better with you!' Treves had forgotten about caution and was now bawling back.

'I've got my rights, damn you, and I'm going to the authorities!'

'Well, go to the authorities . . .' said a bored, silky voice from above them.

Both men wheeled to see the elegant figure of Carr-Gomm regarding them from the top step. When he was quite sure he had struck both of them dumb with amazement he continued. 'By all means do so. In fact, I'll fetch them myself. I'm quite sure they'd be very interested in your story, as well as ours.'

Livid, knowing himself defeated, Bytes glared at Treves, then at Carr-Gomm, then at Treves again.

'Now I think we really do understand one another,' said Treves.

Bytes almost choked on his own venom. 'Right . . . right . . .' he seemed incapable of saying anything else but these words in threatening tones. Slowly he backed down the stairs, his eyes flickering back and forth between Carr-Gomm and Treves. It would have been hard to say which of them he loathed the most at that moment. When he reached the landing a change came over him. His hatred seemed to drop from him like a cloak he had shrugged off. His aspect became casual, that of a man who has decided to cut his losses and search out the next good thing. The look he gave them before he vanished down the stairs was almost cheeky.

Treves and Carr-Gomm were left to stare at each other, both feeling they had been led into territory they had not meant to travel. It was Carr-Gomm who spoke first.

'Singularly unpleasant chap . . .' he said uneasily, 'uh . . . I don't suppose there would be any harm in my meeting your . . . patient, Mr Treves.'

Nothing in Carr-Gomm's manner altered. He spoke in precisely the same tone he had used to dash Treves' hopes a few minutes earlier. His surface remained as it always was, bland, imperturbable, smiling as inscrutably as a Chinese mandarin. It took a moment for Treves to see beyond the manner to the words. When he realized what had been said, he stammered out his gratitude.

'Thank you very much, sir. Shall we say in a few days then?'

'Shall we say two o'clock tomorrow afternoon?' Carr-Gomm replied with a smile.

'Wh . . . whatever is most convenient for you, sir.'

'Two o'clock then.' Carr-Gomm half turned to go, then turned back, troubled. 'You know, Treves . . . it seems this acquaintance of yours has become rather more than just an acquaintance.'

'. . . yes, sir.'

Treves escaped quickly before he could be asked any more questions. Carr-Gomm watched him go, an expression of dissatisfaction on his face. It was aimed entirely at himself, for allowing his disgust for Bytes to lure him into becoming involved where he had meant to remain aloof.

'Elephant Man?' he muttered crossly as he returned to his office. 'I don't *want* to meet an Elephant Man.'

CHAPTER EIGHT

'Freddie—'.

It was the second time Anne had said his name, and now she sighed a little impatiently. From where she sat at her dressing-table she could see his reflection on the other side of their bed. He didn't seem to have heard her.

She wanted him to look up and say how pretty she looked with her hair flowing over her shoulders. The light was dim now, just one flickering gas-lamp, and in the shadows she could still see herself as the Anne Mason who had married the promising young doctor fourteen years ago. Two children and the cares of house-keeping had added a few lines to her face and a couple of inches to her frame, but in the twilight it was possible to ignore these if you wanted to. Soon it would not be possible in any light. Anne felt her youth slipping inexorably through her fingers and tonight she wanted to be reassured that it had not yet all gone. But her husband sat there staring into space, and didn't seem to care for the fresh lace on her nightie or the gleam in her hair.

'Freddie—' she coaxed him again. 'Freddie don't look so glum.'

He made a wry mouth. 'I shouldn't. We made great progress today. I taught him to repeat a few basic phrases. He did rather well too, but I had to lead him every step of the way. Though frankly at times I was unsure of who was leading whom.'

She had to suppress a sound of impatience. This was not what she had wanted to hear. She did not understand him when he talked like this and he knew she didn't, but he continued to do it because her understanding was not important. He simply needed someone there so that he couldn't actually be accused of talking to himself. She wound a drifting blonde curl round her finger and sighed.

'What do you mean?' she said dutifully.

'Are you listening to me?' he looked up and seemed to become aware of her for the first time.

'Of course, darling. Go on about your Elephant Man.' Anne Mason was a headmaster's daughter who had had wifely duty drummed into her by a stiff-backed, stiff-necked mother who considered that she and her husband should live only one life – his. Those lessons were too deeply ingrained to desert Anne even at this moment when she was totally exasperated. So she unwound the curl and settled her face into an expression of deep interest. Treves plunged on as though addressing a meeting of colleagues, trying to articulate what had obscurely nagged at him all afternoon.

'Well, I wasn't sure whether he was parroting me because that's all he was capable of, or whether he sensed that that's all I wanted to hear, and he was trying to please me.'

'But I thought you said that he was rather – simple.'

'He is. I mean – I've always thought he was. I think he must be. Or is that just something I've wished upon him to make things simpler for myself?'

'Frederick, why are you so troubled over this?'

'I don't know.' He ran a hand miserably through his hair. 'I can't explain it. If this is an intelligent man, trapped in the body of a monster, then I'm under a moral obligation to help free that mind, free that spirit as best I can, to help him live as full and content a life as possible.

'But – if he's an imbecile, whose body I can't treat and whose mind I can't touch, well, then my obligation is discharged. They can put him where they will. He won't be bothered, I won't be bothered, but everyone's conscience can remain free and untroubled. And that is my dilemma. What is in his mind.'

She was not a profound woman. Much of what he said was beyond her. But her love for him had detected the undercurrent of bitterness in his voice. She forgot her own annoyance and came to sit beside him on the bed, wrapping her arms round him.

94

'Perhaps you're just polishing a stone,' she said gently. 'Endowing this Elephant Man with qualities he doesn't possess.'

'And what qualities are those?' he said impatiently. 'Intelligence or stupidity?'

She withdrew her arms from him, cold and hurt at what seemed to her a rejection. She had thought her meaning was perfectly plain. It had seemed ambiguous to him only because he was still absorbed in a world from which he shut her out. She went to her own side of the bed and climbed in.

'I'm sure I don't know, Freddie,' she said with her back to him.

He turned to her, contrite. 'I'm sorry. I don't know either. I just don't know.'

She twisted onto her back to look up at him, and said the lame feeble words that were all she could think of.

'Well, these things take time.'

'I've only got until two o'clock tomorrow afternoon, when Carr-Gomm meets him. Somehow, between now and then I've got to make John Merrick at least seem like an intelligent man . . . it's my only hope. Why am I fooling myself? Nothing short of John delivering the Sermon on the Mount is going to sway Carr-Gomm . . .'

His voice, which had become distracted, was cut off abruptly by Anne's hand over his mouth, as she sat up suddenly. With her other hand she reached overhead and pulled the chain on the gas-lamp. In the darkness she put her arms lovingly about him, pressed her mouth against his and tried a remedy that had found no place in Mrs Mason's *Housewive's Almanac*.

'I'm here, Mr Renshaw.'

The clock was just striking one in the distance. Renshaw had almost given up hope of seeing Betty that night. But now here she was standing just outside his cubby-hole,

95

looking as though it would only take a word to make her run for it.

'That's right, Betty.' He slipped out and put an arm round her. 'Don't let's waste any time then. It's this way.'

He drew her down the corridor, into the Receiving Room and out on the other side. She offered no resistance till they reached the last flight of stairs before the Isolation Ward, but then she stiffened suddenly and tried to draw back.

'Mr Renshaw, is he really – ?'

'Horrible, darling,' he assured her. 'That's why you want to see him, isn't it?'

'I dunno—'

His arm had tightened across her shoulders, making retreat impossible.

'You're not going to tell me I've been wasting my time, are you, Betty?' His voice became coaxing but the hint of steel beneath it was unmistakable. 'When I think of the girls I could have brought on a treat like this – I wouldn't like to think I'd been wasting my time . . .'

'No, Mr Renshaw . . .' she gasped.

'That's better. This way.'

Together they climbed the last short flight of stairs and he rammed the door open. Even in the dim light the Elephant Man's deformity was clearly visible. Betty gave a shriek which was echoed by Merrick, and wriggled free of Renshaw's arm. He let her go. She wouldn't go far. He'd find her downstairs, sobbing and crying most likely. And then, of course, he'd have to comfort her, and in the course of doing so he'd naturally claim his reward.

Renshaw could see the Elephant Man making frantic efforts to scramble under the bed. He was laughing as he closed the door and started down the stairs.

Anne found herself alone when she woke the following morning. In the dim light her eyes made out the time – 5.30. She had a vague sense of having been woken by the

96

closing of a door, and a glance out of the window confirmed it. Her husband was hurrying along Wimpole Street as though driven by devils, and even as she watched him he turned a corner and vanished.

She sat by the window for a long time, not consciously thinking, but brooding with a sense of loneliness. She had reached Frederick only briefly the night before; she knew that. Then he had slipped willingly back into that distant world that had started as a fascinating challenge and was rapidly becoming a torment for him.

She sighed as she went back to bed. Often she wished that he could learn to be more cynical, like other men. But then, he would not be the man she loved.

Treves ran through the streets, searching for a cab that would get him to Mile End quickly, but not expecting to find one at such an hour. He could not have stayed at home a moment longer. He felt driven with inspiration. A kind of glorious terror possessed him. He had the answer. It had come to him as he lay awake in the small hours with Anne sleeping quietly beside him.

It was often so. She could not reach his mind with her own, and sometimes that chasm yawned between them. But she could reach his mind with her sweet body. Sated with the gifts she brought him in the decorous darkness, he would find the ideas falling into place in his head, the pieces interlocking neatly as if they had been oiled. In the blue-grey dawn the inspiration had come to him, and he had got up and left her. It wasn't the first time she had woken to find herself alone. He tried to make a mental note to make it up to her that night, then made an impatient noise, because he knew he would forget.

The idea was beautiful in its simplicity. A psalm. He would teach Merrick a Psalm. Carr-Gomm was a pious, God-fearing man with a plain uncomplicated belief in his Maker and a disposition to think kindly of all who worshipped in whatever degree. It was something that sat oddly with the legal precision of his soul. Like so many strands in the chairman's character it plaited badly with other strands. Because of his exposed position of authority, his inconsistencies were more nakedly revealed.

Treves planned to make use of this aspect of Carr-Gomm now. Just let Merrick recite a Psalm convincingly – the Twenty-Third would be a good choice – and in Carr-Gomm's eyes he would have acquired a golden patina that would assure him of the chairman's protection. Treves increased his speed.

It was 6.30 before he reached the hospital. The porter gave him a sleepy shrug. Treves took the stairs two at a time until he was on the top floor. He was heaving for breath and had to lean against the door of the Isolation Ward.

When Treves let himself in, Merrick was asleep, propped up against the mountain of pillows at the head of the bed, his head dropped forward against his drawn-up knees. Treves closed the door quietly and regarded his patient. How could Merrick sleep in that uncomfortable position? He tried imagining it for a moment and at once he could feel the strain on his spine that would turn into an intolerable ache before the night was over. Never to be able to lie down, to stretch out luxuriously – how would it feel?

Bytes' words came back to him – something about Merrick dying from a broken neck if he tried to lie flat. Presumably you could do anything, however uncomfortable, if you knew you'd die if you didn't.

He listened to the heavy wheezing noise Merrick made as he slept, and shuddered.

'John—' he touched him on the shoulder. 'John, wake up. I've come to see you.'

The wheezing turned into a violent snort as Merrick jerked himself out of his sleep and hauled his head up with a force that seemed likely to break his neck. For a moment his eyes were defenceless and Treves was shocked at the

98

naked terror in them. How often had Merrick been startled out of sleep to be kicked or cuffed or jeered at?

'It's all right,' he said quickly. 'It's only me. It's all right, John.'

The fear died away. The eyes became blank again.

'Hallo – my name is John Merrick,' he intoned.

'That's right, John. I want you to say that to someone I'm bringing to see you today – as perfectly as you can. Don't look alarmed—' for Merrick had flinched away at the mention of a stranger. 'It's a friend – someone who'll be kind to you, and I want you to speak politely to him as I've taught you. I'm going to teach you a few more phrases as well, so that you can make some polite conversation. And a Psalm. I don't suppose you know what that is, do you? It's a poem in the Bible, a very beautiful poem. I've got just a few hours to teach you to say it perfectly. Where is the Bible, by the way? It doesn't seem to be here.'

He found the book at last on the window-sill, well away from the table where it had been left. He shrugged. It was natural for Merrick to be fingering the objects in the room.

'We'll start with the conversation,' he said, sitting down, 'and we'll see if we can get you used to that before someone comes to wash and dress you. Then after breakfast we'll start on the Psalm.

'When our visitor arrives I'll show him into the room, and I'll say to you, "May I introduce you to Mr Carr-Gomm?" and you will say, "Hallo, my name is John Merrick." Let's try that . . .'

They were deep in their work when Mrs Mothershead came in at eight o'clock. She looked disapproving when she saw Treves already there but said nothing, and Treves did not invite comment. As soon as he could decently get rid of her he pulled out the Bible. He felt he had done all he could with the polite conversation. If Merrick shaped up as well as he promised to, Carr-Gomm should be convinced.

By one o'clock he felt he had it. He had settled for teaching Merrick the first half of the Twenty-Third Psalm perfectly rather than the whole Psalm imperfectly. It was more important for Merrick to seem to know what he was saying than to be able to recite large chunks.

For the last time Merrick ran through it from memory.

'The Lord is my shepherd, I shall not want,' he enunciated slowly and not too indistinctly. 'He maketh me to lie down in green pastures; He leadeth me beside still waters.' As he heard these words Treves became more than ever convinced that Merrick had no notion of the meaning of what he was saying. Otherwise how could he bear to recite such a grotesque denial of what his life actually was?

'He restoreth my soul,' Merrick continued huskily. 'He guideth me in the paths of righteousness . . . ,' he trailed away.

'Righteousness for his name's sake.' Merrick took up at once.

Treves breathed again. Only one failure of memory was more than he had hoped for.

'Very good, very good. Now when your visitor comes today I want you to say it exactly the way you said it just now. I will introduce him to you, and you will say the words you've learned.

'If you have any trouble with any of the words, I'll help you. I'm sure you'll be just fine. If you do as well for him as you've done for me, then I'm sure our visitor will be very pleased. Now let's go through the whole thing again, shall we? I'll say, "May I introduce you to Mr Carr-Gomm?" And you will say—'

'Hallo, my name is John Merrick,' the Elephant Man came in prompt on cue. 'I am very pleased to meet you.'

They went through it all once more before Treves left, telling Merrick to rest until he returned with Carr-Gomm. As soon as he was on his own, he became sharply aware that he had not eaten yet. Absorbed in teaching Merrick he had no attention to spare for his own needs, but now he was ravenous.

He left the hospital by a quiet side door, hoping not to be accosted by Mothershead wanting him for a patient or

Fox demanding heartily, 'What are you up to, you old dog?', and made his way to a small eating-house nearby. Over a chop he brooded on the coming confrontation.

He had few real fears by now that Merrick could be considered intelligent in the normal adult way. The Elephant Man followed what was taught him with the parrot ability of a bright four-year-old. That was all to the good. With luck he had learned enough to get by this afternoon, and further limited progress would be possible later.

He had no twinge of conscience about the deception he was planning to practise that day. Carr-Gomm did not understand, and where people did not understand they were not entitled to the whole truth. Besides, the chairman had forced the situation on him by fixing this early meeting. Treves' conscience was reserved for the pitiful creature in the Isolation Ward, snatched from his fear and misery and now threatened with an early return to it.

Alone with himself Treves could admit that Bytes' shaft had gone home. 'You wanted the freak to show to all your doctor chums and make a name for yourself.' An instinctive denial had risen up in him at the time, but his hard honest nature would not let him forget that he had gone into that tent looking for something rare, something that would provide the basis for a fine lecture, a learned paper, a book even.

A young doctor had his way to make, and quickly. His post at the London Hospital, his practice in Wimpole Street, these were good solid achievements. But they were not likely to make his name, and Frederick Treves desperately wanted a great and illustrious name in the medical world.

From here he fell to defending himself. There was nothing intrinsically shameful about ambition. Nor was he the only one who hunted down specimens of rare and hideous diseases.

He suddenly felt a small twinge of disgust at where his thoughts had led him. On the very day he was to try and convince Carr-Gomm of Merrick's humanity, he had fallen into the vulgar error of thinking of him as 'a specimen'.

Did all this help, his hours of work with Merrick, amount then to no more than fooling the world that his specimen was a human being, so that he could go on having the use of him as a specimen?

Treves knew himself to be a hard man, even ruthless, as a doctor must often be. But the glimpse he had just received into his own soul shook him. It was like dropping your hand into a pool of clear bright water and finding that you had disturbed a bed of slimy stinking life. He discovered that he had no appetite left, paid his bill and departed.

To quieten the naggings of his conscience, he redoubled his efforts with the chairman as they made their way along to the Isolation Ward.

'It's only a physical problem,' he said, anxious that Carr-Gomm should not be put off by the blurring of Merrick's words. 'He has trouble with certain sounds because of the constrictive deformity of the mouth. His face is entirely incapable of expression. He can try, but he cannot smile . . . But he can talk, and has great eagerness to make contact with people who will let him. So if you have any difficulty understanding what he is saying, just tell me and I'll make it clear.' He knew he sounded overanxious.

'Speaking is one thing, Treves, but can the man comprehend?'

Treves took a long time to answer. Fooling Carr-Gomm in a roundabout way was one thing, but he was reluctant to tell him a direct lie.

'As I said, it's only a physical problem,' he repeated uneasily. 'But I do feel that Mr Merrick is very flattered that you're taking the time and trouble to meet him, and he's most anxious to make a good impression, so he might seem rather nervous.'

'He needn't. I have no desire to cause him any discomfort. Did you make those enquiries we spoke about?'

'Yes. I called on both the British Home and Royal

Hospital for Incurables yesterday afternoon. I'm afraid that they weren't very encouraging, but they said they'd bring it up at their next committee meeting, so we should have their answer shortly.'

'Fine, fine,' said Carr-Gomm heartily. 'You know, your dedication to this patient is an inspiring thing, Treves. But you must remember that this is a hospital, and there are many patients here – patients who can be made well, and you owe them your first consideration. Just don't become so obsessed, old man, that you begin to neglect them.'

Treves was about to protest (quite truthfully) that none of his regular patients were being neglected; but he didn't, because he knew this wasn't really what they were discussing. Carr-Gomm's love of order and moderation had risen up indignantly at the sight of what he considered a lack of proportion in Treves' dealings with the Elephant Man.

Carr-Gomm stood back when they reached the door of the Isolation Ward and allowed Treves to precede him. He did not see Merrick at first, because the Elephant Man was standing right in the middle of the floor, hidden by Treves' form. But then Treves stepped aside and Carr-Gomm found himself just four feet away from a head such as he had never seen before in his life.

Years in the law had taught him to control his feelings, but even so he could not avoid a violent start. Treves noticed with relief that Merrick could not have seen this reaction. His eyes were firmly closed. He was breathing unevenly and seemed to be holding himself rigid. Treves went up and touched him gently on the shoulder, and immediately the eyes were open, gazing trustingly into his. They both turned to Carr-Gomm who lowered his eyes in pity and disgust.

'John,' said Treves steadily, 'may I introduce you to Mr Carr-Gomm.'

'Hallo, my name is John Merrick. I am very pleased to meet you.'

Carr-Gomm was still shaken. Without thinking he

instinctively put out his right hand. Too late he realized that Merrick's own right hand could not take it.

'I'm very – pleased to meet you,' Carr-Gomm sounded unsure of himself. Before he could withdraw his hand, Merrick grasped it with his left. Treves felt a certain half-malicious pleasure at Carr-Gomm's expense. It had only been a tiny awkwardness, but of the two Merrick had coped with it the better. He saw Carr-Gomm staring at the left hand that he held, and felt the older man's shock at its perfect human beauty.

After an uncomfortable silence Merrick removed his hand. Carr-Gomm nervously cleared his throat.

'How are you feeling today?' he asked politely.

'I feel much better.' Merrick's words were clear and assured. Treves began to breathe again. 'Thank you for asking. And you?'

'I'm feeling very fit thank you.' Carr-Gomm told him. 'How is your bronchitis?'

'I feel much better, thank you.'

'Are you comfortable here?'

'Everyone has been very kind. I am extremely grateful.'

Treves looked hopefully at Carr-Gomm waiting for what he had been sure would be the next line. On the odd occasions when he met patients, Carr-Gomm had a fixed routine of polite questions. It almost never varied, and he had counted on it when coaching Merrick. The next stage was always an enquiry about the hospital food.

But no enquiry came. Carr-Gomm was staring at Merrick in a kind of dumb-founded horror. Treves knew that his carefully laid plans would come to nothing if he didn't rescue the situation now.

'Mr Merrick likes the food here,' he said hastily. 'Don't you, John?'

'Oh yes,' Merrick responded on cue. 'It is much better than what I am used to.'

He stopped abruptly. As the silence grew longer, Treves realized with a sinking heart that his memory had failed him. He was growing skilled in reading the expressions in Merrick's eyes. He saw desperation in them now.

'Oh yes?' Carr-Gomm prompted in a polite but chilly voice.

The pause grew agonizing. 'And what was that, John?' Treves encouraged.

'Potatoes . . . ,' Merrick's voice trailed away.

'Yes, potatoes. But . . .' Treves prompted.

It all came back to Merrick in a rush. 'But the variety of food here is very pleasing. I commend you.'

He looked hopefully at Treves, like a dog that has done the trick right at last and waited to be praised.

Carr-Gomm was gazing very hard at Merrick. At last he said, 'I understand that you were beaten.'

Treves stiffened. He had not anticipated this line of questioning, nor had he prepared Merrick for it. Merrick's eyes were flickering helplessly from one to the other.

'Oh no,' he said at last. 'Everyone has been very kind.'

'No,' persisted Carr-Gomm. 'I meant in your former situation.'

A kind of blank despair seemed to settle over the grotesque figure as he felt the firm ground on which he'd thought he was standing turn to quick-sands under him.

'I'm feeling much better now,' he recited mechanically.

Carr-Gomm turned a level gaze on Treves, then looked back to Merrick.

'Tell me, how do you like Mr Treves,' he asked quietly. 'As a teacher.'

Treves ground his nails into his palm and cursed himself for an idiot. How could he have imagined for a moment that this child's deception would fool a man as subtle as Carr-Gomm.

'I – everyone has been very kind to me . . .' Merrick floundered.

'Of course. How long did you and Mr Treves prepare for this interview?'

Merrick looked frantically to Treves for guidance, but his mentor could no longer look him in the eye.

'– everyone has been very kind–' his voice died away.

'Yes, of course,' said Carr-Gomm smoothly. 'Well, it's been a pleasure meeting you, Mr Merrick. Good day.'

Treves recovered his wits sufficiently to say, 'Thank you John. You did very well.' He moved to the door to open it for the chairman.

Merrick watched them go, conscious that his one chance was going with them. He began to talk loudly in a frantic effort to recapture their attention.

'The Lord is my shepherd, I shall not want. He maketh me to lie down in green pastures . . .'

He continued, his voice growing in strength as the two other men left the room. On the small landing outside the Isolation Ward Carr-Gomm confronted Treves.

'It was a nice try, Treves, but the man is obviously mouthing your words.'

He leadeth me beside still waters; He restoreth my soul.

'Yes,' Treves said, too dispirited to attempt to fight back. 'I'm very sorry to have wasted your time sir. I just felt I had to do something I could to protect him.'

He guideth me in the paths of righteousness, for his name's sake.

'I'm sorry, too. He simply doesn't belong here. He'll be much happier somewhere else, where he could be constantly looked after.' His voice became kinder. 'Believe me, Frederick, it's better that it worked out this way. Good day.'

Carr-Gomm began to descend the stairs. Treves watched him go. At the back of his mind he was still registering the sound of Merrick's voice uselessly reciting what he had been taught to an empty room. And then something caught his ear, something very strange.

'Yea, though I walk through the valley of the shadow of death, I will fear no evil, Thou art with me.' Merrick's husky voice floated out to the landing. 'Thy rod and thy staff, they comfort me . . .'

Glancing back at Treves, Carr-Gomm was astonished and irritated to see him standing with his mouth open, gaping for all the world (Carr-Gomm thought) like an imbecile himself.

'What is it, Treves?'

'Thou preparest a table before me in the presence of mine enemies . . .'

Annoyed, Carr-Gomm returned up the stairs to attract Treves' attention, but the younger man was oblivious to everything but the voice coming through the open door.

'Thou anointest my head with oil; my cup runneth over.'

'I didn't teach him that part,' Treves whispered.

He dashed suddenly into the room, leaving Carr-Gomm with nothing to do but follow. In the cramped Isolation Ward they stood and listened as Merrick finished the Psalm.

'Surely goodness and loving kindness shall follow me all the days of my life, and I shall dwell in the house of the Lord forever.'

The three men stared at each other. When Treves spoke, his voice was almost violent.

'How did you know the rest? I never taught you the rest of it.'

'I don't understand,' said Carr-Gomm plaintively.

Treves forced himself to speak more calmly. He had wrecked Merrick's chances once today. If he frightened him now he would wreck his life for good.

'Tell me, John, how did you know the rest of the Twenty-Third Psalm?'

Merrick spoke hesitantly, as though confessing to a crime. 'I – I used to read the Bible every day. I know it very well, the Bible and the Book of Common Prayer. The Twenty-Third Psalm is very beautiful. It is my favourite.'

'It is mine also,' said Carr-Gomm in a quiet voice. 'Who taught you to read, Mr Merrick?'

'I was in a place – like this – many years ago. I was ill – here—' Merrick laid his hand on his left hip. 'They put me—'

'In a hospital,' Carr-Gomm supplied for him. 'And someone there taught you to read? A doctor, nurse – ?'

'No. Someone else who was ill.' Merrick spoke slowly and with difficulty; it was so many years since anyone had required him to talk, and many of the words he needed seemed to elude him. 'He taught me from the Bible – but he died. He said I could have his Bible and his prayer book. I've read from them ever since.'

'And that is all you've read?'

'Sometimes I've seen newspapers – if people leave them about.'

'Mr Merrick – these things you've read in the Bible – do they mean anything to you?' Carr-Gomm was having some difficulty expressing himself. 'I mean – when you speak of goodness and loving kindness following you all the days of your life—' he stopped, too embarrassed to continue to this creature who had known little goodness or kindness since the day of his birth.

'Oh, yes,' said Merrick simply. 'Mr Donner told me it was all true.'

'Who was Mr Donner? The man who taught you?'

'Yes. He'd been a vicar once, but he didn't want anyone but me to know. He used to say he'd "come low" to be in a pauper hospital. But he said it was all true, and I should remember God loved me, even if – even if it didn't seem as though he did.'

'And do you believe that?'

'Oh yes. Else how would Mr Treves have found me?'

'Sir,' said Treves in a strained voice, 'you have several other appointments this afternoon. Don't you think . . .'

'Yes, indeed. I mustn't tire Mr Merrick with too long a visit.' Carr-Gomm put out his left hand, which Merrick took without hesitation. The smile Carr-Gomm gave him was almost conspiratorial. 'It was a great pleasure to meet you, Mr Merrick,' he said for the second time that afternoon.

'I am very pleased to meet you.'

'I hope we can talk together again some time. Good day.'

'I'll be right back,' said Treves hurriedly as he showed Carr-Gomm to the door. He closed it firmly behind him and faced the chairman on the landing. Carr-Gomm's face was pale and he looked shaken.

'My God, how awful!' he said. 'I want to see you in my office as soon as you're finished up here. We've a good deal to discuss.' He started down the stairs.

'Of course, sir. Thank you. Thank you very much, sir.'

Half-way down the stairs Carr-Gomm stopped and looked back.

'Treves, well done.'

'Not me, sir. Mr Merrick. He succeeded in spite of me.'

Treves returned to the Isolation Ward slowly. He was unsure how he was going to face Merrick after the harm he had nearly done him.

'Pride and pomposity,' he thought bitterly. And for good measure he added an even worse sin. 'And having a closed mind from the start.'

He found Merrick back on the bed, propped up against his pillows. He was clearly exhausted by what he had been through. He opened his eyes when the door opened, and the two men looked at each other for a long moment.

'Why did you let me go on like that?' said Treves at last. 'Teaching you what you already knew. Why didn't you tell me you could read?'

'You did not ask me,' said Merrick simply.

The first rule when making a diagnosis ascertain all the facts. To have tripped over that easy hurdle after all this time!

'I never thought to ask. How can you ever forgive me?'

The young man became anxious. 'Oh no, do not say that. I frightened you. You have been so kind to me. I was afraid to say too much. People always want me to be quiet. You wanted me to speak, but I was afraid, I – forgive me.'

Merrick spoke without rancour or blame. He had long ago lost the instinct to protest. He simply accepted what came, day by day. Treves felt that he had never been so ashamed of himself as he was at this moment.

'We do have a lot to talk about, don't we?' he said. 'I have to go and see Mr Carr-Gomm now. I think you should get some rest.' At the door he stopped. 'I'll see you're given plenty to read in future.'

'Could I – ?'

'Yes, go on.'

'A newspaper. I would like to know about the world.'

'Of course. I'll see you get one. Goodbye, John.'

He found Carr-Gomm seated in his leather chair beside one of the tall windows that backed his desk. He had turned the chair so that he could see out of the window, and although he heard Treves' entrance he never moved. He looked as if he had been stunned by an unexpected blow.

'Can you imagine what his life has been like?' he said.

'Yes, I think I can.'

Carr-Gomm swung round. 'No, you can't!' he said with quiet savagery. 'You can't begin to know. No-one can.'

'No.'

Carr-Gomm rose and faced him. 'You're quite right, Treves. This is an exceptional case. And I agree that the Committee should see Mr Merrick – no!' At once Carr-Gomm held up a hand to correct himself. 'Not that way. Broadneck and the others don't like to deal with patients directly. It makes them queasy. Do you have any photographs of Mr Merrick?'

'Well, yes.'

'Excellent. We shall present them, along with the other particulars of the case to the Committee. I want them to see exactly how horribly his body has been deformed. You and I shall vouch for his inner qualities.'

'Do you think they'll go along with us?'

'Of course they will. They're reasonable men.'

Before leaving the hospital that evening Treves sought out Mrs Mothershead and had a private word with her. What he told her and what he requested of her afforded him enormous satisfaction. He would have felt slightly less complacent had he been able to see her after his departure.

Mothershead sat for a long time, her face marked by a frown which seemed to deepen the longer she thought.

Finally she rose and began to climb the stairs to the top of the hospital.

Merrick, dozing gently off, his head against his knees, was startled into wakefulness by Mothershead's abrupt entry. He looked at her apprehensively. She had never been actively unkind to him, but he knew she disapproved of him.

She walked over to the bed and took up the Bible, allowing it to fall open where it would. She handed it to Merrick.

'Read it,' she said.

Slowly his eyes focused on one paragraph and he began to read.

'Thou heardest my voice; hide not thine ear at my breathing, at my cry.'

He realized that she was no longer there. She had begun to back towards the door, a disturbed, almost frightened, look on her face.

'Credit where credit is due,' she said at last. 'You'll have the paper every morning at breakfast.'

She departed quickly. Merrick waited a moment in case she should come back. When he had heard her footsteps fading down the stairs, he looked back at the Bible in his hands. He had been reading from Lamentations.

He sat very still for a long time after she had gone, wondering if anyone else would burst in on him. He strained each nerve to catch the most distant noise. Now and then footsteps would approach the little flight of stairs that led up to the Isolation Ward, but always they passed on and at last he began to relax.

Darkness was falling outside, and all around him he could hear the sounds of a large building closing down for the night. He listened, trying to place them, but his experience was too limited for him to put names to everything he heard. Footsteps he knew, and doors shutting heavily in the distance. All these were familiar from his days in the workhouse. But the voices puzzled him. There were male voices, sober sometimes with responsibility, but always with an undertow of cheerful confidence that held nothing brutal in it. Such voices were totally outside his experience.

Strangest of all was the ripple of chatter from the nurses going off duty. Their voices were young and light-hearted, dispersing sometimes into laughter. In the whole of his life he had never heard such a thing before. He had encountered few young women – sluts in the workhouse, girls hired for an hour or two by Bytes or his other owners, goggling spectators who paid their twopence to see him, and then flung themselves into the arms of their accompanying men when he was revealed – this was his experience of the female sex before he came into the hospital. Since then there had been Nora who screamed when she saw him, and Mothershead with her stern, unyielding competence.

But this other atmosphere that reached him now – of decent good-hearted young women, relaxed and cheerful as they ended their day's work and went to their well-earned supper – had never entered his life before, and it called to him now with the appeal of the rare and exotic.

He felt a yearning to see them and cast hopeful eyes up at the barred window. It was not impossibly high and he felt his determination giving him strength. He edged slowly off the bed and, using his left hand, pulled the chair over to the window. Reaching up he was able to grasp one of the lower bars, and use it to haul himself upwards. From this perch he had a good view of that part of the hospital that formed an L-shape to the building he was in.

Most of the corridors were still well lit, and along them trickled a thin stream of girls in uniforms, going off duty. Now and then slightly older women could be seen coming in the other direction. Their faces were serious and purposeful as they prepared to take up their duties for the night. Sometimes they'd stop and engage some of the departing girls in conversation. Merrick's hand tightened on the bar he was holding as he fought to keep his perch as long as possible.

To his enchanted eyes every girl was pretty. Every normal, properly proportioned face gleamed with youth and health, every smile, however tired, was radiant. Now and then laughter floated up to him like music from another planet.

He longed to stay there forever, watching, unseen. It was so rare that his view of the world could be unclouded by its own violent reaction to himself. He told himself that he must be seeing pretty girls as they appeared to other men, their faces serene and untroubled, not distorted by horror or hardened by the effort to control it.

But the strain of holding himself up to the window was becoming intolerable. As the lights began to dim in the corridors, he edged backwards and began to grope for a way to lower himself to the floor. For a dreadful moment he feared he would lose his balance, fall back and break his neck, but he managed to steady himself against the wall until first one foot, then the other, touched the floor. Almost at once he fell onto the bed. He was breathing hard, but his eyes were triumphant.

He crawled into the comfort of the corner and nestled against the pillows. He felt as close to happiness as he ever had in his life. Treves was kind to him, Treves had promised that he should not be sent back to Bytes, and the other man – Mr Carr-Gomm, the one Treves treated as important – had said he agreed. Merrick did not believe them, it was so long ago that he had lost hope. But he savoured the words, and wondered how long he would be allowed to stay here.

The hospital was growing quiet around him. A distant hollow clang announced the closing of the iron door that barred the rear. It was almost dark, but there was still enough light for him to do what he did every night when he knew himself securely alone. He strained his ears in the silence, and when he was sure no footsteps were approaching, slipped his left hand into the pockets of the baggy trousers and brought out a small object.

It was a photograph, battered and creased, but still

discernible as the picture of a young woman of extraordinary beauty. From its style it had obviously been taken many years ago. Merrick held it propped against his drawn up knees and stared desperately at the face of the woman he *knew*, beyond any shadow of doubt, to be his mother.

How he knew with such certainty was lost deep within him. The memories of his babyhood, vague and confused to begin with had, over the years, hardened into sharpness. Now they never varied. There was always the woman with the beautiful face, cradling her baby gently against her, loving him the more for his deformity, having to part with him (he never understood why, but he knew it was for a good reason), promising to return and claim him soon. And the picture that he had possessed as long as he could remember anything, his only pledge of that long-ago promise.

Many times he had tried to look back into the very beginning, to see his mother's face as he must have seen it then – as though it were imprinted on his mind and by diligent searching he would uncover it. But no memory came to his aid. There was only the picture to remind him, and gradually the printed face had attached itself to his impressions, and when he remembered his mother now it was always with the clear features of the photograph.

He knew – again without knowing how he knew – that his mother had been tragically caught in the path of a stampeding elephant before his birth. She had escaped injury but the creature's slimy trunk had slithered over her and her horror had been so great that it had communicated itself to the child within her, and he had been born with elephant characteristics. For some reason after that they had been forced to part, and this was a great puzzle to which he returned time and time again, for he knew his mother loved him very much and would not willingly have let him go.

Her failure to return for him he explained easily enough. Ugly as he had been as a child, he knew he had become uglier as he grew, until now he was of a monstrousness that

114

far outstripped his deformity as a baby. He knew too that somehow his repellent aspect must be a punishment for some great wickedness. What it had been he could not imagine, but it was so deeply ingrained in him that everybody saw it but himself. And his mother had heard of it, and perhaps blamed him. So she never came back. She was waiting for him to learn to be better. When the time came, she would find him somehow.

As the light failed, the picture darkened to nothing and he slipped it back into his pocket. He wondered if he dared let himself sleep, or if he would be visited again by the bully who had appeared on the two previous nights. He longed to tell Treves and beg that something should be done to protect him, but he did not dare. He trusted Treves, but he did not trust the world. If he mentioned what had happened to him then somehow – he did not exactly know how – somehow the bully would know, and would come for him when Treves was not there. He must just keep quiet and bear it, as he had kept quiet and borne so much in his life.

Within an hour he knew his worst fears were to be fulfilled. The footsteps were heavier this time and approached faster. Renshaw might have been coming on a leisurely sight-seeing trip before, but this time he had a deadly purpose. He burst into the room and stood over Merrick, staring at him malevolently.

'I hear you're 'aving some trouble sleeping,' he said. Then he moved quickly, grabbing Merrick by his thin hair and jerking his head back.

At once Merrick felt himself begin to choke as his supply of air was cut off. He grabbed uselessly at Renshaw with his left hand, wheezing and gasping noisily. Renshaw's little eyes gleamed with sudden understanding.

'Head's too heavy, eh?' he said. He leaned forward, pulling his victim all the way down to the bed so that the constriction in Merrick's throat increased and he had to fight for breath. Renshaw kept on talking in a monotone.

'And I heard a nasty rumour about you. I heard you can

talk. But you can't, can you—?' He jerked again on the hair. 'Can you – can you?'

'Nooooo—' Merrick managed to gasp.

Renshaw looked at him in surprise. Despite the rumours he had heard, he had not seriously expected the Elephant Man to be able to understand and answer him. He gave a wolfish grin of pleasure at his victim's desperation.

'No – no, you can't. Because one word about me out of that stinking cakehole – just *one* word, and you'll 'ave no trouble sleeping. No trouble at all. You understand me? *Do* you?'

'Yyyee-ess.' Merrick managed to croak. He felt blackness descending on him. Just in time Renshaw let him go and strolled casually to the door. There he turned to enjoy the sight of his victim gulping in huge breaths.

'Don't forget,' he said. 'Just – don't forget.'
Then he was gone.

CHAPTER NINE

It took time to persuade the Elephant Man to speak about himself, and even longer for the story to come out. He protected himself from the horrors of his past by locking them away behind an iron door. Any attempt to throw open that door reduced him to the deepest distress, turning him again into a babbling, confused creature, incapable of any communication save a moan of misery. At last Treves decided that it was cruelty to press him, and left off.

But then one morning, about four days after Carr-Gomm's visit, Treves was examining the hip whose disease or injury caused Merrick to limp, and he asked, 'How did this happen, John? Do you remember?'

'Somebody kicked me—' a tense silence followed these words, and Merrick seemed to be holding himself stiff, '—in the workhouse,' he added at last.

'I see.' Treves kept his voice casual, but excitement was taking hold of him. This was the first time Merrick had ever volunteered the word "workhouse". 'And did it hurt a lot after that kick?'

'Yes. For a long time – I couldn't walk properly. So they sent me to hospital.'

'What did the hospital say about it? Can you remember?'

'They said it was cracked – I think. But it was too late to treat it. The crack had got diseased.'

Tubercular complications following a neglected injury, Treves thought mechanically.

'Do you know how old you were then?'

'The – workhouse people said I was seven. I'd been there five years. I was two when my mother left me.'

'Do you remember your mother?'

'Oh yes!' Merrick's face was incapable of expression. Nonetheless it seemed to Treves that a great light broke across it at the mention of his mother. 'She was very beautiful . . . She could not help leaving me there, you must not think badly of her. She didn't know how it would be . . .' Merrick choked suddenly as though he were weeping. '. . . she didn't know . . . or she'd never . . .'

'John, you don't have to talk about the workhouse,' said Treves quickly. 'It's all over.'

Merrick looked at him. 'But you wanted to know,' he said simply. 'You asked me many times to tell you . . .'

'Yes, but not if it's going to distress you so much.'

They left it there, but the following day Merrick again brought up the subject. Treves could tell it was an effort, but Merrick seemed determined to force himself, as though he had decided to refuse his benefactor nothing, whatever the cost to himself. The story took several days to come out, not merely because Merrick constantly grew too upset to continue, but because his difficulty in speaking made it a slow process.

Treves, listening attentively, found himself being drawn into Merrick's nightmare world as though it were his own. He had the sympathetic imagination to put himself in his patient's place and see things through his eyes, and now it was as though his own safe, happy world had flown apart into a thousand pieces, to be replaced by the unending hell of deformity and life as a public spectacle.

There was the grief of abandonment, the freezing sense of being alone in a hostile world. There was food, never quite enough and never appetizing; clothes that were passed on as others grew out of them, clothes that were falling to bits, crawling with lice.

There was 'the difference'. The child's mind, clear and sharp in its dreadful prison, soon became aware that other children survived by banding together and giving each other the care others would not give. But none of these rough-hewn little families wanted him. If he approached he was driven off with jeers and blows. Even in the workhouse children played – but not with him. At meal times he would find himself alone at one end of the table as the others drew away. Often he would have nothing to eat, for the others snatched his food and he was too clumsy to defend himself. He was 'different', but he did not know why. There were no mirrors.

He knew he was ugly, because they said so. He did not know what ugly meant, but he heard it so often that eventually the word 'ugly' became a name to which he would respond. Then they would howl with laughter.

There was the kick – indistinguishable at first from other kicks, but the pain did not stop. At the hospital he encountered people who were seeing him for the first time. Some of them screamed. There was a woman yelling, 'You're not bringing that thing in here,' and the man from the workhouse retorting, 'And I'm not taking him back either, I've got my orders.'

He was dumped, and the paupers' hospital took him in because it had no choice.

In the hospital there was a voice that, if not kind, was not actually hostile. It came from a tall cadaverous man with grey cheeks and despairing eyes, who stared at him and said, 'You look the way I feel inside.'

This was Mr Donner, the clergyman whose drinking and scandalous behaviour had caused him to be unfrocked. Without a livelihood Donner had taken to the road. From time to time he tried to make a new life for himself as a teacher, for he was a man of considerable learning. But as soon as he got two shillings to rub together he turned them into whisky. He had been sacked from job after job. He was dying now, of drink and despair.

He seemed to find Merrick's very deformity endearing. He was the first to talk to him and discover the quick responsive brain that the stumbling speech had hidden. He protected him, taught him to read, taught him to write with his left hand. Above all he taught him his own simple shining faith which had survived, unscathed amidst the destruction of his life.

One night Donner had given the misshapen little boy his own Bible.

'You have it now' was all he said. 'I'll not need it.'

When Merrick went to find his friend the next morning Donner's bed was empty. Somebody thought he'd died in the night. Nobody seemed to know where he might have been taken.

From the hospital to the workhouse – another workhouse this time, run by a man called Cossins. It was Cossins who first showed him a mirror and made him look into it. He was old enough then to understand the difference between himself and others, and he had cried at the sight, till someone slapped him for being a pest.

Then the nightmare of his life really began. Before he had been merely rejected, now he was actively persecuted. He could do nothing right for Cossins. Whenever they met (and it was strangely often), Cossins would fault him for moving too fast or too slow, making too much noise or sitting in 'sullen' silence, for being too greedy or for leaving his food.

The punishment varied. One of Cossins' favourites was to make his victim stand in a prominent place in a corridor beneath a notice that labelled him 'The Fruit of Evil', and anyone who passed by was free to knock some of the evil out of the sinner. Cossins, who was much given to pious exhortations, was fond of declaring that only great deformity of soul could account for such deformity of body, and that it was the duty of a good man to 'drive the devil out' by such methods as might suggest themselves. And the methods that suggested themselves to Cossins' sadistic mind were increasingly ingenious.

He would force the little boy to lie down flat on the floor, knowing that the weight of his head would force his neck back till his windpipe was constricted and he was choking. Cossins would wait until the last moment before allowing Merrick up, then seize the semi-conscious child and tell him that that was what it felt like to die, and he should remember it and mend his ways.

Cossins permitted no brawling amongst the inmates of his workhouse, but anyone was free to attack Merrick. If it was discovered, Merrick would be thrashed by Cossins as a punishment for 'starting a fight'. Once the child attempted to hide, hoping that once darkness fell he could creep out and run away. But when his absence was discovered (as it soon was, there being little else to make life interesting), the hunt was up. Every man, woman and child in the building searched for him, and when he was discovered Cossins thrashed him as a trouble-maker.

When Merrick was sixteen, Cossins died of apoplexy. His place was taken by a man who lacked the inclination to torment, but whose wife insisted that the 'monster' be got off the premises. Merrick was duly sold to a down-at-heel travelling showman whose dancing dog had just died. Because of the extraordinary nature of his deformity, he fetched the relatively high price of £1.15.0.

His life improved to the extent that he was not actually ill-treated. The man did not wish to damage an expensive investment. But the investment proved worthless. The exhibit was closed down in town after town. The 'owner' neglected and starved the Elephant Man, and after a year he sold him to a circus.

He was kept a virtual prisoner, housed like an animal, shut off from the world, which he now saw only through a peephole in a showman's cart. A dozen times a day he would have to expose his deformities before a gaping crowd who would scream and run from him, or stare and poke his growths. When he was not needed for exhibition he would be permitted the only happiness possible to him – to creep away into the darkness and hide. As he crouched there, he would hear the laughter of children outside, enjoying the 'fun of the fair'.

It was in the circus that Merrick had acquired his strange disguise. The black cloak had originally belonged to 'The Great Marvelloso', a magician who used its capacious folds to hide a good deal of clumsy fumbling around with flags and paper flowers. He had discarded it in favour of another of more glorious aspect, and his wife, a motherly soul who pitied the Elephant Man from a distance although unable to look him in the face, had got to work. She ripped out the red satin lining, set buttons in the front, and cut a slit in the left side, for the arm. Then she shortened the cloak by a foot, and with the spare material she fashioned a hat wide enough to take a huge head. From somewhere she conjured up the grey flannel to make a mask that she sewed all round the brim of the hat, with a hole just big enough for seeing through.

Then she went across to the wagon where Merrick was kept, and presented him with his new attire. She managed to explain it all to him without looking at him, and when he tried to thank her she fled.

To Merrick the cloak brought a grain of comfort, not only because it hid him but because it had a capacious pocket that could take his Bible. Somehow he had managed to preserve it all these years, chiefly because no-one else thought it valuable enough to steal. But he lived in terror of losing it, and now he had a place where he could keep it in some kind of safety. When the light was good enough and he was sure he was alone he would take it out and read again and again the words of promise and hope that made his existence tolerable, and that saved him from going mad.

He lived three years in the circus. His 'owner' was repeatedly forbidden to exhibit him, but always the circus moved off in time to prevent the order being enforced. After three years the man decided to strike out on his own. He left the circus, taking Merrick with him, but almost immediately they fell on bad times. He was closed down in one city, then another. He began to look for ways to rid himself of the Elephant Man, at a profit. On the outskirts of London he met a man called Bytes, and they struck a bargain.

When Merrick reached this point he stopped and looked timidly at Treves, uncertain how to take his silence.

Treves was standing at the window, his back to Merrick. He was fighting down a raging anger such as he had never known. Much of the story was as he had imagined, except that it was a thousand times worse, but somewhere in the telling of it he had discarded his professional detachment like a too-heavy coat, and now felt the intensity of Merrick's suffering without any defence.

He was honest enough to admit that part of his anger was directed against himself. Dress it up as he could with worthy phrases about the necessity for medical discovery, the fact remained that he too had used Merrick for his own purposes, and this was very bitter to him now.

'Do you want to know any more?' Merrick asked.

Treves turned at last. He knew his face must show how shaken he had been.

'Not today, John. I don't think either of us could stand it.'

When he had made sure Merrick was comfortable for the night, he went straight to Carr-Gomm. The chairman took one look at him and poured him a large whisky. Then he sat in sympathetic silence while Treves spewed out the savage shame he felt for his own species.

'With the exception of Donner, he seems to have brought out the worst instincts of just about everyone he's ever met. He's had a life that a fiend might have invented in Hell. He's had no childhood, no happiness – nothing to look back on but horror, and nothing to look forward to but more years as a spectacle, and the workhouse at the end of it.

'And yet – the incredible part is—' Treves fumbled for words to express his astonishment at what he had discovered, while Carr-Gomm waited patiently, '—the incredible part is that he has not become brutalized by this life. As a doctor I've seen too much pain and suffering to subscribe to the myth that it ennobles people. Mostly it makes men self-centred and callous to the needs of others. Yet in John Merrick I've met the one man in ten million who could react differently. He doesn't hate his fellow-men, who have done so much to deserve his hatred, nor has he degenerated into a despairing melancholic.

'He's remained sensitive, intelligent – and lovable. His nature is gentle and affectionate. He's without cynicism or

123

resentment, and in all he's told me I've never heard him utter an unkind word about anyone.'

'Remarkable,' said Carr-Gomm in a quiet voice. 'And yet I can believe it. The little I saw of him bears it out. What do you think about this story of the mother?'

'I can't believe it. Whoever his real mother was she obviously dumped him at the first conceivable opportunity. To protect himself from the pain of rejection, he's invented a fantasy figure in her place. Maybe once, a long time ago, some woman was kind to him briefly, and he's convinced himself that that was his mother. He's clung to the memory because he had to cling to something to make his life bearable, and over the years he's endowed her with every virtue. She was beautiful, she was motherly, she loved him – I'm sure he really believes all this, but as far as I'm concerned she's an invention of his own imagination.'

Carr-Gomm sighed. 'I'm afraid you must be right. Well, Treves—' his manner became abruptly business-like, '— we have to marshal our forces. The Committee is meeting in two days' time, and it *must* be persuaded to allow Mr Merrick to remain. Obviously he cannot stay in the Isolation Ward, so I propose to put him into those two little rooms that look out onto Bedstead Square, and which I understand are empty at the moment.'

'Bedstead Square – of course. The ideal place.'

The two rooms in question stood on the ground floor at the back of the hospital, looking out onto a large courtyard which had acquired the unofficial title Bedstead Square because it was here that the iron beds used by the hospital were taken for painting or repair. The rooms were seldom used, being inconveniently placed at a distance from the main wards. But their very seclusion would be an advantage now.

'They'd need some work to make them ready,' Treves mused. 'The smaller one will have to be fitted up as a bathroom because John needs a bath at least once a day.'

'Then perhaps you will be good enough to give the necessary orders. If there is any question, you can say you have my authority. And I should like you to be ready to attend the Committee meeting with all the facts at your command, and some of these.' Carr-Gomm indicated the file of photographs that lay open on his desk. 'As far as I can see the only obstacle might be Broadneck. He has enormous influence over the others . . . not an easy man to impress.' This was Carr-Gomm's diplomatic way of expressing his opinion that Broadneck's mind had long ago scarred over with ignorance and bigotry. 'In any case, if worse does come to worse we still have the British and Royal Homes to fall back on, don't we?'

When Treves did not answer, Carr-Gomm gave him a sharp look.

'Don't we?'

'No, we don't,' said Treves. 'Their committees have informed me that they're unwilling to take Mr Merrick, even if they were supplied with funds. They don't want him.'

'Well,' said the chairman in an unperturbed voice, 'it's up to us then, isn't it? Don't worry, Treves. We'll make them see it our way.' He lifted one of the pictures. 'They've eyes, haven't they?'

CHAPTER TEN

Treves knew that both he and the chairman had miscalculated about the Committee meeting even before it started. He knew it when he encountered Carr-Gomm with Ebenezer Broadneck in the corridor, and Broadneck said briskly, 'Ah, Treves, I wanted to talk to you. Strange rumours going about – patient of yours I understand. Taking úp the Isolation Ward when there's nothing wrong with him. Can't have that now. Still, I expect you can explain yourself.'

The idea that he was to 'explain himself ', as though he were in disgrace was so totally unexpected to Treves that for a moment he was too stunned even to be angry. By the time his temper flared, Carr-Gomm had managed to catch his eye with a silent warning. He also read in the chairman's face a reflection of his own realization that this was a disaster. Instead of being able to introduce the subject of the Elephant Man in his own way, Carr-Gomm had had it thrust on him by Broadneck in a way that put him on the defensive.

'Mr Treves will be coming to address the meeting later, Broadneck,' the chairman put in hastily. 'We have a lot of other business to get through first. Thank you, Mr Treves, don't let us detain you from your patients.'

He steered Broadneck ruthlessly away, keeping him from further observations by the simple expedient of not ceasing to talk himself. Treves could hear Carr-Gomm's voice going on and on right down the corridor and into the Committee Room. He gave an appreciative grin at these effective tactics, but all the same he was worried. Carr-Gomm had previously identified Broadneck as the most likely cause of bother; now it looked as if the problem was to be more serious than either of them had suspected.

Broadneck fancied himself as a leader among men. It galled him that he was not chairman of the Committee, and that his place on it was no higher than that of any other ordinary member. The owner of a string of abattoirs across the country, he was constantly searching for ways in which his considerable wealth could buy him social as well as material advancement. He yearned to be a public man, and his seat on the Committee was intended to be but a step in that direction.

'A status-seeker,' Carr-Gomm had once called him, with all the aristocratic contempt of one whose own status-seeking had been conducted in more genteel circumstances.

Broadneck's immediate aim was to get himself noticed, and to this end he became a trouble-maker. No Committee meeting was allowed to pass off peacefully. The most trivial change of policy would have him on his feet yapping about 'the good of the hospital'. And although most of his fellow Committee members were antagonized by behaviour that made meetings last long past the time that a gentleman would have preferred to depart for his club, their dislike had not made them immune from his influence.

It became plain that afternoon that his influence had already been at work. As he had said, Broadneck had heard rumours, and on the basis of those rumours had got to work on the other members, mostly with success. The Committee men were good, decent Englishmen. They would none of them have kicked a dog or refused a coin to a beggar that stood in their path. But like most decent Englishmen they were nervous of what they did not know. When, after three hours, Treves finally entered the Committee Room, in response to a summons from Carr-Gomm, he knew at once, with a sinking heart, that their hostility had been marshalled in advance against Merrick.

Carr-Gomm addressed the meeting strongly, hoping to recover the initiative from Broadneck. He gave a brief account of Merrick's introduction into the hospital and the piteous nature of his deformities. Broadneck leaned back with a weary air.

'Mr Chairman,' he said, 'the rules of this hospital are quite specific. No incurables are to be admitted. That is a

127

wise injunction. If we were to take in every person with some deformity or other . . .'

'Mr Merrick's misfortune is far from being "some deformity or other",' Carr-Gomm interrupted him. The chairman was normally the most courteous of men, but he was determined not to allow Broadneck to take over the meeting. 'Mr Treves—?'

Treves, who was standing behind Carr-Gomm's chair at the head of the table, knew what was expected of him, and promptly fished out the photographs with which he had armed himself for this meeting. Two showed Merrick full-length, the other three were various views of his head. Treves had carefully chosen the most explicitly horrible pictures. As he passed them round the table there was a shocked silence which at first gave him hope, but it was soon replaced by a rumble, not of pity but of disgust.

Before anyone could recover, Treves, who had returned to the head of the table, began to address them in a tense voice.

'Gentlemen, the London Hospital must not abandon this poor creature. There is no other place for him. Both the Royal Hospital and the British Home have turned him down, even if sufficient funds for his care were provided. The workhouse is certainly out of the question. The patient has an overwhelming fear of returning to the horrors of his past. His appearance,' Treves pointed to the photographs that lay on the table, 'is so disturbing that all shrink from him. He cannot, in justice to others, be put in a general ward of the hospital. The police rightly prevent his being exhibited, and he is mobbed in the streets wherever he goes. What is to be done with him?'

He turned his hands towards them in a slight gesture of appeal. Before it could take effect, Broadneck had cleared his throat and waded into the fray. His piggy eyes gleamed with dislike. His voice, too, had something of a pig's squeal about it.

'I, for one, am sick and tired of this competitive freak-hunting by these overly ambitious young doctors, trying to make names for themselves.' He fixed his eyes on Treves to leave no doubt of his meaning. Treves gave him back stare for stare, but he was conscious of a feeling of unease in his conscience. 'To parade them about in front of the pathological society is one thing, Mr Treves, but to waste this Committee's valuable time with requests for shelter for these abominations of nature is quite another.'

Into the general rumble of agreement round the table, Treves' voice broke passionately.

'Gentlemen, John Merrick is not an animal. He is a man, fully aware of his condition. An intelligent, sensitive, literate man, with an intimate knowledge of the Bible. His horrible infirmities do not reduce him to anything less than what he is, a man; and it would be criminal if we of the London Hospital, his final refuge, the last place on earth where this man can find peace, were to cast him out.'

From his chair at the head of the table Carr-Gomm pounded with his gavel. All eyes swivelled to him. Some were resentful, blaming him for allowing things to go so far. Others beamed to him their expectation that he would put a stop to this nonsense.

'Gentlemen,' he began in his silky voice, 'may I make a suggestion? There are two small rooms off Bedstead Square that are no longer in use and would be admirably suited to Mr Merrick's needs. I also propose to write a letter to *The Times*, appealing to their readers for assistance. Knowing the generosity of the British public, I feel we would have little trouble in raising the funds for his maintenance. Indeed, this hospital's rules do preclude the admission of incurables, but if ever there was an exception to the rule, it is this patient. So therefore, I propose, if Mr Treves is finished, that we put it to a vote. All those in favour of keeping Mr Merrick here?'

Without waiting for their reaction, he raised his own hand. Treves, not being a Committee member, had no vote, and only one man around the table dared to join Carr-Gomm in lifting his hand. Broadneck glared at the man and began to fight back.

'One moment, Mr Chairman.' He waved one of the

pictures of Merrick and looked round the table. 'As far as I'm concerned, this creature has no business being in our hospital.' He glared at Carr-Gomm. 'I think your letter would be an excellent idea, and when you appeal for funds, I think you should appeal for a more appropriate place for him as well. I agree the British public is generous, and I'm sure that somewhere this creature will find a happy and permanent home. *But not here!*'

One of the members mumbled, 'I quite agree.' Carr-Gomm scowled.

'I see,' he said quietly. 'All, then, that move we keep Mr Merrick here?'

Again he raised his own hand, but this time he was alone. He gave an intimidatory look at the one man who had supported him before. The man looked away, ashamed, but kept his hand stubbornly beneath the table. Carr-Gomm exchanged an angry, hopeless glance with Treves.

'All those opposed?' he said formally.

In a moment it seemed that a forest of hands had grown round the table. Treves turned away to hide his contempt. Carr-Gomm remained imperturbable, although his voice had gained a chilly edge.

'I see,' was all he said.

Broadneck was triumphant. 'Well then,' he squealed. 'In the meantime, of course, he needn't be turned out. He may stay in the rooms off Bedstead Square until such time as more suitable arrangements can be made, thus freeing the Isolation Ward for more deserving patients.' He looked round the table as a rumble of assent enveloped him. 'Well then, Mr Chairman, if there is nothing further to discuss, I move that we adjourn this meeting and all go about our normal business.'

In a voice filled with disgust, Carr-Gomm recited, 'I second the motion, gentlemen. This meeting is adjourned.'

Coughs and shuffles filled the room, chairs were scraped hastily back, papers were rustled noisily to put a brave face on departure. Of the men who filed hastily out, only one could look Carr-Gomm in the eye. And that one was Broadneck. As the door closed behind him, Treves slowly released his hands that had balled into fists at the look on Broadneck's face. He felt filled with despair. Carr-Gomm had achieved a very little, a short breathing space for Merrick, but he himself had stood there useless. His eloquence had gone for nothing. They hadn't even listened, these sleek, well-fed men.

Suddenly he picked up one of the photographs. It was lying face downwards, having been slammed down in that position by Broadneck. Turn it over, Trevas thought with bitterness, hide it away, pretend it isn't there. He looked at the hideous face whose eyes now seemed, to his guilty imagination, to be offering him their trust. Then he put it in his pocket. He too could not bear to look at it just now.

'Somehow I don't think they quite understand.' Carr-Gomm sounded sad and resigned, which was rare for him. Years in the law had taught him not to be too perturbed by the outcome of any decision, as there was usually as much to be said for one side as the other. Now, confronted with a situation in which he could see right on only one side, he began to regard this attitude as dreadful cynicism.

Driving home alone that night in a cab, Treves found himself thinking unexpectedly of his elder brother William. Ten years his senior, William had supplied much of the affection he had never received from his father. A good man, William Treves the elder, but dour and withdrawn, especially after his wife's death; much involved in his upholstery business and undemonstrative to his children. To William Treves the younger, it had fallen to be a father to the other children, and with none of them was this more true than with the baby of the family, Frederick.

Steady, solid William had kept the younger boy in check when his violent enthusiasms threatened to carry him away entirely.

'You've got to think, old chap,' he'd said a thousand times in his slow way. 'You always dash along without thinking.'

He'd said it when the fourteen-year-old Frederick had wanted to leave their home in Dorchester and go and live on their grandfather's farm nearby. William understood his brother's yearning to escape the chilly atmosphere of home, but he made it plain that it was no reason to take up a farming career he wasn't suited for.

'You haven't stopped to think, Freddie. All you see is what's in front of you at the moment. But what'll you do in ten years' time with your brain going to waste while you walk behind a couple of horses?'

He was right. Already in his heart the young Frederick knew that what he really wanted to do was follow William into medicine. He stuck out the next four years somehow, and at eighteen had become a student at the London Hospital, blessing William for saving him from a disastrous mistake. He loved the life at once, though it was the practical rather than the scientific aspects of medicine that appealed to him. It was said of him even then that he had 'clever hands' and that he would be a surgeon.

After four years of study he qualified as a member of the Royal College of Surgeons, and after a brief period as a house surgeon at the London he left to widen his experience by joining William, who was an honorary surgeon at the Royal National Hospital for Scrofula in Margate. He had it in his mind that he would make a name for himself in research, and William agreed with him that scrofula, about which little was known, was a good subject.

They had their first and only real quarrel a year later when Frederick threw it all up to become a general practitioner in Derbyshire.

'It's the only way,' he'd argued. 'I can't afford to marry Anne unless I've got a proper practice.'

'Then throw Anne over,' William had said brutally. 'Dammit, Freddie, you're twenty-four. That's much too young to be tossing away a career for marriage. But that's always the trouble with you. You rush ahead without thinking.'

On this one occasion Brother William had been wrong,

Treves reflected. He was happy in his marriage, and it had not harmed his career. By studying in the evenings he passed further exams for the Royal College, and became a fellow of that august establishment. Two years after going into general practice in Derbyshire he was back in London as a surgical registrar at the London. He had progressed rapidly through assistant surgeon to full surgeon at the age of thirty-one. William had been generous enough to admit he'd been mistaken.

But about one thing he had not been mistaken, and even now Treves' brow darkened when he thought of it. He'd continued his research into scrofula after he left Margate, certain that he was on the right tack. At twenty-nine he'd been ready with his book on the subject, *Scrofula and its Gland Diseases*. He had confidently expected this to be the first step towards the making of his name, but William had advised against publication.

'Don't be hasty, Freddie. You've missed something.'

'Such as what?'

'I don't know. If I did I'd write a book about it myself. But there's something wrong, I feel it. You've done it in too much of a rush.'

'A rush? I've spent years on it.'

'But you've rushed it recently, I know. You're too impatient.'

'Don't be an old woman,' Treves had told him amiably. 'This book will make me.'

So he had gone ahead and published. And three months later a German bacteriologist called Robert Koch demonstrated that scrofula was due to the action of a bacillus. Treves, not an expert in bacteriology, had missed the significance of certain little signs that had spoken loudly to Koch. His book had sunk without trace in the vast wash created by Koch's.

He had written other books since, successful books that had brought him the serious attention he wanted. There was *The Anatomy of the Intestinal Canal and Peritoneum*, which had been called the best work on the subject so far.

There was *The Pathology, Diagnosis and Treatment of Obstruction of the Intestine* for which the Royal College of Surgeons had awarded him the Jacksonian Prize.

Yet nothing could quite wipe out the pain of that earlier piece of clumsiness, or obliterate William's melancholy voice, saying, 'You rushed it, Freddie. You didn't look where you were going. You never do. You rush in and never give a thought to the consequences.'

That all came back to him now as he drove home through the quiet streets in the darkness.

Carr-Gomm's letter to *The Times* was written the next morning and delivered by hand. It appeared the following day, featured with gratifying prominence, and was read in many of those homes that might be expected to contain persons of influence. It was read by judges and barristers, by city men and 'men of affairs', it was read by statesmen and royalty, by Lords and Ladies, by those who were rich and titled, and by those who were merely one or the other.

It was read also by William Kendal as he sat in his dressing-room at the Apollo Theatre waiting to go on as Orsino in Shakespeare's *Twelfth Night*. He had already played his early scenes, and now there was a gap before he would be needed again. Orsino was not a long part and it gave him some time to himself.

Mostly he used that time dealing with the numerous affairs that needed his attention as the Apollo's manager as well as its leading actor. There were many who wondered why he chose to put on and appear in plays in which his own roles were often so small and his wife's so large. But William Kendal was an astute man. He knew that it was Madge's stunning beauty and equally stunning acting ability that the town came to see, and he chose plays that would show her to advantage rather than himself. It was good for business, and William liked good business.

Between them he and Madge brought a certain amount of social respectability to a world that was known for its tawdriness and tinsel glitter. Since Madge Kendal was so obviously a lady, it was possible for a lady to be an actress. And since she was too elegant to act in the mannered declamatory style that was usual, she adopted her own natural style, which other actresses soon began to copy.

When the final curtain had fallen, they change together in the dressing-room they shared, commenting on the play, the audience, the state of the box-office, in the casual affectionate way of people who have been happily married and engaged in the same business for twenty years.

He finished first and went off to put some final touches to essential paper-work, leaving her to put out the lights. She yawned and stretched, feeling desperately tired. It had been a long evening and Viola was a demanding role. She made a mental resolution that after this season she would never play it again. After all, she was thirty-nine, and whatever William might say, she could see the lines creeping across her lovely face. She leaned closer to the mirror, examining her complexion nervously.

As she did so, her eye fell on the copy of *The Times* that her husband had left lying there. She dropped into a chair and began to read casually. William would get involved in his paper-work and keep her waiting a long time. By the time she was half-way down the letter page she had become very still.

'Terrible though his appearance is,' she read, 'so terrible indeed that women and nervous persons fly in terror from the sight of him, and that he is debarred from seeking to earn his livelihood in any ordinary way, yet he is superior in intelligence, can read and write, is quiet, gentle, not to say refined in his mind.'

After a moment she fumbled in her bag and took out a pencil and a little notebook. She cast her eyes back over the letter, searching for a name. When she had found it she wrote neatly in the book, John Merrick.

'I'd very much like to meet that gentleman,' she said to herself. 'He sounds almost . . . Shakespearean.'

CHAPTER ELEVEN

It would take two weeks for the rooms off Bedstead Square to be ready for Merrick's occupation. In the meantime it was tacitly agreed that he would stay where he was – which was as much as to say that Carr-Gomm was determined to leave him there and if Broadneck found out and objected, Carr-Gomm would cross that bridge when he came to it.

Treves decided to leave it to the last minute before telling Merrick, whom he knew was beginning to feel at home in the Isolation Ward. The wounds on his body were healing, and with repeated baths his smell became less noticeable. He was even more relaxed in the presence of Mrs Mothershead. Sensing that he had achieved a moral victory in the matter of the reading, he took pleasure in making the most of it.

He would accept the morning paper from her with grave courtesy, enquire about her health and mention something that had particularly interested him in the previous day's news. Treves wondered if Merrick guessed that Mothershead never had time to read the paper, and consequently felt herself at a disadvantage in these conversations. After a few mornings he became certain that he did. It dawned on Treves with a shock that there was more than intelligence in that great head, there was also a lurking humour. It made him wonder for the thousandth time what sort of man nature had intended Merrick to be.

The editor of *The Times* had promised to keep public interest in the story boiling. Treves suspected that Carr-Gomm had some sort of influence on the paper's board, for a couple of days later he was contacted by a reporter for further details of Merrick's condition. He gave them frankly, and for the next few days made sure that some other paper than *The Times* was delivered to the Isolation

The fun-fair on Hampstead Heath...

...and the Elephant Man's first appearance at the London Hospital.

Dr Frederick Treves delivers his paper on John Merrick's tragic condition...

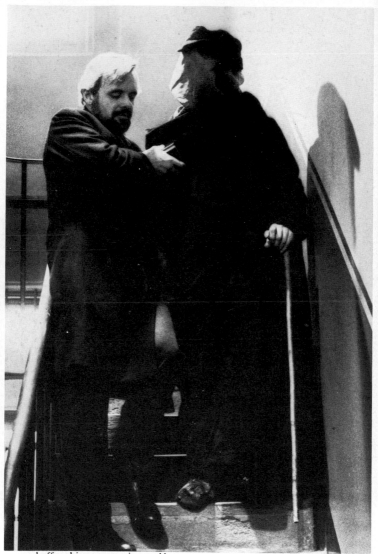

....and offers him compassion and love.

Treves, Carr-Gomm and Mothershead.

The Elephant Man returns from Belgium.

Befriended by Mrs Kendal, Merrick's future seems bright with hope...

...but he is destined, always, to walk alone.

Ward. Whatever Merrick eventually learned about his own condition, Treves wanted it to be directly from himself.

He was less observant, however, about leaving *The Times* lying around in his own home, a piece of neglectfulness that brought Anne's wrath down about his head one evening.

'I am trying to teach the child to be a lady, Freddie, and it isn't made easier by you allowing her to read anything she likes.'

'I didn't allow Jenny to read anything,' he defended himself. 'According to you she just picked it up.'

'It isn't the sort of thing she *ought* to be picking up. It should never have been brought into the house with that kind of thing in it.'

Anne pushed the offending issue of the paper towards him. It was open at page 3, where a good deal of space had been devoted to Treves' comments on Merrick's condition. They were not, he guiltily conceded, ideal reading for a child of ten, but it had never occurred to him that Jenny would be sufficiently alert to pick up the paper or read the piece with any understanding. Remembering his daughter's precocious intelligence, he realized that it ought to have occurred to him. For the sake of domestic harmony he decided to conceal how much pleasure he took in this.

'You little ghoul,' he told her amiably when he went upstairs to say goodnight. 'Why can't you—' he groped around for the phrase Anne had used, '—learn to be a lady?'

She made a face.

'I agree,' he said before he could stop himself.

'I just saw your name in the paper and kept on reading.'

'Did you understand it?'

'Not some of the longer words. What are "fibrous tumours"?'

'Never mind,' he said hastily. 'I'm beginning to agree with your mother.'

'Is Mr Merrick *very* ugly, Daddy?'

'Yes.'

'Why?'

'Because – he grew differently from everyone else. And just kept on growing. Now he's so different that he's – well he's not like other people.'

'Like Alice?'

'Who?'

'Alice in Wonderland. In that book Grandpapa gave me when I was eight. Alice kept on growing bigger and bigger or smaller and smaller. And she wasn't like any of the other people in the book. She kept trying to be, but she was always the wrong size.'

'Jenny,' Treves said urgently. 'Where is that book? Do you still have it?'

'I gave it to Kate but she didn't like it. She said it frightened her.'

'Where *is* it?'

The child's brow puckered. 'In the playroom I think.'

He was in there in a moment, ferreting around among the shelves till he found what he was looking for. It was a large edition, beautifully illustrated in colour and almost untouched, since neither of his daughters had spent much time with it. Treves took it downstairs and stuffed it in his bag which he kept by the door. As he turned to go into the drawing room he found Anne regarding him cynically from the doorway.

'I suppose the two of you sat there and had a nice little scientific discussion?' she accused him.

'No.' He assumed his most innocent air. 'As a matter of fact we talked about Alice in Wonderland.'

'*Alice in Wonderland?*'

It seemed to Treves now that his awareness of Merrick coloured all his perceptions, sometimes sharpening them unbearably. As he went about his daily business, he had the impression that an outer skin had been stripped away from him, leaving nerves raw that usually existed in comfortable padding. At any moment he might be pulled

138

up short in the midst of things he took for granted, and find himself wondering, 'How would this look to him?'

His comfortable home, his casual acceptance of his wife's greeting kiss in the evening, the gentle sound of her breathing beside him at night, the enjoyable arguments with colleagues – he now saw all these afresh from within the head of an intelligent, sensitive man trapped in the body of a monster. As his pity and understanding grew, so did his pain, and he wondered how he could ever have regarded Merrick as merely a specimen.

His mind began to dwell on the fear that enough money would not come in to house Merrick somewhere, and that no home would be offered to him. If that happened, short of taking the Elephant Man to Wimpole Street (which he knew Anne would never allow), he could see no way of providing a home for him. And his dread was growing that Merrick would be returned to a life made ten times more hideous by his glimpse of something better.

While the fear grew daily more real, Treves' own star rocketed into the firmament, and this fact troubled him more than anything else. It was irksome that the growing realization of his ambitious dreams should be spoiled by a haunting sense of guilt. After all, he had done no wrong. But the spectre refused to be silenced so easily. It walked with him always. It whispered to him at night that as much cruelty was committed by single-minded men wearing blinkers as by men of conscious evil. It sat down with him in the elegantly furnished dining room at the hospital, touching the heavy carpet and the walnut panelling, and making the lavish table ghastly to him.

He dined there as little as possible. He hated the air of self-satisfaction that hung over his fellow doctors as they offered him their congratulations with port and cigars; hated the tempting avenue of smugness down which their oiled laughter sought to lure him. But he bore with it all reasonably well until the day after *The Times* printed the item that had caused him trouble at home.

The light-hearted mood that had buoyed him up the

evening before had quite deserted him now. He picked irritably at his food as Dr Stanley persisted in reading the paragraphs out to the whole table, and wondered why it had never occurred to him before that Stanley had a voice like a horse.

'. . . in life until he came under the kind care of the nursing staff at the London Hospital, and the surgeon who has befriended him . . .'

Young Atkins chipped in, 'Good publicity for the hospital, at any rate.'

'Treves comes off well too, eh, Freddie.' Hill was pouring himself another glass of port at the far end of the table.

Treves grunted. He could sense that the atmosphere round this table was partly hostile to him. Some of the older men in particular were affronted at this sudden prominence of a younger colleague. He could see Carlyle now, lighting himself a cigar, his silver hair gleaming in the light from the finely wrought brass lamps above their heads. Carlyle must be pushing sixty. He'd started at the London Hospital and he'd end there because nobody had ever wanted him anywhere else. Carlyle was much given to expounding on the value of consistency, and something he chose to call 'unseen application'. Of late 'shooting stars' had made a mysterious appearance in his conversation, though nobody was so naïve as to ask his meaning. He leaned back now and regarded Treves satirically.

'It was pleasant of you to join us this evening, Frederick.'

'Your Elephant Man dining out tonight?' Hill chimed in.

There was a chuckle round the table and Carlyle added, 'I understand the kitchen ran out of hay this morning.'

The chuckle became a roar in which everyone joined except Treves and Fox. When the noise had died down, Fox indicated Stanley, who was still holding *The Times*.

'Do continue reading, Mr Stanley, please . . .' he said in a quiet, sour voice.

Stanley found his place again. 'It is a case of singular

affliction brought about through no fault of himself. He can but hope for quiet and privacy during a life which, Mr Treves assured me, is not likely to be long.'

There was a short uncomfortable pause, as though someone had made a remark in bad taste. Carlyle tried to ease the atmosphere.

'The Elephant Man. Makes you sound rather more like a zoo-keeper than a surgeon, Frederick.'

Amidst the genial rumble that shook the company, Treves rose to his feet.

'Excuse me, gentlemen,' he said coldly, 'I seem to have lost my appetite. Good evening.'

He walked out without looking at any of them, leaving a chilly silence behind him. Again it was Carlyle who broke it, waving his cigar with an air of injured innocence.

'I say, what's he on about?'

'He's getting a bit of a swelled head, if you ask me,' said Atkins.

'Well no-one did ask you, Atkins,' Fox snapped. 'Frederick Treves is not only the most skilful surgical operator here, he's also a humanitarian of the highest order. You sound like a pack of whining school-boys with your petty jealousies.'

'Look here, Fox, I simply said . . .'

'Oh shut up!'

Treves heard Fox's speech on his behalf from outside in the corridor where he was shrugging on his coat, and was perversely ungrateful. He did not feel like a humanitarian of the highest order and it embarrassed him to be thought of as one. Between those who would applaud him and those who would criticize him, he felt as if he had a pack of jackals at his heels, and he wasn't sure which were the worst.

He slipped quietly up to the Isolation Ward. Now was the time to tell Merrick of the impending move, and also to perform the other task that had been on his mind all day.

The line of bright light coming from under the door

made it clear that Merrick was still up and probably reading, as he read voraciously everything that was given to him. The day before Treves had obtained for him some back copies of the *Illustrated London News* but Merrick, with nothing to do all day but read, had probably gone through them by now.

Treves knocked before entering and waited for Merrick's 'Come in'. He was always meticulous in performing these small courtesies.

'Good evening,' he said when he had closed the door behind him. 'How are you feeling?'

'Good evening. Very well, thank you. And you?' Merrick took pleasure in repeating this exchange of politeness between them. Gravely, Treves replied as he now did every time.

'Very well, thank you.'

Merrick was sitting by the table with an *Illustrated London News* in front of him. It was open at a large picture of the Eddystone Lighthouse with a caption underneath that read, 'A silent shaft of stone on a deserted promontory, the lonely Eddystone is a beacon of aid and comfort to mariners of all nations.' On the facing page was a long article on the history and uses of the Eddystone. Merrick followed his glance.

'It looks very lonely out there,' he said.

'Very,' Treves told him. 'I believe sometimes the light-housemen get no visitors for months.' He sat down by the table and opened his bag. 'I have something for you, John. I'm sure you'll enjoy it. It's very popular.'

He lifted out the *Alice in Wonderland* and laid it on the table. Merrick's face did not change, but he gave a sharp intake of breath.

'Thank you – so much,' he stammered. 'Oh, it's beautiful!'

His good hand began to caress the leather binding, enjoying its soft luxurious feel. He gazed at Treves with speechless gratitude.

'Open it,' Treves told him.

The book fell open at a coloured picture depicting an early scene. Alice, having grown hugely, was trapped in a hallway far too big for her. She lay full length with her head jammed against the ceiling and her foot taking up the whole of the little door. She was giving an imploring look at the White Rabbit, who had stopped to look up at her, appalled. The caption beneath read, 'Curiouser and curiouser . . .'

Merrick turned a few more pages and found himself looking at Alice shrunk too small for her gigantic surroundings. Yet another picture a few pages on showed her grown again, this time in the little cottage. He became very still. Treves watched him intently, wondering for a horrible moment if he'd badly misjudged. Merrick was too intelligent to fail to understand the significance of this book to himself, even at a first glance. Perhaps he would draw from it not the comfort that Treves had intended, but further despair.

Then Treves became aware that Merrick was looking at him with glowing eyes and stretching out a hesitant hand. He took it at once.

'Thank you,' Merrick whispered again.

'Don't thank me,' said Treves hastily. 'It belongs to my daughters. They'd like you to have it.'

'That is very kind of them,' Merrick said with careful formality. 'Please give them my thanks.'

'I came to tell you that I'll be here early tomorrow morning,' Treves said. 'We're moving you to a better place. I'm sure you'll be very happy there, John. So get a good night's rest, there'll be new people to meet tomorrow.' He patted Merrick's arm and got up, closing his bag. 'I must be off home now. Goodnight, John.'

If it occurred to him that there was something mechanical about the reply he received he attributed it to Merrick's absorption in the book. As he hurried down the stairs and out of the hospital Treves was congratulating himself on an ingenious idea, and made a mental resolution to rifle the bookshelves at home. He had a conviction that his elder daughter's taste might prove helpful here, for though Merrick was intelligent he was neither educated nor sophisticated, and the kind of luridly dramatic tale for which Jenny had developed an interest might prove ideal.

His way home took him past the Peacock Public House, one of the more notorious establishments of the Mile End Road, and one which, on a Saturday night, provided a steady stream of minor casualties to the hospital.

A cab passed him as he drew level with the pub, and in hailing it he forgot all else. But as he settled back into his seat he noticed that the pub door had opened to admit a large man that he recognized as Renshaw, the night porter. The man was laughing in a way that suggested this was not his first port of call that evening, and he seemed to be taking great care not to lose something that was tucked under one arm.

Then the cab jerked and was off. Renshaw immediately disappeared from Treves' view and he tried to put the man out of his mind. The moment had made a disagreeable impression on him, but he put that down to the fact that he didn't like Renshaw.

Renshaw's usual crowd of cronies were waiting to welcome him in the Peacock. His sharp eyes took in one or two additions – girls whose highly coloured tatty finery proclaimed their profession. Normally Renshaw had little time for such. It would be a long time, he reckoned, before he had to pay for it. But right now he was in possession of a piece of good fortune that could purchase favours for him without the necessity of cash changing hands. The thought improved his mood, and when he had secured a pint of ale he beamed genially round.

'Here, listen to this!' Having gained their attention he pointed to the copy of *The Times* which he had brought in under his arm, and which was now lying on the bar. 'This is a letter to *The London Times* from the guv'nor of the hospital.' A groan of boredom went up. His audience were not *Times* readers.

'*Listen* will yer?' Renshaw picked up the paper and began to read from it. 'There is now in a little room off one of our attic wards a man named John Merrick, so dreadful a sight that he is unable even to come out by daylight to the garden. He has been called the Elephant Man on account of his terrible deformity.'

Renshaw looked up, pleased to note that he now had the attention of the entire pub. Even the scarlet feather boa round the neck of an excessively blonde young woman in the corner never so much as fluttered. Renshaw continued, speaking slowly so that nobody should miss a word.

'His appearance is so terrible that women and nervous persons fly in terror at the sight of him . . .' Squeals of pleasurable fear trilled from the ladies.

Renshaw grinned. 'And guess who can get you tickets to see him? Your own Sunny Jim.'

'Let's go see him, then,' cried a young male voice from the back of the crowd, and a chorus of noisy approval rose round him.

'Keep your shirts on,' Renshaw reproved them. 'When the time is right. Just now he's in the attic, but tomorrow they're movin' 'im into Bedstead Square – right into my lap. Then – for the right price—' he allowed his eyes to linger on the scarlet feather boa – 'you'll see something you'll never see again in your life.'

He raised his glass to his lips, clutching it to hold it steady under the hail of approving thumps that landed on his shoulders. The atmosphere dissolved into laughter and excited talk. Amid the noise and movement Tony slipped unnoticed out of the door, and made his way hastily back to Turners Road to find Bytes.

Some instinct drove Treves into the hospital early next morning to make a final inspection of the Bedstead Square apartment before Merrick was installed. He was eternally grateful that he had done so.

The rooms were small but pleasant, and to Merrick, Treves thought, used as he was to squalor or the cold impersonality of the Isolation Ward, they would seem palatial. The carpet on the floor was worn but cheerful. An equally bright cloth covered the small round table, and a patchwork quilt lay on the bed. The effect was lively and cosy.

Leading off from the main room was a small one fitted up as a bathroom. Treves looked round this, gave a grunt of satisfaction and returned to look again at the bed, already piled high with the extra pillows Merrick needed. In this room Merrick could be happier than he'd ever been – if only he were allowed to stay.

Treves was about to go when something over the mantelpiece caught his eye and he drew in his breath sharply. He stood there for a moment, shocked. Only the day before he remembered he had been reflecting to himself how Merrick's needs were colouring his whole view of life, and here was something so simple, so obvious, that he had lacked even the common sense to notice it. In another minute he had got to work.

Mrs Mothershead, coming into the room a moment later, stopped on the threshold, doubting the evidence of her own eyes.

'Mr Treves – what on earth are you doing?'

'I'm taking this down.' With a nod of his head Treves indicated the mirror in his arms as he just managed to set it on the floor without dropping it. He was breathing hard. The mirror had been a lot heavier than it looked. 'I never want there to be a mirror in this room – of any kind. Not even the smallest,' he said emphatically. 'There's no need to remind the poor creature of his tragedy every time he lifts his head.'

Mothershead looked grave. 'I should have thought of it before,' she said abruptly. 'I am extremely sorry.'

'*I* should have thought of it,' he told her. 'Don't blame

146

yourself. After all, we're none of us used to this situation. We must just try to think of these things before they occur.' He dusted himself down. 'I'm going to get John now. Can you have a porter remove this before I get back.'

'It'll be done.'

As soon as he reached the bottom of the small flight of stairs that led up to the Isolation Ward he knew there was something wrong. The noises coming from inside the ward were reaching him even here, and already he could hear that they were sounds of anguish and desperation. He stopped outside the door, knocked and called to Merrick. But the only answer he received was a tide of whimpering moans that reminded him of the day he had rescued Merrick from Bytes. Concerned, he entered without waiting any longer for an invitation.

Merrick was crouched on the bed, apparently asleep, his head drooped over his knees. He seemed to be in the grip of a nightmare. His good hand made feverish clutching motions at his bad hand and he was bathed in sweat. Only part of his mouth was visible, and from it came a series of gulps and coughs and half-formed words. His back was tensed with fear and his whole body writhed as if in rebellion against some terror.

Treves approached him with caution, anxious to wake him gently. But as soon as he touched him, Merrick uttered a great cry and jerked up with such violence that his head was thrown back. For a moment he fought uselessly for breath until Treves' hands took hold of his head and eased it forward. Merrick supported it in his hands and sat still, breathing heavily.

'What is it, John? A bad dream?'

'Yes,' Merrick gasped.

'What was it?'

Merrick fought for the word. 'Wo – workhouse.' He made an effort to recover himself. 'Now I'm awake – I shall be all right.'

'Good. Can you get up now? I've come to take you to your new home in Bedstead Square.'

147

He was aware of the other's sudden flinch of alarm, and patted his arm encouragingly. It was natural that Merrick should be reluctant to leave a room where he had known some sort of security, even for a few days.

He helped him on with the long cloak, and adjusted the grey flannel curtain round his head. Merrick moved uneasily to the table and drew *Alice in Wonderland* towards him.

'I'll carry that if you like,' Treves offered.

'And I should like to take this . . .' Merrick pointed to the *Illustrated London News* that he had been reading the day before. It was still open at the picture of the Eddystone Lighthouse.

'Take them all,' said Treves.

'No – just this.'

Treves collected up the *News* and added it to *Alice*. Then he handed Merrick his stick and offered him his arm. As soon as Merrick took it he could feel that he was shaking, but he decided to leave questions and explanations till later.

They moved slowly down stairs and along corridors, retracing the steps they had taken less than two weeks ago until they came down into the hall near the main front entrance. Merrick's hand tightened, he seemed to shrink back, but Treves guided him firmly to one side and into a corridor that led to the back of the hospital. Within sight of the rear entrance they turned aside again, and a few more steps brought them to the door of the little apartment.

'Wait here,' said Treves. A quick look inside reassured him that the mirror had been removed. 'All right. Come in.'

He stood back as Merrick edged his way slowly into the room, looking around the walls in apparent confusion.

'This is your new home, John.'

Merrick pulled off his hood and stared at the room which he could see better now. His eyes were bewildered.

'This – is my new home?' he whispered.

'Yes.'

Merrick turned incredulous eyes on him. 'This hospital?'

'Of course. What did you think?'

Merrick's answer was to turn back to the room and begin running his good hand over some of its objects in tentative wonder. And for the first time Treves realized what had been going on in his mind. Merrick's own story, told to him in bursts of confidence over the last fortnight, could have given him the key if he had thought to look for it. A life without peace or rest, being shunted about from pillar to post, from workhouse to owner, and from owner back to workhouse. This was what 'moving' meant to Merrick. And the man who called himself his friend had never given it a thought; had said glibly, 'We're moving you to a better place,' and assumed that Merrick would understand the word as he himself understood it.

Again he was made sharply aware of the wide gulf between Merrick's experience and that of the rest of the world, and the need to cross the narrow line that stretched across it with the care of a tightrope walker.

Merrick was almost sobbing in his joy and relief. 'How long will I stay here?' he stammered.

'I promise you,' said Treves slowly, 'you will never see the inside of that horrible place again. You will never, *ever* go back to the workhouse – or that man.' Even as he spoke he felt mocked by his own helplessness. He had no positive plan for aiding Merrick if sufficient funds did not come in to keep him here. To cover his fears he forced himself to speak heartily. 'It's a splendid room, don't you think?'

Merrick had begun to inspect everything in more detail, running his fingers along the mantelpiece, the backs of the chairs, the tablecloth. Two small prints on the walls that showed a little boy sleeping in one and praying in the other caught his attention for a long time, but he turned away without saying anything.

It was the window that seemed to give him the most pleasure. Tall and wide, it was sufficiently near the ground for him to sit and look at the outside world – or at least that part of it that was comprehended by Bedstead Square and the men who were working in it. Beyond the houses to be seen on the far side of the square rose the tall noble spire of St Philip's Cathedral. Merrick stood at the window for a long time gazing up at it, his whole attitude one of awe and disbelief. Coming to stand behind him Treves saw how resplendently the early morning sun touched the spire, drenching the weather vane at its peak with gold, and heard the quick intake of Merrick's breath.

'When I'm next moved,' said Merrick softly, 'may I go to a lighthouse? Or a blind asylum?'

Treves longed to say, 'You will *not* be moved. Despite them all I will find a way of keeping you safe here.' But the burden of the Elephant Man's growing trust in him was becoming oppressive, and he left as soon as he could.

He went straight to Carr-Gomm and waylaid him at the door of his office.

'Has the response picked up?' he demanded.

'Frankly, Treves, it's not what I expected. A few small cheques, well-wishers. Don't worry. These things undoubtedly take time.'

'But he's so afraid he's going to be carted off to the workhouse.' Treves gave Carr-Gomm a level look. 'I once promised him he'd never have to go back there again.'

Carr-Gomm fell silent for a moment. He seemed to be experiencing some awkwardness.

'Well—' he said at last, 'I'll let you know if there's something in the afternoon post.'

'Please do.'

But when the afternoon came there was nothing.

CHAPTER TWELVE

'Frederick, *no*! Please understand, once and for all, that I absolutely refuse.'

'It would only be for one afternoon – for a few hours—'

'I refuse to have that – creature – in my house. That is final.'

Treves ran a hand distractedly through his hair. He had anticipated Anne's objections to his plan, but not their violence. She had never opposed him with such persistence before. And, since he had always allowed her to be the final authority in matters concerning their domestic life, he found it hard to insist on having his own way now. He was reduced to pleading.

'Anne, he is not a creature, he is a man, a human being like you and me. He just happens to look different, but that isn't his fault, it's his misfortune . . . .'

'Freddie, listen to me – I've had the problems of John Merrick brought into this house morning, noon and night. I've heard about his deformity, his wonderful mind, his wicked owner . . . I've heard about Broadneck and the Committee and Mr Carr-Gomm till I'm tired of all of them. And now you actually ask me to let him come here for a visit – what does he want to pay us a visit for? What good can it do him?'

'I told you, he wants to visit "a real house". That's what he calls it. He's never been in one in his life. He's never known anything but workhouses, the hospital and show-men's carts. His only impression of the way people live is gained from the books I've been taking him—'

'I was going to ask where all my Alexandre Dumas books had gone, but I suppose I have the answer.'

'He likes lurid adventures,' Treves said apologetically. 'The more romantic the better – beautiful heroines – dashing escapes – he lives them all as he reads them. We take it all for granted, but it's a new world to him. He actually cried over the ending of *The Three Musketeers*.'

'Good heavens, why?'

'I'm not sure, I've never read it. But he said something about the heroine dying. John prefers them to get married and live happily ever after. He's a great romantic. I was going to ask you if you could get him some love stories . . .'

'I'll get him all the love stories you want, Freddie, but I will not have him in my house. Have you forgotten that we have children?'

'I wasn't thinking of the girls meeting him. Though actually Jenny would love to. She's said so. She isn't as squeamish as you.' He said this because he couldn't resist annoying his wife, though in truth he had no intention of letting his daughters see the Elephant Man.

'Freddie, I said no.'

The argument ended there for a moment while they had dinner. Treves was wondering how he could bring up the subject again when Anne said, as she poured his coffee, 'If John Merrick has formed his impressions of the way people live from reading Alexandre Dumas and the like, what sort of idea does he have of this house?'

'Rather unrealistic, I'm afraid. He dreams of a grand residence with huge rooms and easy chairs into which the hero can "fling himself". Heroes always seem to be flinging themselves into chairs in the books he reads. They never just sit, apparently. Not heroic enough.'

Her lips gave an involuntary twitch, but she controlled it before he could see. Against her will she was softening to him, but she was determined not to give in.

'I've tried to explain to him that No. 6 Wimpole Street isn't Versailles,' Treves went on. 'I've told him we don't have the armies of menials and powdered footmen that he's read about . . .'

'I should think not, indeed. Cook would give her notice if anyone called her a menial.'

'Nor do we have the white marble staircase, or the gilded mirrors and the brocaded divans . . .'

She gave a small choke, but refused to meet his eye.

'I think I managed to convince him that we lived in a more modest way, something along the Jane Austen style. He's read *Emma*, so I believe he understands.'

She still had not given in when she went to take a last look at her daughters. She stood regarding them for a long time, seeing them with the new eyes that her husband had forced on her. There was Kate, a happy uncomplicated child, with a mind that seldom looked below the surface of things. 'Trivial', her mother had sometimes said with disapproval; but Kate already showed promise of that beauty which in adult life would make people forgive her almost any amount of triviality.

Jenny would have more trouble. She would never be a beauty, and her sharp, clever brain would probably cause her more problems than benefit. But she had a lively, witty personality that would draw people to her despite the ordinariness of her face.

Both her daughters, Anne realized, had something that the world would call attractive, and the world would be accordingly kind to them.

She returned to her room to find her husband already in bed, looking at her anxiously. She went across and kissed him.

'When does the Elephant Man want to come?' she said.

The day of Merrick's visit to Wimpole Street was also the day Nurse Kathleen Darrell was conscripted for 'Bedstead Square duties'. She was informed she'd volunteered, but as she privately told Nurse Nora Ireland, it was the kind of volunteering where everyone else steps back quickly and leaves you standing there. Nora felt a certain sympathy, but only said, 'You'll get used to it.'

She and Mothershead between them bathed Merrick for the visit, with Nurse Kathleen looking on. When they finally left the bathroom, Nora noticed that her new helper was looking a bit queasy.

Mothershead followed them out, turning to say a few last words to Merrick who was still in the bathroom.

'There now, you're all dry,' she told him kindly. 'Now get into those things.' She closed the door and smiled at the two girls. Nora wondered cynically if Mothershead's benign aspect was induced by the prospect of having less to do with the Elephant Man in the future.

'Well, I think I can safely hand the duties over to you girls now,' said Mothershead. 'Mr Merrick will require a bath every day, that way he won't pong quite so much. Nora, you can instruct Kathleen on the finer points of Mr Merrick's bath. You two will be on your own tomorrow.'

They tried to look bright and failed.

'Don't look so glum, girls,' Mothershead told them. 'Such enthusiastic volunteers should be more cheerful.' At the door she turned. 'And don't forget, either of you. Under no circumstances are any mirrors to be brought into this room – even if he asks. If he does ask, I want you to let me know.' She departed.

'He's so – ugly,' said Kathleen after a silence.

'Ugly or not, you're going to help me,' said Nora firmly.

The door of the bathroom opened and Merrick came slowly into the room. He was dressed in clothes that for him would have to pass as 'Sunday best'. The billowy white shirt and baggy black pants had once belonged to a very large man who had died recently in the hospital. His family had not known what to do with his clothes, and had jumped at the bargain Treves offered them. Mothershead had got to work shortening the trousers and generally making the clothes fit Merrick's unusual shape, and the Elephant Man now had something that could be called a wardrobe. Strange as his present garb looked, it was at least clean and freshly pressed.

Both girls offered him forced smiles, but he was unable to look at them.

'Feeling better now, Mr Merrick?' queried Nora politely.

'Yes.'

Kathleen's eyes went wide at the sound. Merrick had

not said a word during his bath, and she had come to believe that the story of his conversational powers was a myth.

'You look very nice in your new clothes,' Nora persisted.

Merrick looked down at himself. 'Thank you very much,' he said in a pleased voice.

'Well, if there's nothing more—' Nora began to edge towards the door, 'I suppose we'll be leaving you now.'

She and Kathleen departed hastily. Merrick began to walk round the room, moving this way and that to get the feel of his new clothes. He liked the sense of them against his skin. They felt finer than anything he had ever worn before.

A knock on the door announced Treves, dressed for departure.

'You look splendid, John,' he said in a hearty voice.

'Thank you very much.'

'When one is invited to tea, one must look one's best.'

But there was still the enveloping disguise, which even on this day must protect the world from the sight of him. Treves helped him on with it (it was a good deal cleaner now, thanks again to Mothershead's efforts), and the two of them went out to the waiting cab.

Anne, alone in her house, waiting for the arrival of her husband and their guest, was near to screaming. She could not take her eyes off the clock, and each faint movement of its hand towards four heightened the tension within her.

She had done everything Frederick asked. She had made sure that the house looked its best and most welcoming. She had put on her prettiest dress. She had spent hours studying the photographs so that the Elephant Man's appearance should not come as a shock to her, and now she began to wonder if she had been wise to do so. She had stared at those nightmare pictures till they seethed in her brain with a horror that grew every minute. The thought of that 'thing' coming into her house – polluting it, was the way she thought of it – drove her hands to clench and her throat to constrict, and she wondered how she could bear it.

She began to walk about touching small objects, while her mind went round like a mouse in a treadmill. The children were safely dispatched to friends, the pictures of Merrick were safely cleared away so that he would not know how she had studied to become accustomed to him, every mirror in the house had been removed, the tea was all ready, and it was a splendid tea such as would be prepared for an honoured guest. She wondered if she might even have overdone it. It was possible, she was so anxious to please Freddie.

To please her husband had been the only motive in this, because he cared so desperately about what happened to Merrick, and had asked her to help him. She felt a small stab of resentment somewhere within her – that he should care so much about this, should talk about Merrick constantly, bring his problems, and even himself, into their home. Treves' work at the hospital involved him so deeply that Anne always felt she had to fight for that part of him that was hers. And now she wearily admitted to herself (for she was an honest woman) that some part of her feeling about Merrick was jealousy, and she wondered how much longer it would be before she hated him totally.

She was upstairs when they arrived. From behind the lace curtains she was able to see the shrouded figure descend from the cab with Treves' help, and walk clumsily across the pavement to the front door. Her first thought was that he looked small and pathetic. For some reason she had pictured him as huge.

She moved to the top of the stairs and stood where she had a good view of the hall below, but knew she was unlikely to be seen. She tensed as Treves helped Merrick off with the disguise, revealing the great head, then let out her breath slowly. It was bad, but she had got over the first moment alone. She believed she could control herself now.

She heard Treves' voice saying, 'Make yourself comfortable, John,' as he showed Merrick into the sitting room. Then she could delay the moment no longer, and she began to descend the stairs. Treves was standing at the bottom, looking up at her with a reassuring smile.

'Come and meet our guest, my love,' he said, in a voice designed to reach Merrick in the sitting room.

He gave her hand a squeeze as she reached the bottom step. The door of the sitting room stood wide open, and through it she could see Merrick clearly. He had his back to them and was looking round the room with an air of wonder and delight that was unmistakable. Nothing escaped his attention. The furniture, the ornaments, the pictures on the mantelpiece, he touched them all gently and reverently with his left hand. The pictures seemed to hold his attention the most.

Anne, watching him, thought again, 'He's so small.' Then she squeezed Treves' hand back and together they went in. Merrick turned as he heard them coming and immediately lowered his eyes. With her nerves sharpened to a fine edge, Anne saw at once the way his eyelids dropped, and instinctively she understood it.

'He is afraid of me,' she thought. 'He is afraid he will see horror and revulsion in my face, so he protects himself by looking away first. He fears me more than I fear him.'

'John Merrick, I'd like you to meet my wife, Anne Treves,' her husband was saying.

Without further hesitation Anne walked boldly forward and extended her left hand to Merrick. Her smile was charming and without any hint of strain.

'I'm very pleased to meet you, Mr Merrick.'

He took her hand and raised his eyes slowly to meet hers. Her smile held.

'I'm very . . .' Merrick's voice wavered, 'I'm very . . .'

The next moment, to the horror of both his hosts, he had burst into violent sobs. He drew his hand out of Anne's and covered his eyes, turning away from them and weeping piteously. Anne watched him, helpless. Instinct told her that she was watching the crying of a lonely child, but she could not bring herself to enfold that shaking figure in her arms as she would have done with any other child. It was Treves who put his hand on Merrick's shoulder and spoke gently to him.

'John, what's the matter? Why are you upset?'

Through his sobs Merrick managed to say huskily, 'I'm not used to such kindness – from a beautiful woman—'

Then Anne did look away from him, lest he read the sudden shame in her eyes at this mention of her "kindness". For the first time she saw how this meeting must look to him, what it must mean to him after the whole world had rejected him – 'As I did,' she thought.

'Would you like a nice cup of tea, Mr Merrick?' she offered.

'Yes – thank you,' he said huskily.

'Yes,' Treves said, relieved, 'a cup of tea would go nicely.' While Anne escaped to see to the making of tea, he went on talking in a hearty voice to cover the fact that Merrick's sobs were not yet under control. From the kitchen Anne heard him suggest a look round the house and then the two men, moving off slowly up the stairs. By the time the three of them met up again in the sitting room both she and Merrick were in better command of themselves.

She could look at him more easily now, with eyes that pity was blinding to his ugliness. She noticed that, though shy, he was not tongue-tied, and though he slurped his tea a little he was not, as she had feared, disgusting.

'How is your tea, John?' Treves asked, to keep conversation going.

'It's very good. I'm enjoying my visit with you very much,' he said politely. 'It's so very kind of you to have me as a guest in your home. I'm sorry I made a spectacle of myself.'

'Not at all, John.' As he spoke Treves looked intently at his wife, urging her to help keep the balloon of small talk in the air. But she was struck dumb. Merrick did not appal her quite as much as he had done, but she was still unable to think what to say to him.

'I love the way you've arranged your pictures on the mantelpiece. Is that the way it's done in most houses?'

'Oh, yes,' said Treves heartily.

'Who are they of?'

'Oh, our relatives – the children.'

'The children? May I see?'

'Of course.' Treves took some of the pictures down from the mantelpiece, hoping Merrick would not notice the faintly discoloured outline where the mirror had once been. He handed a picture of his daughters to Merrick, who took it reverently, regarding it as if it was an icon.

'The children—' he said slowly. 'Where are your children?'

'Oh they're gone for the day—' Treves said hastily, 'with friends.'

He wondered unhappily if Merrick would understand and resent such an obvious ploy to keep the little girls out of his way, but Merrick only repeated, 'Friends, ah yes, friends. How nice,' as though the word gave him the greatest pleasure.

Anne found her tongue and pushed another of the pictures towards Merrick. 'And here is one of Frederick's mother.'

'How lovely.'

'Yes,' said Treves lamely.

'And here—' Anne found another picture, 'are my mother and father.'

He looked at the couple in the frame for a long moment before saying, 'They have noble faces.'

Anne stared at him. 'I've always thought that myself,' she said.

'Oh yes,' he repeated gravely, and set down the picture under Anne's startled eyes. When next he spoke it was in a timid voice, and his words astonished both his listeners.

'Would you – would you like to see my mother?'

'Your mother?' said Treves. He had known about the dream figure of his mother that Merrick had built up, but never for a moment had he suspected that it might be backed up by a picture.

'Here.' Merrick reached into his pocket and brought out a small battered picture of a very lovely woman, which he handed gently to Anne.

'Why, Mr Merrick' – Anne studied the woman's young, delicately formed face – 'she's beautiful.'

'She has the face of an angel,' Merrick said simply. 'She *was* an angel. She would hold my head and sing to me. She was so kind' – his voice trembled – 'so kind to me. You must not think ill of her. It's not her fault, for in the fourth month of her maternal condition she was knocked down by an elephant. I'm sure I must have been a great disappointment to her.'

'Oh no, Mr Merrick,' said Anne softly, looking at him. 'No. No son as loving as you are could ever be a disappointment.'

'If only I could find her. If only she could see me now, here, with such lovely kind friends. You, Mrs Treves, and you, Mr Treves. Then maybe she would love me as I am. I've tried so hard to be good.'

Anne could no longer see his face for her eyes were blurred with tears. The yawning sadness in Merrick's last words had moved her unbearably and she saw the piteousness of his tragedy unclouded by revulsion for his looks. She tried to fight back the tears but they would not be restrained. They coursed down her face, distorting it, so that she dropped her head. Without knowing what she was doing, she held out a hand to Merrick and he took it at once, everything forgotten but his desire to comfort her. He understood why she wept and he wanted to tell her that there was no need, but all he could do was to repeat huskily, 'Please – please—'

They sat there together, the beautiful woman and the ugly man, their intense communication of sympathy wiping away all difference between them. Treves watched them in wonder, but made no attempt to interrupt. He knew they had both forgotten him.

CHAPTER THIRTEEN

'It seems we may have to revise our ideas about the mother,' Carr-Gomm mused, turning the photograph over in his hands. 'Possibly she existed as he remembers her.'

'Possibly, but I'm still not convinced,' said Treves. 'There's no proof that this picture is of her, and no way of knowing how he got it. He says he's always had it, but that may simply mean he picked it up so long ago that he's forgotten.'

'That's true, I suppose.'

They were sitting in Carr-Gomm's office the morning after the tea-party at Treves' house. The chairman had insisted that Treves come along as soon as possible and let him know how it had all gone, and Treves had been able to do so with a certain amount of pleasure. Despite some of the disconcerting events of the day before, he felt Anne's meeting with Merrick could be called a success.

'On the other hand,' he said, 'it may be as you say. She may be his mother and his memories of her may be substantially correct. I doubt if we shall ever know now. At any rate I haven't hurt his feelings by letting him know my doubts.'

'Very wise. And you've also allowed him to continue believing that his mother was charged by an elephant, apparently?'

'I haven't mentioned my own scepticism to him. I saw no point. If it comes to that I don't know for certain that it isn't true. She may have been, although I doubt very much whether it would explain his condition. I certainly don't believe the "African isle" part of the story, and I think John's just repeating what he's heard from Bytes and others like him.

'I haven't said all this to John because I think the truth would be hard for him to bear. It's just about tolerable for him to think his condition is caused by a tragic accident when his mother was carrying him. But to tell him that nature made him that way . . .'

'I see. Yes, of course.' Carr-Gomm nodded and stared again at the picture. 'I wonder where he got such a good frame for this.'

'I can tell you that, sir. My wife gave it to him just before he left us. She took one of our own photographs out of it, and said the best gift she could give him was a way to protect his mother's picture. He was so overcome I thought he was going to break down again.'

'Mrs Treves bore the visit well then?'

'Extraordinarily well. They seemed to understand each other quickly in a way that took me weeks to achieve. John constantly surprises me. I thought he'd told me everything, but I'd never suspected the existence of that picture. Yet he brought it out to show Anne at the first meeting.'

'A woman's sympathy will often have that effect, while the most up-to-date medical science will fall short.' Carr-Gomm handed back the picture. 'You'd better return this to Mr Merrick. I'm sure he doesn't like to be parted from it.'

Treves rose to go. 'Sir, was there anything in the mail this morning?'

'Very little, I'm afraid. But I haven't given up hope. I cannot believe that the British public, whom I have always believed a kindly people, will refuse to come to this man's aid. I shall speak to *The Times* again and let you know if anything comes in. In the meantime, please convey my kindest regards to Mr Merrick.'

Nora was beginning to regard her duties with the Elephant Man as a test of her suitability as a nurse. On the day of her first encounter with him, when she had screamed and dropped the tray, she had waited for a moment alone with Mothershead and apologized for her unprofessional reaction.

'It was just seeing it . . .' she explained.

Mothershead had regarded her with stern kindness. 'Patients here are not "its". They are either "he's" or "she's". But that's all right, Ireland. This one is going to be more work for all of us.'

Since that day Nora had tried her hardest to see the Elephant Man as a 'he'. She had tried to tell herself that he was an ordinary human being, inwardly just like any other. In fact, inwardly he was better than many others, if what she was now hearing was to be believed. And while she was not in his presence it was easy to convince herself that he was nothing but a much injured man who was entitled to her kindness.

But all the good resolutions dropped away from her whenever she entered his room and saw that ghastly head again. Then it would be as it always was, and she would have to struggle to maintain the composure and smiling face that Mr Treves had told her was essential and that her own kind heart also prompted.

After all these weeks she was easier in his presence, but not so much easier that she felt it made much difference. This morning she had volunteered to take his breakfast tray up to him instead of delegating the job to Kathleen, because she had imposed it on herself as a duty. If she could not force herself to do distasteful things then she was no use as a nurse, and this thought haunted her.

As instructed she knocked and waited for his husky 'Come in', then pushed the door open. He was sitting at the table, his hands occupied with some work that in her preoccupation she did not notice fully.

She set the tray on the table, managing to avoid lifting her head and looking directly at him, while despising herself for this piece of cowardliness. But as she began to lift the plates off and set them on the table, her eye fell on a cardboard box which he hastened to move out of her way. Its sides were covered with carefully drawn windows and arches. Many of the lines were shaky, but the whole thing bore evidence of hours of ingenious work.

'Good morning, Mr Merrick,' she said politely.

'Good morning,' he responded in the same formal tone. He did not look at her, nor did he seem at ease, and Nora was shrewd enough to realize that this was because of her own unease.

She busied herself in the invariable morning routine, removing a clean towel and blanket from the cabinet where they were stored, but as she headed for the bathroom with them she stopped and looked again at the cardboard box. Merrick was working on it again, holding it clumsily in his right hand while his good left one grasped the pencil to make marks on the side of the box. His breakfast stood there, ignored.

Curious now, she moved a step nearer and stayed watching until he became aware of her presence and leaned back, looking up at her timidly, as though awaiting reproof.

'What is this that you're doing?' she asked. When he did not answer, she pointed at the box. 'What is it?'

He indicated the window and her face lightened.

'What? Oh, I see. It's St Phillips. Oh, of course. Why – why it's very good. I mean, you've got the windows and arches just right.'

'Yes,' he said, pleased at her tone, but not offering further information.

'But it's so good, I mean—' she floundered, aware that it would hardly be tactful to say what she was really thinking – that it was good considering his condition. 'It's so very good,' she finished lamely.

'Thank you – very much.'

'Where did you get this box?'

He pointed to the door. He was not sufficiently relaxed with her to speak unless it was absolutely necessary.

'The hallway?' she said, puzzled. 'Oh, the wastecan?'

'I meant no harm,' he said anxiously. 'It was the only place where I could find cardboard. I thought it had been thrown away.'

'It's all right. It was thrown away. No-one wants it. It's just that it's a little dirty, that's all.'

Forgetting everything now but her curiosity, she set down the towel and blanket and leaned closer. Through the awkward drawing of a man who could use only his left hand, she was beginning to perceive real skill and meticulous observation.

'What's this?' she said, pointing to a circle drawn on the top.

'The main spire.'

'The – oh, the spire. How silly of me, it's as plain as day. Mr Merrick, where did you learn to do this?'

He longed to talk to her, to answer her questions fully and draw her into conversation. Then perhaps they could sit and chat as people did who have suddenly found each other interesting. But instinct warned him that her suddenly kindled warmth would be extinguished just as suddenly if he dared presume on it. So he contented himself with saying vaguely:

'I learned a long time ago.'

'Oh, but how will you finish it? You haven't any more cardboard.'

'I'll have to find some more.' He shrugged, at a loss. The movement of his shoulders made Nora aware of his body, and she drew back. He was the Elephant Man again.

'Yes, well—' she felt suddenly uncomfortable. 'Good day, Mr Merrick.'

She hastened from the room, forgetting the towel and blanket which she had left on the table. Merrick made as if to call after her, but thought better of it. With difficulty he scooped them up himself and took them into the bathroom. He arranged the towel neatly over the back of the bath, and the blanket over the back of a chair. Then he stood back to admire his work. There wasn't a line out of place.

He was becoming adept now at eating. His meals always arrived ready cut for him so that he could manage them easily with just a spoon or fork in his left hand. Today he got through his breakfast quickly, anxious to resume work as soon as possible on the cathedral. As he ate, he gazed out of the window on the original. This was his favourite time of day for looking at it, the moment when the morning sun climbed the spire till it seemed like one glowing finger pointing upwards. Watching it he felt part of that glow, part of the eternal hope to which it aspired. As the day wore on and the sun moved away he would give a faint sigh of regret, and count the hours till he would be given his vision again.

He wondered if Nora would return for his breakfast things. He hoped so. For a moment as they talked that morning he had looked up into her face and known that she had forgotten his ugliness in the interest of their conversation. It gave him a chance to study her features, which were not turned away from him but open and friendly, and he had thought how pretty she was. He would have sat there all day, watching the movement of her lips, the soft peach-like colour of her complexion and the flickering movements of her dark eyes, had she let him. But their moment of communication had passed almost as soon as it had begun. He had seen the awareness of him creep back into her eyes, and hoped he had concealed his hurt.

His pain had caught him unawares; it was so long now he had thought himself innured to it. That wound had been inflicted so often during his life that it seemed like a natural part of himself. But now – his mind ran back over the weeks he had spent in the hospital – he'd been protected and cared for long enough for the wound to begin to heal, and any new infliction hurt as bitterly as that first pain, long ago in his childhood, when the truth about himself had begun to dawn.

It was easy in this room without mirrors to forget what he was, and think that a pretty girl might talk to him at her ease, might smile and laugh, and that he might see reflected in her friendly eyes the image of the man he longed to be. For the moment that hope was crushed. All over the hospital – all over the world – there were pretty girls like the one who had fled him this morning, as they would all

166

flee him, no matter how hard they tried to pretend, and in fleeing they would force him back into hell.

With a desperate intensity that took his breath away, he yearned for beauty to feed his senses which had been starved since the moment of his birth. Why, he thought – what was he? Ears that had heard no music, eyes that had seen no loveliness, hands that had touched no softness, a heart that had known no love, save once so long ago that it seemed a dream. There was beauty all around him in the world – and it fled from him.

He rose and moved over to the window. There was a constriction in his heart that was like a choking pain. He would have wept if weeping were easier. He stood by the window a long time, gazing out on the spire glittering in the sun, until the ache in his throat had subsided. At last he went back to the table and sat down again to his work.

A nurse came to take away his breakfast things. It was not Nora. He greeted her politely but did not look up at her. Half an hour later two others came to give him his bath. Again neither of them was Nora and this time he was glad.

Lunch came and went. He ate it quickly and returned to his cardboard cathedral. He wanted to do as much as possible before the light became poor, and he was pleased with the way it was going.

Late in the afternoon, just as he was beginning to think he must finish for the day, there came a knock on the door.

'Come in,' he said mechanically, thinking it was the evening meal.

But it was Treves, with an air of suppressed excitement and apprehension.

'Good afternoon, John.'

'Good afternoon.'

'John, there's someone here who would like to meet you. Would that be all right?'

'Yes – of course.' Merrick was flustered, as though Treves' nerves had communicated themselves to his. He wondered if his visitor was another senior member of the staff, someone like Carr-Gomm.

Then Treves stood aside and Merrick saw his visitor standing in the doorwway. He caught his breath. He truly believed he must be looking at the most beautiful woman in the world.

'John,' Treves said, 'I'd like you to meet one of the brightest lights of the British stage, Mrs Kendal. Mrs Kendal, John Merrick.'

'Good day, Mr Merrick.' Madge Kendal's voice was deep and husky.

He recovered himself enough to remember his manners. 'Good day . . .'

She moved into the room and came to stand before him, gazing directly into his eyes. Nothing in her expression betrayed the awful revulsion that swept over her. After seeing one of Treves' photographs she had believed herself prepared for the worst, but no photograph, she now realized, could prepare anyone for the piteous outrage of nature that was John Merrick. But Madge Kendal was not an actress for nothing. She fought now for control of her features and her eyes, and achieved it. Merrick became the recipient of the most dazzling smile at her command.

'I've brought you some things,' she said. 'I hope you'll like them, Mr Merrick. I hope you don't think it too forward?'

'Oh – no,' he scarcely heard her words or his own reply. He could not take his eyes from her.

'I knew you'd understand. Here.'

She took something from under her arm and handed it to him. Dazed he looked at it and saw that it was a framed photograph of herself, looking as elegant and fashionable as she did now. He could not speak. The ache was back in his throat, but this time it was from joy. He was terrified of bursting into tears again. Looking closely at him, Mrs Kendal understood everything that was passing through his mind. To break the tense silence, she spoke archly.

'I want you to know that I don't go about giving my pictures to just anyone.'

He managed to speak at last. 'Oh, no. I would never think it! It's so beautiful. You are so – I'll give it a place of honour here, next to my mother.'

He stepped back and lifted the portrait to the mantelpiece where the newly framed picture of his mother stood.

'She's very pretty, your mother,' said Mrs Kendal.

'Yes.' Merrick looked from one picture to the other, as though unable to decide which one gave him the most pleasure. Then he turned, as though remembering the proper behaviour of a gentleman to a lady paying a visit.

'Would you care to sit down?'

She thanked him and seated herself, taking the chance to lay on the table a large book she was carrying. She had got her second breath now and was able to look at him more easily.

Treves waved Merrick to the only other chair, refusing to take it himself. He stood watching the two of them, smiling with pleasure at the apparent success of his plan.

'I see you're constructing a – church?' Mrs Kendal regarded the cardboard box.

'A cathedral – yes. I have to rely on my imagination for what I can't actually see . . .' He hesitated before coming back to something that was puzzling him. 'Mr Treves says that you are in the theatre. Do you live there?'

'Oh no, Mr Merrick. I just work there.'

'Well, even to work there would be wonderful. Is it beautiful?'

'You've never been?'

'Alas, no.'

She studied him curiously. The old-fashioned word had taken her aback. Despite what Treves had told her about Merrick's intelligence, she had somehow believed that 'intelligence' in this case meant little more than the cleverness of an animal. Physically, Merrick had surpassed her worst nightmares. But now, as she forced herself to talk to him, she found herself confronted by a wistful, gentle personality whose words, though a little indistinct, were courteous and even charming. It disturbed her to discover that mingled with her pity was a liking for the person he was.

'Well, you must go,' she said, trying valiantly to carry on the conversation. 'It is one of the most beautiful places on earth. Of course, I'm rather partial.'

'Tell me about it, please,' he begged.

'It's very difficult to put into a nutshell, but I should say the theatre is the shrine of the imagination, where one may suspend disbelief and travel anywhere in the world, to any time you desire.' She was not blind to the shine that came into his eyes. She went on, uncertain whether she was doing more harm than good, but not knowing what else to say. 'You may look over the shoulders of kings unobserved, battle with ruthless tyrants and marry the beautiful princess, all in the space of a few hours.'

She smiled, and her voice took on an added gentleness. 'On stage you may be whoever you wish to be, do anything you please, and always, always live happily ever after. The theatre is all the brightest and best things of the world, Mr Merrick. It is lights and music, gaiety and joy. It's – well, it's romance.'

'Romance . . .' he whispered longingly.

'That's one thing the theatre has in great store. Which reminds me . . .' She turned to the book she had brought in with her. 'I have something else for you.'

The book was bound in fine leather, and gold lettering announced it to be the complete works of William Shakespeare. Merrick could hardly hold it in one hand. He quickly put it down and began to leaf through it, touching its pages with reverence.

'Have you read it?' she asked politely.

'No, but I certainly shall,' he flicked over some more pages until he came to a play whose title caught his eye. '*Romeo and Juliet.* I know *of* this . . .' He began to read from half-way down the page, saying the words in his thick lisping voice, but with perfect comprehension of their meaning.

'*If I profane with my unworthiest hand,*
This holy shrine, the gentle fine is this:
My lips, two blushing pilgrims ready stand,
To smooth that rough touch with a tender kiss.'

Embarrased by the last words, he stopped. He had not seen the astounded look Mrs Kendal had given Treves, nor the equally disbelieving one she turned on him. If what Merrick had told her was true – that he had never seen these lines before – then he was reading them for the first time; and sightreading them with an ease and flexibility that many a professional actor would envy. She stared, and the true tragedy of a man with such quick perception and sensitivity imprisoned in this ghastly cage almost reduced her to tears in front of them.

But she recovered herself in time to halt Merrick as he began to close the book. She put her hand on his, and huskily began to recite back to him Juliet's lines, which she knew by heart.

'*Good pilgrim, you do wrong your hand too much,*
Which mannerly devotion shows in this;
For saints have hands that pilgrims' hands do touch,
And palm to palm is holy palmer's kiss.'

He paused just long enough to search her face to see what she wanted him to do, then dropped his eyes back to the book and continued reading.

'*Have not saints lips, and holy palmers too?*'

'*Aye, pilgrim,*' she replied at once. '*Lips that they must use in prayer.*'

'*Oh then, dear saint, let lips do what hands do.*
They pray, grant thous, lest faith turn to despair.'

His voice faltered on the last words, but she tightened her hold on his hand, urging him on.

'*Saints do not move, though grant for prayers' sake,*' she said quickly.

'*Then move not, while my prayer's effect I take.*
Thus from my lips, by yours, my sin is purged.'

171

Merrick came to the end of the speech and, without stopping to think, read straight on to the stage direction. '*Kissing her . . .*' He stopped, afraid he had gone too far, and lowered his head. Mrs Kendal was shaken with pity. She forgot that he was hideous. She remembered only that he had nothing. Very deliberately she removed her hand from his and reached up to touch his face.

'*Then have my lips the sin that they have took,*' she continued the lines of the play.

After a moment's confusion he managed to go on, '*Sin from my lips? Oh, trespass sweetly urged! Give me my sin again.*'

Very slowly she leaned forwards so that her face was close to his, aware that he had frozen in startled fear. But she had made up her mind that he should have the only gift it was in her power to give – the knowledge that he was not so different from other men that it was impossible for a woman to kiss him. He would never know what it cost her.

She put all the gentleness and tenderness of her woman's soul in the effort to lay her lips against the corner of his distorted mouth. When she drew away his eyes were closed, but he opened them immediately and they looked at each other for a long silent moment.

'Why, Mr Merrick,' she said in a soft voice so that only he could hear, 'you're not an Elephant Man at all.'

'Oh – no?'

'Oh, no, no – you are Romeo.'

His eyes filled with tears. Treves, who had forgotten everything except what was happening in front of him, pulled himself together abruptly and remembered his patient. The plan had succeeded beyond his hopes, but now he began to fear that Merrick had been subjected to more emotion than he could stand. Belatedly it occurred to him to wonder what the interview had done to Mrs Kendal.

'Mrs Kendal has to leave, John. She is due at the theatre.'

She rose thankfully and said her goodbyes, extending

them as much as possible to cover the fact that he could hardly reply.

'I'll come and see you again, John,' she said from the doorway.

In the corridor she took Treves' arm, almost collapsing.

'Mrs Kendal?' he said, alarmed.

'I'm fine, Mr Treves. Would you mind if I were alone for a minute?'

'Of course. I'll see you to your carriage.'

When he had left her, she went to the wall and stood staring at a large portrait of one of the hospital's founders. She had no interest in the man and his features made no impression on her. But if she stood like this no-one could see the tears that were coursing down her face.

CHAPTER FOURTEEN

Prompted by Carr-Gomm, the editor of *The Times* was doing everything in his power to light the spark of public interest in the Elephant Man, but the paper's efforts produced no more than a thin stream of offerings. Some well-wishers, moved to deep compassion, sent repeated offerings, but these, though steady, were usually small in size, indicating that those whose generosity was the truest had the least to give. From wealthy homes the donations were meagre. And the next meeting of the Committee was drawing inexorably nearer.

It would never have occurred to Treves or Carr-Gomm to appeal for help to *The Ladies' Gazette*, chiefly because they were unaware of its existence. But when, a few days after Mrs Kendal's visit, a representative of that little magazine knocked on Treves' door, the doctor spoke to him courteously enough. He was willing to talk to anyone about Merrick if it would help.

The Ladies' Gazette was a publication that lived on the doings of famous and glamorous people. Society, royalty, the stage, these were the breath of life to its pages. It was often read by the very people it wrote about, but the greater part of its readership lay in those middle-class homes for whom it provided a window onto the glittering world they aspired to, yearned for, and knew in their hearts they could never enter.

Its frivolous pages were scanned in the virtuous home of Mrs Annabel Jameson, a well-to-do merchant's wife of unimpeachable respectability and dullness. For a week, until the next issue came out, it would be her bible and her comfort, after which she would dispose of it into the waste-bin, from where it would be rescued by the equally respectable governess to her children, Miss Elizabeth Ireland.

From Miss Ireland it usually passed on down to the kitchen maid, but there came a day when the maid searched Miss Ireland's room in vain for the week's discarded *Gazette*. The magazine was by now on its way to London, accompanied by a letter from the governess to her sister Nora at the London Hospital.

'I noticed the mention of the hospital's name,' she wrote, 'and, reading further, discovered a description of the man I think must be the one you wrote to me about – the one who frightened you so. If so, do write and tell me. Did you actually *see* Mrs Kendal? I can't wait to hear from you.'

When Nora had read the item, her first thought was to check the magazine's date. It was now four weeks old. She stopped in the corridor on her way to breakfast, feeling a gleam of satisfaction. Much had happened in four weeks, and the letter she would send back to her sister Elizabeth would be full of news of the most surprising kind.

Over breakfast she yielded (without much difficulty) to the entreaties of the other young nurses at her table to read from the *Gazette*.

'Mrs Kendal,' she read, 'always at the forefront of fashion and form, was seen leaving The London the other afternoon. No, dear readers, the most facile actress of our day has not been taken ill, but rather said she was 'visiting a friend'. And who was the lucky recipient of this attention? Quick enquiries proved it to be none other than Mr John Merrick, the Elephant Man, of whom our readers may have heard. After a chat of three-quarters of an hour, Mrs Kendal was kind enough to leave Mr Merrick an auto-graphed portrait of herself.

'Owing to a disfigurement of the most extreme nature, Mr Merrick has never been properly presented to London society. But knowing that wherever Mrs Kendal goes, others inevitably follow, the question arises – will London society present itself to him?'

Amid the little ripple of excitement that shook the table Nora announced with some pleasure, 'I told you there was a whole load of toffs going in there, didn't I? Every day for

175

nearly a month. Now we know. And it's not just Mrs Kendal's picture he's got – oh Lord!'

This last exclamation was drawn from her by the sight of Mothershead bearing down on the table. As if by a signal, every one of the young nurses suddenly remembered that she was due on duty any minute. Mrs Mothershead watched the mass exodus with grim humour. But when they were gone and she picked up the magazine that Nora had dropped in her haste, the humour vanished from her face to be replaced by an expression of anger.

It had been seething inside her for some time now as she watched Merrick's room fill up with a succession of photographs and trinkets, for his new visitors seldom came without bringing a gift in addition to the pictures – an elegant neck-tie, a set of studs, a watch; they seemed, thought Mothershead crossly, to have a genius for offering Merrick what was useless to him.

Her anger did not touch Merrick himself, who, despite his disturbing quickness of mind, she still regarded as a child to be cared for. She would never be close to him or touch his heart as Treves had done, but his plight, his gentleness and, above all, his need of her care had aroused the protective instincts she usually kept deeply buried within her. These days she often stopped Treves to enquire how fast the donations were coming in, and shared the sinking of his heart at their slowness.

She seldom did the menial tasks of nursing Merrick now, but she supervised them constantly to see that his care was kept up to standard, and this morning she went herself to collect his used breakfast things.

He looked up timidly at her polite greeting. He had finished eating and was making marks on his cardboard cathedral which had grown very little recently. Shortage of cardboard was one reason, but the other was the sudden dramatic up-turn in his social life.

'The nurses will be along for your bath soon, Mr Merrick.' Mothershead said as she piled plates onto the tray.

'Oh, yes. Thank you. It's very important – today.'

'More visitors? You had two lots yesterday, didn't you?'

'Yes. Lady de Grey came in the morning. Look.' He pulled forward a photograph of the famous aristocratic beauty that showed her sitting on a hammock, leaning enticingly to one side, one hand clasping a fan which she held just behind her head. In contrast to the stately poses of many of the women who now crowded Merrick's mantelpiece the picture of Gladys de Grey was openly flirtatious. Mothershead just stopped herself clucking her disapproval.

'It doesn't do her justice,' Merrick said gravely. 'She is much more beautiful in the flesh. Mr White said so, too.'

'Who is Mr White?'

'I don't exactly know. He came with her – she called him "Lukie".'

'But he's not the lady's husband?'

'I didn't like to ask – but I don't think he can be. Did you say something?'

Mrs Mothershead had said 'Hrrmph!' before she could stop herself, but she judged it wisest not to repeat it. She had her own opinion of married women who went visiting with other men, but this wasn't the place for it.

'Who came in the afternoon?'

'The Countess of Warwick. Look.'

The Countess' pose was statuesque and almost in profile. The photograph had evidently been taken when she was ready to go riding, and showed off the tightly-corseted hour-glass figure to perfection.

'Did anyone come with her?' demanded Mothershead.

'Oh, yes. Lord Charles Beresford.'

This time Mothershead yielded to temptation. 'And where are the husbands of these ladies when they come visiting you with other men?'

'I don't know. I couldn't ask them, could I? What was that? You *did* say something.'

'I said Hrrmph!'

'I don't understand. What does it mean?'

'It means you're making some very funny friends, my lad.'

'They're very kind to me. Lord Charles gave me this.' Merrick handed her a solid gold cigar case inscribed with the Beresford coat of arms.

'Delightful of him. What does he think you're going to do with it?'

'Well, he used it to keep cigars in. I shall keep it as a memento of a friend.'

'John,' said Mothershead curiously, 'do you feel these people are really your friends?'

'Of course. They take so much trouble to come and see me, and I really do appreciate them giving up their time. They all have so many other engagements, but they manage to visit me.'

She was silent for a moment before she said, 'Who's coming this afternoon?'

'Lord and Lady Waddington, at five o'clock.'

'Well then, I expect you'd like some tea delivered. I'll see to it.'

'Thank you.'

In the hall downstairs she encountered Treves in a hurry.

'Sir, I'd like to speak—'

'Can it wait a while, Mothershead? I'm due to see Mr Carr-Gomm and I'm a bit late.' Half-way up the stairs he turned and called back. 'Is anyone coming to see John today?'

'Lord and Lady Waddington. That was what—'

'Of course, I'd forgotten. You'll see them in if I'm not here, won't you, Mothershead?'

'Yes, sir.'

Carr-Gomm dismissed Treves' apologies for his lateness with a wave of the hand. He was in sober mood.

'If the contributions don't pick up soon, Treves, I'm afraid we're going to have a difficult time with the Committee.'

'How much longer before they meet?'

'A fortnight.'

'Can't you find a way of putting it off, sir?'

'I *have* put it off – three times. I've stalled until I've run out of ways to stall. Not un-naturally Broadneck has become thoroughy suspicious. He is now threatening to get together a quorum and call a meeting against my wishes. I am afraid that he can do that. That would be a disaster. I would have even less influence over such a meeting than I can see I'm going to have anyway. So I asked you to come and see me because I wanted to tell you myself that the meeting will be in three days' time, and I want you most particularly to hold yourself free to be there.

'Our last hope may be that you can influence the Committee by telling them how our friend has developed over the past few weeks, and what an insane piece of cruelty it would be to throw him out with nowhere to go but the workhouse.'

'I honestly believe,' said Treves slowly, 'that John will find a way of killing himself before he goes back there. It *must* not happen. It would have been bad enough to send him back weeks ago when he first came in here – but *now*, when he's beginning to believe in himself as a human being, as a man . . . if you could see the change that's come over him.'

'I should like to visit him again. You must make me an appointment. From all I hear, Mr Merrick's days are crowded now.'

'Ever since Mrs Kendal came to see him he hasn't stopped having visitors. She came back for a second visit the other day. That pleased him more than anything else, I think. Most people don't come a second time, but when they go away they tell their friends about him and the friends come. So there's always a new stream of guests. He receives them like royalty. Mothershead found him a tea-set from somewhere, and he's even learned to pour tea with his good hand.'

'But what on earth do they talk about?' said Carr-Gomm, puzzled at the picture that was being conjured up for him.

'Mrs Kendal talks to him about the theatre. He loves that. He sees the theatre as a child would see it – a magic place where you can dream of being or doing whatever you like.'

'Dangerous . . .' muttered Carr-Gomm.

'What?'

'Nothing. Go on. They talk about the theatre. What else?'

'They – er – read Shakespeare together.' Treves stopped abruptly, feeling the impossibility of describing the strange and touching scene when Mrs Kendal had been Juliet to Merrick's Romeo. He himself had been an intruder at that moment. Carr-Gomm gave him a sharp glance but did not press the matter.

'And the others?' he queried.

Treves grinned suddenly. 'Mr Merrick is getting adept at the niceties of conversation,' he told Carr-Gomm. 'He asks them to tell him about their lives and he tells them about his. Since their experiences are so widely different there's usually plenty to talk about.

'What pleases me most is that he's losing his shyness – not just with his formal visitors, but with everyone. He spends a lot of time at the window during the day, and the men who work in Bedstead Square have got used to him. They pop across to chat to him as though he was just anyone, and gradually I think that's how he's beginning to think of himself.'

'But surely, that's not possible. Every time he sees himself . . .'

'I don't allow mirrors of any kind in that room, sir. Since he can't see himself and people treat him so normally, he's starting to forget, or at any rate to think that his deformity isn't so very dreadful.'

'Let us hope that nothing happens to remind him violently that it is.'

Both men fell silent as though a shadow had fallen across

them. After a moment Carr-Gomm seemed to force himself to speak cheerfully.

'So Mr Merrick is now used to conversing with the very cream of society. How exceedingly dull he will think me after the Countess of Warwick who, I understand, came calling yesterday.'

'That's right. John admires her greatly, though not quite as much as the Duchess of Manchester.'

'*What*! Are you telling me, Treves, that one of the most notorious women in London has been visiting here?'

'Yes, and she brought Lord Hartington with her.'

'Good grief!'

In an age when the indiscretions of the aristocracy were successfully concealed from anyone outside their own immediate circle, the German-born Duchess Louisa had flouted convention to an extent that could not be kept a secret. She had been married for nearly thirty years to the Duke of Manchester, and borne him five children. But this had not prevented her, when a young woman, from having an affair with Lord Derby, in the course of which she extracted a written promise from him that should he ever become Prime Minister he would get her appointed to the Queen's household as Mistress of the Robes. In due course he had become Prime Minister, and been as good as his word; something which, when she discovered it, infuriated Queen Victoria so much that she excluded her Mistress of the Robes from the invitation list to the Prince of Wales' wedding – an incredibly open snub for a woman of the Duchess's rank and position.

Louisa's most blatant indiscretion was a long-standing love affair with Lord Hartington, or 'Harty-Tarty' as society called him. For her sake he remained unmarried, ignoring his duty to provide an heir to the Dukedom of Devonshire, which he would one day inherit, and it seemed that nothing, not even age – for Louisa was now in her fifties – would shake him from her side. Even now she was still a considerable beauty, and her picture was one of the most prominent on Merrick's mantelpiece.

Under the urbane exterior of a man of the world, Carr-Gomm concealed a puritanical soul. It caused him now to say, 'It seems to me, Treves, that you have contrived to turn this hospital into a way-station for all the notorious riff-raff of London society.'

'Well, John doesn't know they're riff-raff, sir. And it means a lot to him to see them.'

'Oh, very well. Who is it today?'

'Lord and Lady Waddington.'

'Well at least they're decently married – and to each other,' said Carr-Gomm, unconsciously echoing Mothershead.

It was Mothershead who showed Lord and Lady Waddington to Merrick's rooms later that day. As soon as she saw them, she feared the worst. They were young, attractive and empty-looking. Lady Waddington twittered aimless pleasantries until Mothershead produced a photograph of Merrick. It was Treves' instruction that all visitors must be made familiar with their host's appearance before going in so that they could experience their initial shock where he could not see them. Treves was determined that there should be no repetition of the day when Nora had come upon him unawares.

When Lady Waddington saw Merrick's picture, Mothershead thought she was going to faint.

'I can't, Charlie,' she fluttered prettily. 'I just *can't*. Oh, do let us go away.'

He coughed. 'Impossible my sweet. What would people say? I mean – everyone knows we're coming, you know.'

Mothershead's lips tightened.

'If her Ladyship doesn't feel up to the visit,' she said at last, 'it really would be better if it were not made. If Mr Merrick sees that his appearance upsets people—'

'Oh no, no.' The girl recovered elaborately. 'Charlie's right. We've told so many people we're coming, and besides,' she made a noble effort, 'one must be kind to these poor unfortunates, must one not?'

182

With difficulty Mothershead restrained herself from hitting her.

'If you'll follow me then.' She led them down the hallway to Merrick's door and knocked.

She hated Lord and Lady Waddington for the eagerness in Merrick's voice as he called 'Come in'; hated them even more when she saw him standing there ready to greet them, dressed in his best clothes, the window carefully open so that the last of his lingering smell should not offend them; hated them totally for the joy in his eyes when they controlled themselves sufficiently to simper forwards and shake his hand.

'I'll get you some tea,' she said gruffly, and departed.

She sent Nora along with the tea, but returned herself half an hour later to see how everyone was managing. Her sensitive nose for atmosphere warned her as soon as she entered that the young couple were both on the verge of screaming, although smiles were fixed onto their faces as though held on by steel rivets. To all this Merrick was happily oblivious. He was examining a ring that just fitted onto the little finger of his good hand, and a silver-tipped walking cane that rested against his chair.

'Thank you for your kind gifts,' he was saying. 'I can't say enough about this ring. And this walking stick is ever so dashing. So much more elegant than my old one. More tea?'

They nodded shakily, beyond speech. John reached over and lifted the tea-pot to refill the lady's cup. She sipped delicately and seemed in control of herself, but as she replaced the cup it rattled against the saucer.

'If you have a chill I can close the window,' Merrick offered.

'Oh no, no – I'm fine. Please – I mean, thank you–' she floundered to a standstill.

'I don't get out as often as I'd like to, for some people do find my appearance disturbing. Of course, I can't fault them,' he went on. 'People are often frightened by what they don't understand. And it is hard to understand, even for myself, for you see, Mother was so very beautiful.'

'When you're ready to leave,' Mothershead told the couple, 'Mr Treves would like to speak to you.'

'Oh yes – well – perhaps it is time we were going.' The young man jumped to his feet and the girl followed suit. Their relief was palpable. Merrick made his farewells in the same courteous, gentle tone in which he had greeted them, and if their replies were a little hurried he did not seem to notice.

Mothershead delivered the Waddingtons into Treves' care, glad to do so before she forgot her manners. She returned to her desk in the Receiving Room, relieved to have them out of her sight. But they reappeared about ten minutes later as Treves ushered them out of the front entrance and said goodbye on the step.

'I regret that I must leave you here, M'lord and M'lady,' Mothershead heard him say. Thank you so much for coming. It was an act of the greatest charity.'

Now Lady Waddington was all ease and graciousness. 'Oh no, Mr Treves. The pleasure was all ours. Good day.'

From her desk Mothershead watched the whole scene with undisguised annoyance. She had a clear view of the Waddingtons' faces as they turned away, and the speed with which their smiles slipped to reveal the disgust beneath drew from her the muttered comment, 'Watery-headed bunch!'

She wondered how far Treves was aware of the truth behind these visits. Did he know that what he called kindness was no more than a society version of the very life from which he had rescued Merrick? 'Oggling the animals in the zoo' was Mothershead's contemptuous verdict, and in her stern judgement Treves was either ignorant or had wilfully blinded himself. She respected him for the brilliant doctor she knew him to be, but she considered that he had no more common sense than men usually had, and his first words as he approached her, after seeing off the Waddingtons, confirmed it.

'Incredible, isn't it?' he said cheerfully. 'Well, I must be off, Mothershead. I've got a lecture at the college.'

She rose as he prepared to pass on. 'Excuse me, sir, I'd like to have a word with you.'

'Oh? Well, quickly please, Mothershead. I'm overdue.'

She moved closer and lowered her voice. 'I can't understand why you let these people go in there, sir.'

'Now, Mothershead, you have to understand that this is very good for John. He relishes contact with people outside the hospital . . .'

'But you saw them, sir,' she interrupted him, urgency making her ignore etiquette. 'They couldn't hide their disgust. They don't care anything for John. They're just trying to impress their friends.'

'Aren't you being just a little harsh, Mothershead? You yourself hardly treated John with much loving kindness when he first arrived.'

She faced him squarely. 'I bathed him, didn't I? I fed him and cleaned up after him! If loving kindness can be called care and practical concern, then yes, I did treat him with loving kindness, and I'm not ashamed to say it.'

'You're right, Mothershead. Please forgive me. Of course, I appreciate everything you've done for John and I'm glad that you are concerned about his welfare. But I'm the physician in charge and I must do what I think best.' He hurried on before she could interrupt again. 'I'm also very late, so please excuse me.'

He started to go, but she moved quickly and placed herself in front of him. 'If you ask me, sir, he's just being stared at all over again.'

He gave her an astonished look. 'You really must excuse me, Mothershead. I can't discuss this any further.'

He went to his office and collected the things he needed for the lecture. The college adjoined the hospital and he contrived to go across without passing again through the Receiving Room. He was irritated and annoyed. He had had his judgement disputed before but not by nurses, and never on the subject of Merrick, about whom everyone now deferred to him as the uncontested expert.

He delivered his lecture with the upper part of his mind only, while the rest dwelt on the injustice of Mothershead's accusations. He remembered Merrick's room as he had seen it last, crowded with mementoes of his society visitors. The mantelpiece was now overflowing with photographs of the ladies who had followed Mrs Kendal's example. The atmosphere of the room had been gay, clean and cheerful, a cosy little home over which its imprisoned monarch could reign happily. How different from the circumstances in which he had found the Elephant Man.

The faces of Merrick's visitors floated before Treves' eyes as he talked on and on in the lecture hall. They were not the faces he himself would have chosen for companionship. Beautiful as many of them were their aristocratic, well-fed complacency would have bored and infuriated him. They were so familiar they might have come out of one mould; all with a high-nosed air about them, the inevitable result of the tension they felt.

With a sense of dismay Treves confronted the thought he had been edging closer to without knowing it. Their tension was caused by their reaction to John and the effort to control it. 'You saw their disgust.' Mothershead had accused him, and it was true. He had been aware of it many times, but discounted it for the sake of the benefit that John could take from these visits. And he believed, with total conviction, that John was unaware of the way his visitors regarded him. Many folk in the past had been horrified by his appearance, and he had grown used to seeing them scream and run away. People whose breeding (or whose curiosity?) demanded that they control their feelings and present an appearance of smiling complacency were outside his experience, and he accepted their politeness at its face value.

It seemed to Treves that several weeks cocooned in his mirrorless rooms were making Merrick forget that he was different from other men, and this was the effect that gave him the most satisfaction.

Was it not better to allow him to continue in this happy ignorance, even at the cost of a small deception? Treves knew what Mothershead would say, but Mothershead did not know John as he did himself. Just the same, by the end of the evening he was admitting to himself that her challenge had disturbed him.

He was far from proceeding to an actual admission that she might have been right, but before he went home for the night he slipped back to the hospital and made his way to John's rooms. Like a mother hen guarding her chicks he wanted to look in and see for himself that John was settled and happy. He might stop for a chat, hear about that afternoon's visitors and admire their gift. Then the nagging little voice within him would be stilled.

Before he reached Merrick's door he could hear the sound of a low plaintive murmur coming from inside. Probably another nightmare, he thought, although it was quite different from any sound Merrick had ever made before. Quietly he opened the door.

Merrick was not in bed, but seated at the window with his back to the door. In his hands was a large white pillow which he grasped tightly to his chest. Part of it was brushing against his cheek, and as he rubbed his face against its softness he whispered urgent words. Treves could make none of them out, but the tone reached him clearly enough. It held a melancholy, a yearning for delights once known and lost forever. It was the voice of a lover.

Beside him was the table on which the portraits of Mrs Kendal and Merrick's mother occupied pride of place. But the mother's picture had been turned face down. Only Mrs Kendal's remained, her dark sweet eyes gazing on Merrick in the darkness.

For a long time Treves stood there, frozen with shock, his mind refusing to take in the implications of what he was seeing. When he could force himself to move, it was to close the door and turn quietly away.

He left the hospital as un-noticed as he had entered it. He tried to believe that the storm inside him was not his conscience, only the tiring effects of a very long day. But the honesty that lay at the bottom of his character would not permit this escape, and on the long walk home in the darkness he faced the fact that it might take all his life for him to find forgiveness for what he had inadvertently done.

He let himself quietly into the house and went directly into the sitting room. It seemed to him now that almost no time had passed since Merrick had been in this very room, overcome with emotion at Anne's friendly greeting, the pretty smile on her face. The words came back to Treves – 'I'm not used to such kindness from a beautiful woman' – and he wondered how he could have missed the danger that stared him in the face.

Automatically he went to Anne's bookshelf and began hunting through it. It gave him something for his hands and mind to do, and he needed that now to still the fear within him. After a few minutes he had a small pile of books on the table. The last one that came to hand he quickly replaced on the shelf. It was *The Hunchback of Notre Dame*.

There was a soft movement behind him and Anne appeared in the doorway, dressed for bed.

'I thought I heard you come in. I've been waiting for you upstairs,' she said. She smiled when she saw what he was doing. She never grudged the time he gave to Merrick now. 'More romances for John?'

'Hmmmm?' he only half heard her. She came further into the room and studied his face.

'Freddie, what's the matter? You look half dead. Was the lecture very tiring?'

'No, it isn't that. I've just been thinking about something – about Bytes.'

'Oh, Freddie, what put that wretched vampire into your head?'

'Something I—' he made himself stop. He could not tell Anne the implications of what he had seen earlier that night. But he had to tell her some of what was churning in his mind or he would go distracted. 'I'm beginning to think I'm very little different from him.'

'Bytes! Oh that's absurd.' She began to poke the fire into life again.

He sat down feeling deathly tired. 'Is it? Mothershead said much the same thing.'

'She said you were getting like Bytes? I don't believe it.'

'She implied it – that I've set John up as a curiosity all over again, except that this time he's in a hospital, with all the accoutrements of science rather than a carnival. But still the people come to stare. At least, that's what Mothershead thinks. Oh they don't pay a tuppence admission any more. No, now it's pictures, curios and precious books. All for a chance to see the terrible Elephant Man.'

She ceased working on the fire. She had been listening to him only superficially, sure that he was using her as a sounding board as he often did, without expecting any response. More often than not there was no response she could give, for many of the things he 'discussed' with her were above her head. But now it was suddenly borne in on her that her husband was not talking as a doctor or a scientist but as a man in trouble, and that he was asking her help. There was an unhappiness in his voice that she had never heard before when he was talking about a medical problem. She laid down the poker and came beside him on the sofa.

'But it's all to make John happy,' she reminded him. 'It's not as if you're getting anything out of it.'

There was the dreadful bitterness of self-knowledge in his voice as he replied. 'Oh, no. I'm not getting anything out of it. My name is constantly in the papers. Carr-Gomm praises me to the heavens. Patients have begun asking expressly for me.'

'Frederick, now you are being absurd. You're an extremely talented man. Of course the patients ask for you. And as for John . . .'

'Yes. John Merrick *would* still be crouching in filthy shops and broken-down circuses if I hadn't happened along that day and seen what a splendid paragraph my diagnosis would make in the journal. And it paid off, didn't it? All I had to do was say, 'Step right up, ladies and gentlemen. Step right up and see your worst nightmares personified, your worst fears made flesh! Turn him around! See the horror of London, the terror that I, the good doctor, bring you. Turn him around, the terrible Elephant Man! See the monster made fashionable, see the outcast. See the freak!'

He would have said more but she broke in, unable to bear his self-laceration any longer. 'Oh no, Frederick, that's all wrong! John is happier and more fulfilled now than he ever has been in his entire life. And that is completely due to you.'

'Yes, it is. And what did I do? I opened a door and let a condemned man see paradise, knowing that his chains would never let him cross the threshold. How could I do it? What was all this for?'

'Frederick, just what is it that you're saying?'

'Am I a good man or am I a bad man?'

'Oh, Frederick.' She put her arms round him, trying to reach him with her love, knowing that there was a grief inside him she could not touch.

'You're a good man, a very good man.'

He said, so softly that she barely heard it, 'I feel so ugly.'

CHAPTER FIFTEEN

Medically Merrick needed little help these days. The damage to his hip would never be any better, but his wounds had healed and his bronchitis had disappeared with good nursing. Keeping him clean, fed and warm was a job that could have been left to the nurses with Treves dropping in once a week, but he continued his daily visits, knowing that John would miss them. Treves now felt a deep sense of guilty responsibility for the life he had taken over for his own purposes and changed in a way that might not be for the better.

He remembered reading somewhere that in ancient China, if one man saved another's life, the one he had saved became his property and his responsibility. He knew now how that burden must feel. John had given himself trustingly into his hands, and Treves had no doubt that he would have been amazed to learn of his benefactor's sense of guilt. He was, as Anne had said, happier than he had ever been before in his life. But the guilt was real nonetheless.

He had another reason for his daily visits. He had become honestly fond of the gentle, sensitive man he had discovered beneath the shell of the monster. When he looked at John he no longer saw his shape.

Because Merrick's medical needs were now slight, and they must talk of something, Treves drew him out to discuss the books he had read. He discovered that Merrick had gone through the whole of Shakespeare in an astonishingly short time.

'I like the sonnets best though,' he said one day. 'I think poetry is so beautiful.'

That evening Treves went on a hunt through his bookshelves at home and discovered two volumes of poetry. They belonged to Anne, who offered them willingly, and

Treves made a point of mentioning that Anne had sent them when he handed them over the next day, knowing that any attention from a pretty woman charmed Merrick.

They read the poems together. Despite his thick speech Merrick had a natural gift for the feel of a verse that would often lead him into its heart, while Treves was still puzzling over its meaning.

That morning he returned several times to the same poem, as though sensing that it had a significance for him that it would only yield up with study.

'*When will the stream be aweary,*' he read, '*of flowing under my eye?*

When will the wind be aweary of blowing over the sky?

When will the clouds be aweary of fleeting?

When will the heart be aweary of beating, and nature to die?'

Treves took up the refrain:

'*Never, oh never, nothing will die.*

The stream flows, the wind blows,

The cloud fleets, the heart beats,

Nothing will die.'

They were silent for a moment. Treves waited to see if Merrick wanted to read anything else, but he closed the book with a small sound that might have been a sigh. His eyes passed over the room and came to rest on the picture of the child sleeping. He gazed at it for a long time.

'I wish I could sleep like normal people,' he said quietly. Before Treves could think of a reply, Merrick turned and looked at him levelly. 'Mr Treves, there is something I've been meaning to ask you for some time . . .' He seemed not to know how to go on.

'Yes, John,' Treves encouraged him gently.

'Can you cure me?'

Treves was taken aback. It was the last question he had expected, and now he wondered why it had never occurred to him that John might wonder about this. It was so obvious to himself that the condition was incurable that he had forgotten that John knew nothing of such things.

Mingled with his surprise was a renewed sense of remorse. This is the result, said the little voice inside, of allowing him to forget that he is so unlike other people. He *has* now forgotten it, and he begins to hope with a cruel hope that will destroy him.

'No, John,' Treves said after a moment. 'I can't. I can care for you, but I can't cure you.'

Merrick did not seem disturbed or disappointed by this answer. 'I thought as much,' he said simply.

He got to his feet and moved to the window. Treves followed him with his eyes and saw how Merrick turned to face him. And then something happened which he was afterwards never able to explain.

Merrick was standing, gazing in his direction, and it seemed to Treves that those features, which had never before been capable of expression, wore one now. It was a calm, knowing look, almost a benign smile that contained in it forgiveness. Treves stared in disbelief, and as he did so Merrick was lit up by a blinding flash of light that seemed to come from the window behind him. Treves blinked against the brilliance of it, unable to comprehend what he was seeing, or even to believe his eyes. When he looked again, the moment had passed. Merrick had turned away and was moving towards the bookcase to find a place for the precious new volume. He seemed unaware that anything unusual had happened.

'John—' Treves was thoroughly confused, but he was interrupted by a knock on the door.

'Come in,' called Merrick, turning round. He was back to his old self. There was no light and no expression on those set features. Treves might have begun to believe he had imagined everything, but he knew that he was not a fanciful man.

The arrival was Nora, holding a brown paper parcel tied with string. Merrick said nothing. Since they had talked together about his model cathedral more than a month ago he had seen her very seldom, and never alone.

'Are you looking for me, Nurse?' asked Treves.

'No, sir. Mr Merrick.' Nora seemed nervous, but she approached Merrick and looked him in the face. 'I have something for you.'

A slight tilt of his head indicated his surprise, and she turned quickly to the table and opened up the parcel. It contained several squares of new cardboard, a cutting knife, a paste-pot, a few brushes and some paint.

'I thought these things would be helpful with your cathedral,' she said, smiling at him.

'Oh yes – thank you – thank you—' he began to stumble over his words in his efforts to express his thanks. But it was more than thanks and they both knew it. It was his joy and relief that she had returned in spirit to the moment when she talked to him with interest and without reserve. Treves looked from one to the other, touched by the girl's gesture and by Merrick's reaction, but realizing there was something here he did not understand. It was not like Merrick to lose his composure these days. If anything, he was growing famous for the elegance of his social address.

Merrick began to examine the materials. Then he laid them carefully aside and at once began to pull the crude spires from the model he had been working on. He could do them so much better now. Nora gave him a smile of total understanding and departed quickly.

'The cathedral is coming along nicely,' Treves observed.

Merrick answered without looking up. He was absorbed.

'Yes, soon I'll start the main spire, but I must finish these columns first. How kind of her.'

Treves leaned forward to get a better view of what Merrick was doing and found, as Merrick shifted slightly, that he was looking directly at the back of his head. What he saw there made him freeze with dismay. The growths were larger – significantly larger. They must have been growing all these weeks but so slowly that he had never noticed.

'How blind of me,' he murmured.

'I beg your pardon?' Merrick looked up.

'Nothing, John.'

Merrick must never know what he had seen, Treves decided at once. If it really did mean a deterioration of his condition, and possibly the approach of the end of his life, there was no need to worry him with it. But what was left of that life must be made as happy as possible. And suddenly the dread that he would start to hope for too much became irrelevent.

'Is there anything else, John? Anything at all that I could get for you?'

Merrick looked up quickly, his eyes alight. 'Oh, no, there is nothing. I have everything. You have given me everything I could possibly want. I am happy every hour of the day. I only wish there was something I could give to you.'

'Please, John, it would give me so much pleasure to give you something. Something just for yourself. Isn't there something you would like to have?'

Merrick was silent for a moment. Then he rose and went over to his cloak, reached into its pocket and pulled out a folded piece of paper that seemed to have been torn from a newspaper. He handed it to Treves, who examined it closely.

It was an advertisement for an elegant gentleman's dressing-bag. It boasted ivory brushes, silver fittings and Moroccan silk linings. In its finely wrought luxury it was the epitome of everything for which Merrick could have no possible use.

'You want a dressing-bag, John?'

'You don't think it's too gaudy, do you?' Merrick asked anxiously. 'It's really very dashing. It says here it's something no gentleman should be without. I'm inclined to agree.'

Treves got up and went to the door. 'So am I,' he said with decision. 'I should have thought of it before. Leave it to me, John. If I can possibly get one I will.'

In the corridor he began to examine the advertisement again, and became so engrossed in it that he almost walked into Mothershead. She was carrying a parcel.

'Mr Treves, some more books arrived for Mr Merrick.'

'I wish they'd stop sending books and start sending money.'

'No better news?'

'No. And there's barely a week to go till the next Committee meeting,' he sighed. 'Have the books put in my office, please. John's got enough to keep him occupied for the moment.'

'Yes, sir,' her eyes fell on the paper which he was holding low enough for her to see. 'What's that?'

'A dressing-bag,' he said, showing her.

'Very smart indeed.' She looked bewildered.

'Yes. John wants it.'

'*A dressing bag?*'

'You don't think it's too gaudy, do you?'

'Well—'

'John thinks it's very dashing. Something no gentleman should be without. I'm inclined to agree.'

As he walked off he had the satisfaction of knowing that for once he had totally deprived Mrs Mothershead of speech.

Anne, into whose hands he gave the job of acquiring the bag, was similarly speechless, though not for long.

'But what on earth is he going to *do* with it, Freddie? It's completely useless to him.'

'He doesn't see it that way. I've come to realize that he has another life, one that goes on entirely in his head and which makes his real life tolerable.

'In his dreams he's – oh, everything nature meant him to be when she formed his character.' Treves sighed heavily as he added, 'and that includes a ladies' man.'

'Oh, Freddie, no.'

'I'm afraid so. He's a young man in his early twenties and if he has one tragedy that's greater than all the others put together it's that his reaction to women is entirely normal. Mrs Kendal's first visit made him very much aware of himself as a man, and now he falls – very humbly – in love with every lady that comes to see him. Imagine those feelings inside a body that makes a woman want to run from him.

'He mentioned once that he'd like to go to a blind asylum. Since then I've sometimes wondered if it was in his mind that a woman who couldn't see him might come to love him.'

She was silent for a while, and when he looked he could see tears falling gently down her face. He slipped his arm round her and held her close to him.

'And this dressing-case—?' she said at last.

'It's part of the fantasy. In his dreams he's not only a great lover but a terrific swell. But he needs some props to help him keep the character up. It's like that time Jenny put a bit of tinsel on her head one Christmas and wrapped one of the dining-room curtains round her? Do you remember we found her parading up and down telling everyone she was a countess?

'Well, it's the same with John, only he's a bit limited about the "props" he can use. A real dandy would wear a top hat and a dress suit, but he couldn't get into them. You couldn't put a proper shirt on him or squeeze his feet into patent leather shoes. It's true he's got the silver-topped walking cane and the ring Lady Waddington gave him, but they're not enough.

'When he has this case it'll complete the character. He can sit in that room and feel himself to be a dashing young spark. He can't use the silver-backed brushes and the comb because he's got very little hair to brush. The razors will be useless to him because he can't shave. An ordinary toothbrush is no good to him, and neither is a cigar case. But he'll have them – and he'll *believe* it, don't you see?'

'Yes, I begin to,' she said in a sad voice. 'Leave it to me, Freddie.'

The Committee meeting neared with the slow, massive

unstopability of a juggernaut. Those who feared it watched its approach with a mounting sense of horror, but the one man who had the most cause to fear being crushed beneath its wheels remained oblivious. Treves, Carr-Gomm and Mothershead were united in keeping him in happy ignorance till the last possible moment.

The chairman, encountering Broadneck in the corridor one morning, seized his chance to do a little subtle manipulating.

'Ah, Broadneck, you'll no doubt be pleased to know that we've received a smashing response to my letter.' It was a lie, but in the circumstances Carr-Gomm's soul wasn't troubled. 'It's all very heart-warming, though several letters do mention how beastly it would be to part the poor fellow from Mr Treves and the staff, but since the Committee insists . . .'

'Good day, Carr-Gomm,' Broadneck scowled and passed on down the corridor, leaving the chairman to reflect on the uselessness of applying subtlety in opposition to brute force.

On the day of the meeting Mrs Mothershead went early to Carr-Gomm's office. She did this every day now, immediately after the post's arrival, and together they looked through the disappointing mail. It never took long.

'A few small cheques,' Carr-Gomm sighed. 'But no offer of a home. Nobody wants him.'

'But what'll happen to him after today, sir?' Mothershead demanded. 'If the Committee refuse to let us keep him—'

'I'm afraid they will. There's not the slightest doubt of that.'

'Then where is he to go?'

Carr-Gomm's only answer was a sigh and a long look at his hands. Neither of them spoke, but the word 'workhouse' hung between them. Both had heard the story of Merrick's life only at second-hand, but somehow his horror of the workhouse had communicated itself to them so that now it was almost a tangible thing.

There was a knock on the door and Nettleton entered,

stiff with importance. Without a word he handed the chairman something he bore in his hand, the mere touching of which seemed to inspire him with awe. He positively crept out of the room.

A glance at the object Nettleton had handed over explained his behaviour. It was a letter, but not such a letter as Mothershead had ever seen before. The paper was thick like parchment, and heavily embossed in a shape that she might almost have mistaken for a royal coat of arms – if she hadn't known it to be impossible.

The envelope crackled noisily as Carr-Gomm opened it and drew out the sheet of paper within. This too was embossed and bore only a few short lines, but those lines cleared the worry from Carr-Gomm's face and replaced it with a look of disbelieving delight.

'What is it?' said Mothershead urgently. 'What *is* it?'

Without a word he handed it to her and stood watching as her face assumed the same look as his own. When she looked up their eyes met, but for a moment neither could speak.

At last Carr-Gomm found his voice. 'Mrs Mothershead, I want your promise that you will say not a word of this to anyone.'

'Even Mr Treves sir?'

For once in his life Carr-Gomm's pale eyes gleamed with a humour that was almost roguish.

'Especially Mr Treves,' he said.

From his office window overlooking the front entrance, Treves had watched the Committee members arrive. To him they all looked like executioners. They would vote to return John Merrick to Hell, and then go home to supper with the easy consciences of good men. He hated every one of them.

Carr-Gomm sent to him before the meeting began, so that they could go in together.

To his amazement Carr-Gomm looked relaxed, almost

cheerful as he led the way to the Committee Room. Treves wondered for a moment if he could possibly have forgotten what was to happen today, or did he just no longer care?

'Sir,' he said urgently under his breath as they went in, 'if there is any way we could defer . . .'

'Steady on, Treves,' Gomm interrupted him. 'Have a seat.'

Reluctantly Treves went to his seat. Carr-Gomm took his place at the head of the table and rapped his gavel. When he was sure he had their attention, he began to speak.

'Gentlemen, I know we begin every meeting by reading the minutes, but in the interest of speed I think we should conclude a matter discussed previously, to wit, that of Mr John Merrick, the Elephant Man . . .'

The very sound of the name brought Broadneck exploding to his feet. Carr-Gomm's only reaction was to offer a smile to Treves, who was feeling too grim to answer it.

'Mr Broadneck?' Carr-Gomm beamed at Broadneck in a way a more sensitive man might have been wary of.

Broadneck began to yap. 'Mr Chairman! I was under the distinct impression that we had concluded discussion of this disagreeable matter. Had we not ascertained that an Elephant Man is *not* acceptable as a patient? Have we not, very generously, allowed the creature to use two of our rooms until such time as he could be properly disposed of? Have we not made every effort to interpret the hospital's rules benevolently in the name of charity?'

His swivelled gaze round the table produced the expected rumble of agreement. The Committee members were beginning to feel harrassed by Carr-Gomm. More than one of them silently offered thanks that Broadneck was available to do the dirty work.

Confident that he had the majority with him, Broadneck expanded. 'Which brings to mind my next point. The rules, gentlemen, the rules. In a society such as ours, it is of paramount importance that we not stray from the established order. Has that order not already been fearfully strained by allowing this . . . this . . . sideshow exhibit to take up residence, however temporary, in two very useful rooms, the purpose of which would be far better served in accommodating *treatable* patients, patients to whom this hospital was originally dedicated? I believe we have a duty . . .'

Treves felt he might vomit if he stayed. How could Carr-Gomm sit there, that inscrutable smile on his face as if he expected the heavens to open any minute and a *deus ex machina* to descend and make everything right? Didn't he understand that he'd ruined their chances by bringing matters to a head prematurely? Or had he, too, secretly joined the ranks of the uncaring? Was this his way of reneging on his word, getting rid of John Merrick and allowing Broadneck to take the blame?

For a moment Treves seriously considered the possibility. He knew Carr-Gomm to be a well-meaning man, but a subtle and devious medical politician. He was about to hurl caution to the winds and throw himself into Merrick's defence when he looked up suddenly and caught Carr-Gomm's eyes on him. He had the feeling that the older man had read his every thought and was trying to tell him something. The pale eyes looked directly into his own with a message as clear as words.

Leave it to me, I know what I'm doing.

Treves leaned back against his chair and his hands unclenched. He was still troubled, but Carr-Gomm's remarkable power of instilling trust as if by hypnotism, had been stronger than his fears. His shoulders sagged tiredly. He became aware that Broadneck was still ranting.

'. . . In light of these facts, our course is clear. The question is not whether to accept this creature as a patient. The question is when will those rooms be vacated for use by better qualified, more deserving cases? I move that this Elephant Man be removed from the premises immediately. We have a sacred duty to cure the sick, not care for circus animals. That is my last word on the subject, Mr Chairman. Shall we vote?'

He threw the last words directly at Carr-Gomm, as a challenge. Carr-Gomm did not immediately reply, but he checked his watch then cleared his throat.

'I take it, Mr Broadneck,' he said gently, 'that your mind is fixed on this matter?'

Broadneck's already high-coloured face turned puce. He seemed unable to believe what he had heard.

'Mr Chairman, don't you have ears. I am *unalterably* opposed to any . . .'

Treves had ceased to listen. His ear had been caught by the sound of a faint commotion far off in the building. His mind said automatically – 'Accident case – emergency.' But his abnormally acute hearing had picked up a new tension in the distant noise, a sense of pleasurable excitement, intangible but unmistakable. He made a conscious effort to shut out Broadneck's voice and listen more intently. Carr-Gomm, too, was paying no heed to Broadneck's blustering. His eyes were alight with expectation and Treves knew, without knowing how he knew, that Carr-Gomm's confidence that day was somehow linked with whatever was happening in other parts of the building. The chairman's eyes were on him again.

Leave it to me, I know what I'm doing.

'No,' Broadneck howled. 'My mind is made up on this.'

Whatever the commotion was it was coming near. It had resolved itself now into footsteps.

'You shall not sway me,' Broadneck persisted.

The footsteps were in the hall immediately outside the Committee Room.

'May we *now* vote, Mr Chairman, at long last?'

Carr-Gomm checked his watch again and began to rise to his feet. He was smiling broadly. The door had begun to open.

I know what I'm doing.

The door was flung wide. Two footmen entered quickly and took up position on either side of it. One of them announced in a loud voice, 'Gentlemen, Her Royal Highness Alexandra, Princess of Wales.'

The next moment a tall, slender and very lovely woman stood in the doorway.

'Good morning, gentlemen,' said a soft, utterly feminine voice.

At forty-two Alexandra had retained much of her extraordinary beauty, although time and her husband's frequent infidelities had drained the joyousness from her face and left a wistful sadness behind.

But if she had lost Prince Edward's interest, she had strengthened her hold on the affection of the British people. They pitied her unhappiness, admired her looks and the way she had kept her elegant figure after six children, but mostly they loved her for the warmth and kindness of her heart. Alexandra had never been known to refuse an appeal to her sympathy.

She stood now in the doorway as the men round the table rose hastily to their feet and stared at her, too stunned to speak. She knew precisely the impression she made and she enjoyed it. Alexandra had always liked being the centre of attention; she liked the glitter and the pageantry that went with her position. She savoured now the sensation she had made by her entrance.

'I hope I'm not interrupting?' she asked in the gentle voice that had lost most of its Danish accent, but still managed to be charmingly not-quite-English.

Carr-Gomm seemed to pull himself together. Even he, the only one who had expected the Princess's appearance, had suffered a slight shock at the sight of her. He stepped forward.

'Indeed not, Your Highness. Your presence is always greatly appreciated. We were just about to put the matter of Mr Merrick to a vote.' He turned back to the other Committee members. His eyes sought Broadneck who, understanding how he had been out-manoeuvred, was trying to control the workings of his face. 'The Princess is very interested in Mr Merrick's fate,' he said with unmistakable emphasis.

Alexandra's lips twitched faintly. She knew perfectly the

role she was being called on to play and she responded to Carr-Gomm's cue without hesitation. 'Indeed I am, sir, as is the Queen. I have a brief communication from Her Highness which she has requested I read to you.' She moved forward.

Carr-Gomm stood back to make his place at the head of the table available to her and she came to stand there. Instead of sitting down, she took a piece of paper from her reticade and began to read from it.

'To the Governing Committee, London Hospital. I would very much like to commend you for the charitable face you have shown Mr John Merrick, the Elephant Man. It is laudable that you have provided one of England's most unfortunate sons with a safe and tranquil harbour, a home. For this immeasurable kindness, as well as the many other acts of mercy on behalf of the poor, of which Mr Carr-Gomm has kept me informed, I gratefully thank you. Signed, Victoria, Empress of India, Queen of the United Kingdom of Great Britain and Ireland.'

Alexandra folded the paper and looked round the table. Her gaze came to rest on Broadneck, the man who had been standing when she entered, and therefore presumably the author of the unpleasant squeals of anger and outrage that had reached her down the corridor. She felt a flinch of distaste for his violent face and hard, piggy eyes. But she allowed none of this to show. Instead she gave Broadneck the full power of her magnificent eyes, and although her words took in the entire Committee it was to Broadneck she spoke.

'I am sure you gentlemen may be counted on to do the Christian thing.'

Then she seated herself with the air of someone prepared to stay there all day if necessary. With a small nod of her head she indicated that she wished them, too, to be seated.

Carr-Gomm replied quickly, 'Thank you very much, Your Highness. You may be sure we shall.'

Alexandra exchanged a conspiratorial glance with him. She had an intuitive gift for understanding atmosphere and she understood this one exactly. She and Carr-Gomm had never met, but already they were like actors playing predetermined roles in a drama. Treves watched the whole performance, as stunned as any man there, hardly able to take in the immensity of what had happened. It was too soon yet for joy.

Broadneck sat down quickly, because his legs were collapsing under him. He was thoroughly unnerved. He realized that much of his outburst must have been audible down the corridor. He felt a fresh surge of hatred for Carr-Gomm, who had tricked him into this.

The chairman continued in a smooth voice: 'Well, then, I move that Mr John Merrick be admitted to the London Hospital on a permanent basis, on condition that the hospital shall receive a yearly payment equal to the cost of occupying one bed, and that the funds for his care shall be clearly separate from hospital funds. All those in favour?'

He raised his own hand at once. For a dreadful moment it was the only hand raised. The other members, puzzled, stared at Broadneck, as if awaiting his lead. Their action seemed to give him a last stab of courage, for his hand remained stubbornly down. Red-faced, he stared at Carr-Gomm, then at Treves, then at Alexandra. She beamed back at him with eyes as apparently innocent as a child's.

Before that gaze he retreated, seemed to deflate in front of them all. Slowly his hand was raised, and after it came the hands of all the others, confused by the loss of their leader.

After that there was nothing for it but to close the meeting at once. Broadneck had no heart for any further business, and the royal guest must be attended to. Carr-Gomm escorted her to his office, followed by Treves. Formalities followed, Mothershead was sent for to make her curtsey, tea was served, polite conversation was made. Through it all, Treves was in agony, longing to get away to tell Merrick the good news, but unable to move.

Alexandra made him tell her the whole of Merrick's known history. The version Treves offered up was suitably edited, but still sufficient to draw from her expressions of horror.

'Mr Treves,' she said at last, 'I should very much like to meet the Elephant Man. But not—' she added hastily, as a note of alarm covered his face before he could stop it, '—not, perhaps this afternoon. It would scarcely be kind of me to walk in and take the poor gentleman by surprise.' Her eyes twinkled. 'We have seen to what shocks that can lead, have we not, gentlemen?'

Treves began to understand why people loved Alexandra. He was immensely relieved that he did not have to put Merrick on display before giving him an extra bath.

The Princess had taken out a little notebook and was scribbling in it with a gold pencil.

'Shall we say – next Wednesday afternoon?' she asked, and again her eyes shone with laughter. 'That is – unless Mr Merrick has any conflicting engagements. I hear he has a crowded social calendar.'

'I can assure Your Royal Highness that Mr Merrick has no "conflicting engagements" next Wednesday afternoon,' said Carr-Gomm, who had not the slightest idea whether he had or not. 'We will be honoured to welcome you.'

It seemed that the entire staff of the hospital, plus any patients that were on their feet, were gathered in the front windows to watch the Princess's departure. Before getting into her carriage, she turned and gave them all an elegant little wave, and a cheer went up. Within minutes the whole story of the Committee meeting had gone round the building.

When the carriage had rumbled out of the gate, Treves and Carr-Gomm turned to each other jubilantly, but the chairman, as always, expressed his joy in deceptively moderate terms.

'If anyone,' he said, 'has got to Mr Merrick and denied me the pleasure of being the one to tell him the good news, I shall be excessively angry.'

'Then we'd better hurry, sir.'

Their route took them past Treves' office, outside which

Carr-Gomm stood and fumed impatiently while Treves darted in to collect something.

'Was that really necessary, Treves?' he demanded, looking disparagingly at the wrapped parcel that Treves had tucked under his arm.

'Yes, sir. Absolutely necessary.'

At the door to Merrick's room they found Mothershead standing guard.

'I've made sure no-one went in till you came, sir.'

'Thank you, Mrs Mothershead. Perhaps you would like to come in with us,' said Carr-Gomm.

Treves led the way inside and went straight up to Merrick, who rose apprehensively.

'Good afternoon, John. Mr Carr-Gomm has something he would like to say to you.'

He deferred to Carr-Gomm, who took centre stage with a beaming face.

'Mr Merrick,' he said formally, 'it is my greatest pleasure to welcome you, officially, to the London Hospital. The Governing Committee have voted, unanimously, to provide you with these rooms on a permanent basis. This is your home now. I'm so very, very pleased for you.'

He finished by bending his head forward in anticipation of Merrick's reply. But the Elephant Man was speechless, whether from joy or disbelief no-one could tell. He only looked around them – from Treves to Carr-Gomm to Mothershead, who was smiling at him.

'So you see, John,' Treves encouraged him, 'there's no need for a lighthouse. All your friends are here.'

'Welcome home, John,' said Mothershead.

At last Merrick spoke. 'My – home—?'

'Yes, John,' said Treves.

'You—' he looked at them all by turn, '—did all this for me?'

'Yes,' said Treves again.

Merrick pulled himself together. 'Please – please thank the Governing Committee for me. I will do my utmost to merit their kindness.'

He turned away from them slightly and looked at the room as if seeing it for the first time. Treves could sense that only now was it beginning to dawn on him that at last he had a real home, a place of his own.

'My home.' Merrick lingered over the words.

'There is one more thing, John,' said Treves. 'Here.' He laid the wrapped parcel on the table, and stood back, indicating for Merrick to open it. He thought he had never known such pleasure and satisfaction as he felt watching Merrick pull off the paper and open the dressing-bag. It was plain that the Elephant Man was overjoyed by his gift. He lovingly handled the articles, the brush, the comb, the tooth-brush, taking them in and out of their compartments, opening and closing the bag with a dazed air, as if he could not believe what was happening to him.

'Mr Treves—' he said huskily. 'Thank you, my – friends.'

Treves raised his eyebrows to Carr-Gomm in a silent question. The chairman understood at once and signalled to Mrs Mothershead to leave.

He followed her, stopping briefly at the door to say, 'Once again, Mr Merrick, welcome to the London Hospital as our permanent guest.'

Then he was gone, leaving Treves alone with Merrick.

'It's getting late,' said Treves in a deceptively casual voice to cover the fact that he knew Merrick was weeping quietly. 'I keep forgetting that winter is so far advanced until the light starts to fade so early in the day. Look at it, dark already.'

He kept up this small talk until Merrick had recovered his composure. Then he smiled at him.

'I hope you like your present, John. Anne chose it.'

'Please thank Mrs Treves for me. I hope she didn't go to any trouble.'

'She did, because she wanted to – because it was for you.'

He was momentarily afraid this might set Merrick off

208

again. The Elephant Man had had as much as he could bear.

'Mr Treves – thank you for what you've done for me. I know it was you who made them keep me here.'

'It wasn't me at all, John. It was – a very kind lady who I'll tell you all about tomorrow. Not tonight. You've had enough excitement for one day. Goodnight.'

CHAPTER SIXTEEN

There was a good crowd in the Peacock tonight. Jim Renshaw's "parties" were getting known in the district and the demand was growing. So far the porter had confined his sightseeing trips to Bedstead Square to five or six persons. It was easier for him to keep control that way. But confidence and greed had combined to make him think a larger expedition practicable, and this evening he was planning on twelve.

He stood in the centre of the bar-room, jingling the night's takings in his pocket and trying to see through the smoke that hung, fog-like, over the customers. A sheaf of raised arms stabbed the air to catch his attention and Renshaw surveyed them with lazy pleasure, enjoying the feeling of power their supplications gave him. A good number of the drinkers were ladies of the town who did the rounds of the pubs last thing to drum up trade. Renshaw knew most of them by now. His "parties of pleasure" always included at least one whore who paid her entrance fee in kind. Renshaw found these occasions more rewarding even than he had hoped. He had discovered that the horror and revulsion that a sight of the Elephant Man always induced did something to a woman, shook her with a physical frenzy that she had to work off with a man afterwards.

Secretly this rather shocked Renshaw. Buried deep down amidst his brutality and sentimentality, he kept a half-recognized strain of puritanism where female behaviour was concerned. It wasn't "nice" that a woman who'd had a nasty shock should be sexually excited by it. But he profited by the fact just the same.

He passed over tonight's collection of whores, searching for a new face. At last he found what he was looking for – two new faces, sitting at a table with a raffish-looking young man who seemed to be coping well with both of them, for the moment. The boy had an air of tawdry prosperity.

'Here now,' he called to Renshaw, 'these lovely ladies ain't never seen it.' Renshaw gave the two girls the briefest glance – enough to assure him that either (or both) of them would do. The fair-haired one was a choice piece.

'You're on, mate,' he said. Turning back to the other customers, he raised his voice. 'All right, all right. That's enough for this performance.' Amid a chorus of disappointed moans, he yelled, 'Hang on, hang on. There's always tomorrow night. Not to worry.'

He began to round up his little flock, shooing away a couple of hangers-on who tried to slip in at the back.

'Not tonight, ladies,' he told them genially. 'Sally, you oughta be ashamed of yourself. You've seen it twice already. What's got into you?'

The blowsy red-head he'd addressed gave him a knowing look. 'I really couldn't say, Jim Renshaw. But I know what gets into me afterwards – and so do you.'

He gave her a chuck under the chin. 'Not tonight, Sal. I've got me 'ands full. Hop it now. Go and earn an honest penny.'

Turning away from her, Renshaw found himself confronting a man in a twisted stove-pipe hat and a five-day growth of greying beard. Renshaw regarded him curiously, conscious that this stranger had been studying him silently from a seat by the bar all evening. Several times he had looked over to the bar, and always the man had been sitting there, drinking gin and never moving his pale eyes. But he never spoke, and amidst the racket of the other customers the silence that surrounded him had been almost tangible. Renshaw would have died rather than admit he'd been unnerved by it; but he did not, as he would otherwise have done, tell the stranger briskly to get out of his way. There was something about the man that killed such words on his lips.

'Room for one more?' Bytes enquired in a soft voice that

mysteriously reached Renshaw easily despite the row going on around him.

Only a moment earlier Renshaw had declared "house full", yet now he found himself saying, as though hypnotized, 'At the right price . . .'

Bytes held out a hand that contained several coins, but his gaze never left Renshaw's face. With difficulty Renshaw dragged his eyes away and looked at the money. He stiffened with shock when he saw the amount. Whoever this cove was, he wanted to see the Elephant Man badly – badly.

'There's room,' he said.

'Well, let's be off then,' said Bytes.

The giggling procession moved on its way. They might have been a party of cheerful holiday-makers, enjoying a well-earned day out. Renshaw had already slipped an arm round the waist of the blonde whore, whose name turned out to be Jess. Her male companion seemed disposed to resent this, until a closer look at Renshaw made him think better of it and turn his attention to Beattie, the other whore. But he still nursed a sense of grievance. He'd paid for all three of them.

Bytes wandered out alone at the back and followed the gaudy crowd quietly at a distance. As he walked he was considering his position.

The money he had handed over was almost the last of a dwindling stock. Much of the rest had gone on the hire of the horse and cart that Tony was now minding in a backstreet near the hospital. He had offered Renshaw a purposely generous contribution to ensure that he would be included in the party this very night. Otherwise the hire of the cart would be wasted, and Bytes' money was fast running out.

His fortunes over the last few weeks had fluctuated wildly. Destitution had threatened, following the loss of his prize possession, and Bytes had been forced to ease his financial circumstances by a little quiet burglary.

Burglary had once been his trade in an on-and-off sort of

way. He had never really taken to it, preferring less energetic forms of roguery when they presented themselves. He was forced back to it only by the most pressing need.

Alas, his professional judgement had failed him. He had fallen foul, not of the law but of the competition. The shop he had chosen to rob lay in the heart of a well-defined 'patch' that was considered the exclusive preserve of the local criminal fraternity. Bytes got away with enough cash to tide him over comfortably for a few weeks, but found himself a hunted man. His only protection was that his pursuers did not know for certain that he was their quarry. Just the same, Bytes deemed it wise to retire from London for a while – for his health.

He had vanished from the metropolis, never knowing that Tony was searching for him with news of the Elephant Man. When he returned a month later, hoping the dust might have settled as his pockets were again nearly empty, he found Tony still waiting impatiently to deliver the message.

Bytes, a superstitious man, considered that Providence had smiled on him. As he walked on through the darkness towards the hospital, he reflected that it must surely be Providence that had brought him back at this moment, with just enough cash left on him to arrange for the recovery of his property.

It was not until he was safely alone that Merrick felt able to relish the full joy of his dressing-case. He knew his little audience were on his side – Treves, Carr-Gomm, even Mothershead now. But any spectators, no matter how sympathetic, were a restraint on the free flow of his imagination. The case was a vehicle for dreams, and dreams could only be savoured in happy solitude.

Alone at last he could be himself, the true self that nature had meant him to be, the self that would use such a dressing-case as a matter of course. He studied its contents, removing each one and laying it gently on the table. They lay there in a neat row, but after a moment the order displeased him and he began to re-arrange them.

He held up the tooth-brush and considered it. He had never used such a thing, but the debonair young gad-about that lurked hidden inside his body would have used one every day to maintain the dazzling smile he turned on the ladies. It was the same with the comb and the ivory-handled razors, accessories a gentleman could not afford to be without.

He wondered how he might have obtained the case. He would have preferred it to be a gift from a pretty woman, but was it likely? Merrick's knowledge of etiquette was almost nil, but some instinct told him that no well-bred young woman would give such a personal gift to a man not her husband.

A wife then? And into his mind rose the charming face of Anne Treves. She epitomized the little he had ever seen of domestic bliss but – was it not a little soon to be thinking of domestic bliss? Marriage cramped a man's style. Even a betrothal got in the way of those delightful little saunters in perfume-scented gardens, whispering languorous delights into small feminine ears. Reluctantly, he decided he had bought the case for himself.

His situation settled, he began to consider how best he might spend the evening. A night out on the town would suit him. Dressed in the height of elegant fashion he'd saunter along to – here Merrick's knowledge failed him – to wherever dashing young blades did saunter to on these occasions. A theatre-party perhaps, to see *Twelfth Night* at the Apollo? The idea pleased him. He'd send Mrs Kendal a bouquet of red roses with compliments on her performance. A note would be delivered to his box, inviting him to a select supper at the Kendals' house afterwards. There would be champagne – ladies . . .

He began to prepare himself for the night's revelry, taking up one of the silver-backed brushes and stroking forward his thin hair till it lay neatly across his monstrous skull. To check the effect he lifted the picture of Mrs Kendal and used the glass to give him a reflection. The ugliness of his own face staring back did not disturb him. He did not see it.

With difficulty he used his fin-like right hand to slip the ring onto his left. Then he opened the cigarette-case and shoved a cigarette into his right hand. All that was needed now was the walking stick, and his accessories were complete. He twitched the stick up into his left hand and began to circle the room in a casual saunter. He could feel the admiring eyes cast upon him, drawn by his matchless elegance.

Before Mrs Kendal's picture he stopped and inclined his head towards her.

'Hello, my name is John Merrick,' he said courteously. 'I am very, *very* pleased to meet you.'

He gave her a small bow, then he turned and repeated the movement in the direction of the other ladies on his mantelpiece. He felt his heart might break with happiness.

The thunderous opening of the door behind him shattered his fragile world like crystal. On the threshold stood Renshaw grinning tipsily.

'*Curtain time!*' he announced in a voice that drink had made carelessly loud. Then his jaw dropped as he took in the sight before him.

Merrick's mind was racing, wondering wildly how he could have so mistaken the time. He knew the nightly dreaded visit must come, but he had believed later – much later. But while his thoughts whirled, his body froze. He stood immobile, a grotesque figure in his finery, and for almost half a minute Renshaw had an uninterrupted view.

It was Renshaw who broke the silence first, laughing hysterically as some part of the truth began to dawn on him. The sound galvanized Merrick into action and he made frantic, useless efforts to clear away the articles from his dressing-case. When he fumbled for the ring, Renshaw took two steps into the room and seized him by the cloak.

'No, no, you look lovely,' he crooned. 'Don't change a thing, darling. You look like the bleedin' Prince of Wales.'

He seized Merrick by the neck and thrust him at the window, kicking it open. Out in the square his audience waited expectantly.

'My friends—' he declared, '. . . the Elephant Man.'

He moved quickly as he spoke, stripping off the cloak with one brutal movement and shoving Merrick forwards to where the light was better. A noise rose from the audience, gasps of horror from those who were witnessing the spectacle for the first time, cheering and clapping from those who were back for a second or third visit.

The young man with the two whores, who had regained Jess in Renshaw's temporary absence, stood with an arm round each one.

'Horrible,' he neighed, 'I told you it was horrible – just horrible.' As if in confirmation he bestowed a smacking kiss on each one.

'Perhaps,' said Bytes, speaking softly behind him, 'the ladies would like a closer look.'

The young man began to laugh, edging the girls forward, ignoring their half-hearted resistance and sniggers of 'Come on, Jack – no don't – Jack . . .'

The window ledge was just low enough for them to scramble over, and before they knew it they were in the room. Renshaw had pulled Merrick back to allow them to enter. The Elephant Man was no longer struggling, but stood rigid with terror, sensing that this time a worse ordeal than usual awaited him. Renshaw held him in a tight grip, his head turned towards the girls who were making faces of disgust.

Jack had scrambled in behind them and was surveying the room. His eye fell on the mantelpiece with its multitude of pictures.

'Cor – he's a real ladies' man,' he exclaimed. 'Come on, give the ladies' man a kiss.'

The last words were addressed to Beattie, and as he

spoke them he seized her wrists and held them behind her, edging her forward.

'Come on,' he said in her ear. 'You'll give him a kiss.'

'Go on, Jack,' she protested, still half-laughing, unwilling to believe him serious.

But a madness had descended on Jack and Renshaw at the same moment. It was as if they were the same man. As Jack pushed Beattie forward, Renshaw held Merrick in place for the approaching kiss. His eyes were glittering as he watched Beattie come closer, her face distorting with fear and disgust as she realized what would happen. The crowd outside was leaning in through the window, egging them on, crazed with excitement.

Jack began to bring Beattie's arms to the front, raising them into the position of an embrace. As she touched Merrick the girl began to scream and struggle, but Jack pressed her forward even harder, while Renshaw and the crowd roared with laughter. Merrick's wails of fear went unnoticed.

'Here, that's enough romance . . .' said Jack. 'Now into bed.'

Beattie's struggles became wilder as her disgust gave her strength. By the time Merrick had been manhandled onto the bed she had managed to escape. Renshaw let her go. His attention was drawn by Jess, who had been watching the whole scene from a corner, her eyes wide, her face pale. Her beauty and her petrified terror seemed to bring a fresh charge of life to him. At any other time he would have taken her on the spot. But now a different desire – monstrous, thrilling – surged through him.

'A prince needs a harem,' he said, grabbing her and tightening his arms against her instinctive struggles. His blood seemed to be running twice as fast as he lifted her in his thick arms and jammed her, face downwards, onto Merrick. She screamed and screamed without end, and Renshaw thought if he could just get rid of the other quickly he'd enjoy her ten times as much after this.

Merrick had backed away on the bed as far as he could,

but as the girl's bawling face approached his he tried to escape again. Too late he felt his head slip backwards out of his control and his cries burned to frantic wheezing. Somewhere over his head he heard Renshaw's voice say, 'Mind his head – you'll kill him.'

Through the haze that was coming down over him he could just sense that the room was filled with people. Most of the rest of the crowd had jammed into the room, laughing and screaming and trying to see what was happening on the bed. Renshaw pulled the Elephant Man's head up, hissing frantically,

'Quiet down . . . quiet down. You'll have the whole place down on us.'

The noise dropped suddenly and in the comparative silence that followed Merrick heard the voice he would know and fear to the day of his death.

'Bring him out then, so we can all see him.'

Merrick began to look round frenziedly to see where Bytes' voice had come from, but Bytes was not in the room. The crowd was dispersing now, clambering back through the window until Merrick was left alone with Renshaw. He felt himself propelled to the window again.

Suddenly one of the crowd, emboldened by drink and excitement, reached out and caught Merrick's good hand, pulling him half out of the window. In a moment the others were on him, yanking him from Renshaw's hands over the low window-sill and out onto the cobbles of the square. The clumsy movements knocked Renshaw off-balance and, groping to save himself, he cannoned into the cardboard cathedral which clattered to the floor and disintegrated. He swore furiously as he clambered up, tearing at the bits of cardboard which seemed to be everywhere.

He found himself alone in the room now. Merrick was outside, on his hands and knees on the cobbles. No-one was near him. Revolted by the touch of him, the crowd had let him go and were staring at him from a few feet away. An uneasy hush had fallen over them and a little chill wind stirred the women's hair.

Quickly Renshaw scrambled out and hauled Merrick to his feet. He looked round to see if the noise had roused the hospital, but could see no sign. The crowd were moving in again.

'Give 'im a drink,' said a man, moving forward with a bottle of gin. He grabbed Merrick and poured some gin into his mouth, then pushed him away. At the same moment Renshaw released him so that he went reeling. The porter was beginning to enjoy himself again.

Merrick was caught by another man, force-fed more liquor, shoved again. A woman caught him this time and shoved him hard into the arms of another woman. The audience took up the rhythm of snatching and shoving till Merrick was whirling around them faster and faster until he fell to the floor, dizzy and sick. His head lolled to one side and he gasped for breath. The first man was standing above him, emptying the remains of the gin bottle over his head.

They were silent now, circling him like a pack of dogs closing in on a terrified rabbit. He swept his eyes round the circle that had formed around him, seeking some spark of human mercy in any of them. But they were animals.

Without knowing it he began to wail, a high pitiful endless sound that seemed to delight them, for they joined in, imitating him, then bellowing with laughter as they came for him, seized him and threw him above their heads. They tossed him higher and higher, then spun him round, ignoring his feeble flailing.

At last Renshaw intervened, not from pity but because he wanted to regain control of the situation. It irked him that the crowd should enjoy his exhibit in any way but the one he offered them. And he was beginning to fear for Merrick's safety. It would be a shame to lose such a prime source of wealth.

'Here now – here now—' he called, pulling at the crowd. 'He's had enough. Show's over.'

With grunts of disappointment they lowered Merrick to

the ground, where he was grasped by Renshaw just in time to prevent his collapsing.

'Meet you at the Peacock,' he called, to encourage them to go.

'Bring your friend,' called a male voice.

Renshaw laughed drunkenly. 'He's had 'is fill for one night.'

He stood where he was, holding up the exhausted Merrick, while he watched them move reluctantly towards the iron gates of Bedstead Square. It was safest to make sure they'd really gone. In the moonlight he could just make out a dark shape beyond the iron gates. It might have been a horse and cart but it was hard to be sure.

It occurred to Renshaw that it was some time since he'd last seen the man with the stove-pipe hat, who had paid him so generously, but he shrugged. If a fool parted with his money and then didn't stay to see the show, that was his look out.

He helped Merrick climb clumsily back in through the window and put him on the bed. The room lay in a shambles about them. Renshaw began to pick up some of the pieces of the cathedral. He had a vague idea of making everything tidy again so that no questions should be asked, but after stumbling about for a few moments he realized he was only making things worse. His mind was too fuddled by now to care.

He grinned at Merrick. 'I did real well tonight.'

From his pocket he fished a coin which he flipped onto the floor in front of the Elephant Man.

'An almond for the parrot,' he said. 'Here – buy yourself a sweet.'

Merrick neither moved nor spoke. He sat petrified, his eyes fixed on Renshaw as the porter made his way to the window and climbed clumsily out. Still he sat immobile, listening as the brass-heeled boots clinked across the cobbles and out of the gate, grew fainter in the distance . . . and died away . . .

It was silent now and almost completely dark. The ordeal

was over. The agony of it had shattered him, but still beneath his suffering pulsed the thought that he had survived. Tomorrow he would force himself to say something about these visits to Treves, or perhaps there would be no need to speak. Treves would see the shambles and ask questions, and the burden of terrifying decision would be taken from him. After the scene that afternoon, Carr-Gomm's announcement that he could stay forever, it was easier to feel that he could be protected.

Somewhere far back in his mind lurked the memory of Bytes' voice, but it was fading. He supposed it must have been an illusion, created by his terror. He had seen nothing of Bytes, and now it was all over. Slowly he let his breath out in relief and lay back against the cool pillows. Their softness brought blessed relief. He relaxed against them, offering himself to exhausted sleep . . .

'My treasure . . .'

The voice was soft and husky and seemed to float out of the darkness, but it had the effect of making Merrick's eyes flash open. He could see nothing, but he *needed* to see nothing. Already he knew that he had been wrong. Bytes' voice had been no illusion, but a frightful reality. Bytes had not gone away. He was here, now, in this room. Even as Merrick strained to see, Bytes appeared out of the shadows by the window where he had been hiding ever since he had crept in, unnoticed, during the commotion. He was smiling a horrible smile.

'Aren't you glad to see me?' he asked, caressingly.

'Bytes . . .' Merrick could only utter the word in primeval terror, as a man might repeat the name of a fiend that haunts him. He was beyond conscious thought, beyond reaction. He only knew that his worst nightmares had risen to engulf him.

He had no strength to resist Bytes, and his brain was too stunned to give him the determination to try. He submitted as in a trance to a will stronger than his own, whilst all the time his mind was silently screaming despairing appeals for help to an uncaring world.

He knew, as if he were seeing it happen to someone else, that Bytes had pulled him off the bed and wrapped his cloak around him, was grunting into his ear.

'Now we're ready to go. Don't waste time about that.'

These last words were jerked from Bytes by the sight of Merrick reaching towards the little table where stood the framed picture of his mother. He had almost reached it when Bytes impatiently knocked his hand aside and shoved him towards the window. The picture fell to the floor with a clatter, and lay face up in the darkness. Merrick gave a whimper and tried to pick it up, but Bytes stood firmly in front of him, muttering, 'Get on with you I said.'

Then Merrick made no further attempt. He had submitted totally to the despair that engulfed him, for he knew that Hell waited for him again, but this time twice as dreadful for the glimpse he had had of another world, and there was no hope anywhere.

There was only the darkness, and fear, and Bytes voice whispering, 'We're moving on again, my treasure.'

The bright morning sun gave a cold edge to the wreck of Merrick's room. Treves, standing in the doorway, took in the smashed cathedral, the picture of Merrick's mother lying face up on the floor, and – strangely – a penny lying beside it. He determinedly fought down the cold grip of horror in his stomach. It was too soon yet to think . . .

As a last hope he flung open the door to the bathroom, but it was empty as in his heart he had known it would be. To the last moment he clung to the possibility that Merrick might have damaged the room in the frenzied grip of a nightmare, but when the Elephant Man was nowhere to be found Treves knew he was dealing with something evil.

Within a few minutes he knew the worst. In the corridor he was stopped by Nettleton, who had a story to tell. Nettleton slept on the hospital premises, in an attic room overlooking Bedstead Square, and last night he had been roused from his slumbers by a commotion below.

'Why the hell didn't you do something?' Treves raged, 'Call somebody – rouse the hospital – something?' Frustration choked him.

'I didn't know what to do, Mr Treves,' Nettleton said miserably. 'You weren't there or I'd have called you and – I didn't know what to do—'

'You just let him be taken away and never lifted a finger to help him . . .'

'No, honest, Mr Treves, I never saw him being taken away. Last thing I saw he was going back inside, through the window. I thought he'd be all right after that so I went back to bed. I never knew about anything else happening – honest.'

He was telling the truth, Treves realized. Nettleton was thick-headed and lacking in initiative. He worked within the rules and when the rules did not tell him what to do he was lost. But he was not vicious. Blaming him would help no-one.

'Are you sure you recognized Bytes?' Treves demanded wearily.

'I dunno his name, but I seen 'im before. He come in one day and slipped through the Receiving Room when he thought no-one was watching 'im. I went after 'im to stop 'im, but I heard you and 'im having a shouting ma— talking, so I reckoned it was all right if you knew 'e was there.'

'And you saw him again last night? You're sure of that? You were a long way away.'

'There was a good moon, Mr Treves, and you can't mistake that 'at of 'is.'

'All right. That'll be all, Nettleton.'

'I'm sorry, Mr Treves—'

'All right, all right, I don't blame you.'

Treves had been vaguely aware of Mothershead passing down the corridor towards Merrick's room. Now he saw her reappear and stand as if stunned. But he had no time to explain anything to her now. He had urgent business.

At this time of the morning he should find Renshaw building up the furnace in the operating room stove.

He covered the distance at a run, flinging the door open and standing stock still on the threshold as his eyes took in exactly what he had expected to see. Renshaw was applying a bellows to the old coals which were still hot, causing a vile smoke to rise from them. He looked hung-over, but sleek, contented and satisfied with life. The sight of that smug brutal face filled Treves with a coldly murderous rage such as he had never known before. He knew now how men killed for the joy of it.

Renshaw became aware that he was being watched, and looked up. Treves' face, black with fury, told him that he hadn't got away with the previous night's antics, and the doctor's first words reduced his innards to pulp.

'*Where is he?*' Treves shouted.

Renshaw found that his mouth would form no reply, and all that came out of it were spluttering sounds.

'*Where is Mr Merrick?*'

'I – I don't know what you mean, sir.'

Treves stalked over to him like a hunter sizing up the prey. Renshaw backed slightly.

'Don't lie to me,' said Treves in a voice in which the savagery was barely suppressed. 'I know all about it. You were *seen*. You're in this with Bytes, aren't you? Where did you take him?'

Renshaw wondered if he was going mad. He no longer understood anything that was being said to him.

'Take him?' he squealed. 'Now wait – I didn't take him anywhere. I don't know no Bytes. We were just having some fun. We didn't hurt him . . . just having a laugh, that's all.'

'*He's gone!*' Treves bawled into his face.

'When I left him he was in his bed, safe and sound.' Renshaw declared with a touch of conscious virtue.

Treves felt his last thread of control snap. '*You bastard*. You tortured him. You and Bytes *tortured him*. You bastard. *Where is he?*' But he knew he was raving helplessly. The

224

true horror of the situation was filtering through to him. If Renshaw and Bytes had not acted together, the porter had no way of knowing where Bytes had taken his captive. Merrick might have vanished for ever.

Renshaw had recovered some of his confidence now as his own temper slipped away from him. He didn't appreciate being bawled at when he had a hang-over.

'*You're not listening to me*,' he bawled back. 'I don't know no Bytes and I ain't done nothing wrong. People pay to see your monster, Mr Treves. I just take the money.'

'*You're the monster. You're the freak! Get out. You're finished!*'

Hardly knowing what he was doing, Treves seized Renshaw's arm and began to drag him out of the operating theatre. Renshaw was filth, Renshaw polluted the place just by being there. Treves acted on instinct, to dispose of him as he would have done any vermin.

But Renshaw threw him off and whirled round with his back to the door, seizing the poker from the stove. Neither man noticed Mothershead standing quietly just outside the door.

'Have a care, Mr Treves,' Renshaw said in a low, intense voice. 'I ain't afraid of you. You and your bleedin' Elephant Man. I'm glad of what I did. And you can't do nothing. Only Mothershead can sack me.'

In another moment he would have been dead, as Treves, demented by rage, seized the poker from Renshaw's hand and raised it with murderous intent. But before he could bring it down on Renshaw's skull, he found the porter had vanished. There had been a loud crack like a hand striking an ear with all the force of hatred, and Renshaw was on the ground clutching his head and barely conscious. Mothershead stood over him rubbing her hand, a look of grim satisfaction on her face.

'Done,' she said.

Treves' visit to the shop where he had first found Bytes

and Merrick was as unproductive as he had known it would be. He had not really imagined that Bytes would hang around to be followed. Such enquiries as he could make in the neighbourhood elicited the information that Bytes and Tony had vanished, nobody knew where.

Carr-Gomm was sympathetic but firm.

'I'd like to think I felt no less for John than you, Treves, but face the facts. The man has disappeared. Very likely to the continent. There's no question of your going after him, you're desperately needed here by your patients. Remember, Treves, you did everything in your power – everything in your power.'

CHAPTER SEVENTEEN

At the start he could tell one day from another. On the first day there was the long dreadful journey in the cart, with Tony driving and Bytes sitting with him in the back, unwilling to lose sight of his reclaimed "treasure". He shuddered away into the furthest corner to escape Bytes' evil presence, but it was always there, gloating over him.

About evening the cart changed to a train. He allowed himself to be hauled onto it unresisting, stunned by grief and hopelessness. Already it seemed as though he had always known that this life would one day engulf him again, and that the brief weeks in Treves' care were nothing but a vision sent to torment him, a vision that seemed to recede further with every moment.

They travelled all night on the train, and in the morning the air had a fresher smell and there was the sound of birds calling wildly. On the quay Merrick just caught a glimpse of a sign that said "Dover", and a vast expanse of water, before closing his eyes and settling back into the darkness within his mask. He could no longer bear to look out onto the world. To retreat within himself, his consciousness bounded by the walls of grey flannel about his head, was the only solace left.

Tony guarded him while Bytes disappeared on some business of his own. When he returned, a conversation pierced Merrick's darkness.

'I've got the tickets. They'll take us as far as Ostend' – that was Bytes' voice.

'Where the 'ell's that?'

'Belgium. There's a better market for our kind of merchandise in foreign parts, Tony. They ain't so squeamish over there.'

'Is it far?'

'It's a good bit in a boat.'

'Howd'you get them tickets? Thought you'd run outa money, Mr Bytes.'

'Didn't say anything about buyin' 'em, did I? Gentleman over there was very careless coming out of the booking office, barged right into me. He *was* going to rush on without apologizing – even tried to say *I'd* run into *him*. I was forced to detain him and put the matter right. He got so flustered he never noticed he'd dropped his wallet. It just happens to contain three tickets to Ostend and enough money to take us by train to Brussels.'

'Why Brussels, Mr Bytes?'

'The bloke I bought that thing from was planning to join up with a circus that was leaving for Brussels. He made it sound like a good place to do a bit of honest business.'

The two of them assisted Merrick's clumsy footsteps up the narrow gangplank with many a loudly voiced comment about 'our poor friend – sea air – quick recovery'. Once aboard they took him hurriedly to the most inconspicuous place they could find and sat him down. Merrick shivered. It was a long time since he had been outdoors for any length of time and the air was chilly.

He had thought that his despair was complete, but when he felt the boat begin to move he knew that he had not experienced total desolation till this moment. While on land he had somehow clung to the dream that something might happen to enable him to escape and make his way back to London and Treves. He knew that his crippled hip made escape practically impossible, but he had held onto the illusion with a tenacity that he only understood now, when its last shreds were torn from him. With that strip of water between himself and England widening every second, all possibility of rescue was gone. He did not even comprehend where he was being taken.

Through the small window in his flannel mask he peered out at the only thing he could see – a seagull perched cockily on a large funnel. It seemed totally at home. In the air above, other members of its kind wheeled and screamed as they followed the boat out to sea. A small boy came into sight and reached out to make a grab at the seagull. But it was too swift for him. It eluded the hand that would have captured it and swooped into the air. The little boy grabbed upwards, but the seagull avoided him easily and rose high, shrieking abuse. Merrick raised his head cautiously to watch the bird's progress. As he stared, the seagull wheeled freely in the air and headed back towards the land.

Merrick leaned his head forward on his knees and cried wearily.

The journey was terrible. A violent wind blew up, making the boat toss. Merrick was sick and terrified, but even his prayer that the danger might claim him and his life be ended was denied. When they reached Ostend he was half-unconscious, but alive.

At Ostend there was another train, on which he fell asleep, and there his perception of days ended. When he woke up, the train had stopped and he was being hauled out. He did not see the name of the station, but he gathered from the talk that they were somewhere near Brussels, wherever that was; the words meant nothing to him.

Bytes fell in with a circus and joined his lot to theirs. He had been right in his estimation of the continentals as less squeamish than the British. The circus had a large, permanent freak section, and it was always this that attracted the biggest crowds.

The days became one day, the weeks ran together. He lived in an old wagon that Bytes had managed to buy from one of the circus families. Here he slept, ate and exhibited. His days were an endless round of 'performances', his nights a torment of memory. He prayed constantly for death.

The comforts that had made his life bearable before were lost to him now. The picture of his mother, his Bible, his prayer book, all these had been left behind in London. These days he had but one solace, a small visiting card on which were printed the name of Frederick Treves and the London Hospital. It was the card he had taken in Treves' room one day, long ago. He had kept it ever since in the pocket of his cloak, and there it still was. In his moments alone he would take it out and draw what little comfort he could from it. It had now the sense of a message signalled from a distant star that had spun off into space and left him stranded. It spoke to him of a life that increasingly he felt he must have imagined.

He was kept a semi-prisoner. Bytes never allowed him to go far from the wagon, but he placed little restriction on who came to see him there. And Merrick had a surprising number of visitors.

They were not spectators, for they lived in the circus and they came between shows. They were the other freaks, interested to see the new addition to their numbers. They, too, backed a little when they first saw him, so that Merrick discovered that he was a freak even among freaks. The knowledge would have hurt him if he had not been beyond hurt by now.

But they recovered themselves quickly. Their eyes were not blinded by what was 'normal'. To them the abnormal was normal, and within a short time they had accepted Merrick into the fellowship of the deformed. For the first time in his life he was one among equals. It was something even Treves had not been able to give him.

Few of them spoke much English. They were French, German, Belgian and some Slavs. They had crossed Europe to find this little refuge in a place where freaks could band together and find the solace of companionship. They communicated with Merrick in pidgin English and signs, but mostly they offered him their silent sympathy.

They became his friends, insofar as the life permitted him to have friends. He discovered in them deformities and mutations so strange that for once it was he who looked in wonder.

There were the pinheads, a brother and sister called Tip and Top, whose heads were cone-shaped and elongated. To emphasize their oddity they shaved their heads and left just a small tuft growing out of the tops. There was a hermaphrodite called Sammy, who had the shape of a woman, the genitals of a man, and one well-developed breast. As long as the genitals were hidden the overall impression was female, but Sammy was known to have the strength of a man and to be prepared to use it on any unwary male spectators who showed too much interest in his female half.

George and Bert were among Merrick's most frequent visitors. Two men down to the waist, and one man beneath that, they were the first creatures he had ever met who struck him as possibly worse off than himself.

Then there was the Lion-Faced Man, a man with a large growth of yellow hair on his face, who had decided to make the most of it. He constantly combed it to produce the right effect, and had been known to express the opinion that exhibiting for money was better than working for a living. He had struck up a close friendship with another of the same mind, Fred, who appeared entirely normal until he pulled at the skin of his face and demonstrated the incredible distance to which it would stretch.

His new friends did much to make Merrick's life slightly more bearable, but there was one difference between himself and them that no bridge could cross. They were their own masters. Not one of them had been bought and sold as he had. They had the normal use of their limbs and could defend themselves against anyone who tried to take advantage of them. Even George and Bert, physically handicapped as they were by possessing only half a body each, were in possession of two shrewd brains that had largely protected them from exploitation, except on their own terms. Many of the freaks were their own managers. They paid the circus a percentage of their earnings, but otherwise they were free. Those who were managed by others had struck bargains out of which they did very well. There was not one who, like Merrick, was treated as a possession. Even Marcus could give as good as he got.

Marcus was a dwarf who continually went about in a plumed hat, trailing a little wooden ark on wheels, drawn by a string. Merrick often wondered about that ark, as it seemed to add nothing to Marcus's grotesqueness, which consisted only of being small and ugly. Marcus never spoke of his ark, but he would not be without it.

He spoke, in fact, very little to anybody. To Merrick he had never addressed so much as a word. But he was constantly looking at him, frowning. Sometimes he came over to watch Bytes put the Elephant Man on exhibition. Merrick first noticed him one day when the show was drenched in a thunderstorm. It seemed to make no difference to the crowd's appetite for horrors, for they huddled round the freak wagons almost as much as ever.

Bytes would deliver his patter just as he had always done, regardless of the fact that most of his audience probably could not understand a word. The back of the wagon was covered in the painted canvas poster, and before this Bytes would stand, gabbling through his words and waving Merrick's silver-topped walking cane. He had had time, while hiding in Merrick's room, to look round him and pocket most of the expensive gifts, including the gold cigarette case and the ring. They had all been sold by now, but Bytes kept the cane, both for its usefulness and because he liked its elegance. He felt it gave him an 'air'.

At the appropriate moment Tony would haul up the painted canvas and reveal Merrick standing in the back of the van, his head larger now, his few hairs turning grey. The crowd would gasp and shriek as crowds had always gasped and shrieked, and Bytes would swing into the full performance.

'Turn round – hurry up—'

Merrick turned slowly; he found movement more diffi-cult now. Pain seemed to cover his body like an extra skin, and the increased weight of his head was hard to manage.

'Dance,' Bytes commanded.

Merrick began a series of awkward lifting movements, the closest he could get to a dance. Without his walking stick he could hardly manage to keep his balance, but he obeyed blindly, blanking out his mind from all consciousness save the oft-repeated prayer that death might come soon. Somewhere on the fringe of the crowd he was aware of Marcus, frowning, with a savage look in his eyes.

Merrick faltered suddenly and came to a stop, wheezing. But Bytes was not satisfied. This shortened performance would bring meagre takings. So he hopped nimbly into the wagon and managed to jab Merrick with the stick, catching him in the back out of sight of the audience.

'*Dance!*' he rapped.

Merrick could not contain his groan of pain. As he began again making the awkward movements the audience began to throw coins. Some of them hit him, but most of them landed on the floor, where Tony busily scooped them up into a hat. Marcus had vanished.

After the afternoon performance came the meal, potatoes and slops, doubly revolting after the better food he had become used to. Bytes stood over him in the back of the wagon, to make sure he left none of the muck. The sharp deterioration in Merrick's condition worried and angered him. It would be just like the spiteful so-and-so to starve himself to death just when he was paying dividends.

'Eat, my treasure,' he enjoined. 'You always liked it before.'

Merrick looked wearily at the bowl but made no move to touch it.

'Eat,' said Bytes angrily. 'I said eat.'

Merrick closed his eyes. The quiet movement gave Bytes the feeling of having been simply put aside, which enraged him.

'*Eat, damn you!*' he yelled. He knelt and grabbed the bowl, jabbing it at Merrick as if he would have liked to ram it down his throat.

'I said *eat.*'

But Merrick did not move, and Bytes, oblivious to everything but his own temper, hurled the contents of the bowl at him. Merrick lapsed into a coughing fit, and Bytes abandoned the attempt for the day.

When morning came, Merrick found himself violently

hungry, hungry enough to try the revolting potatoes. But after a few mouthfuls nausea overcame him again and, despite a hefty kick from Bytes, he could eat no more.

He grew weaker. When Bytes tried to vary their performance by making him stand on a wooden stool in the centre of the crowd he could barely keep his balance. Bytes walked round him, jabbing his exhibit now and then with the stick, while the crowd pressed in for a closer view, and Merrick turned round and round obediently, sometimes seeing Marcus's frowning face on the edge of the circle, sometimes not.

When it became obvious that Merrick had not the strength to keep upright on the stool Bytes abandoned this method and reverted to using the back of the wagon. But even these performances were becoming too much for him. The simple movement of turning round involved slow, agonizingly painful movements. Dancing became impossible. His attempts at rhythmic movements faltered into cumbersome lunges that left the audiences disappointed and hostile.

Bytes was becoming desperate. His takings had fallen off and it was this creature's fault. One day he threw caution to the winds and brought out the stool again, thrusting it up onto the wagon beside Merrick.

'Up! Up!' he rapped.

Already exhausted, wheezing and coughing painfully, the Elephant Man made futile efforts to climb onto the stool, but he could not manage even that little ascent. The audience shouted its disapproval, booing and hissing both the Elephant Man and his exhibitor. Bytes swore and banged with his stick on the wagon floor. Again Merrick tried to mount, but again he failed.

Frantic to save his failing show Bytes climbed into the wagon and grasped Merrick by the arm, forcing him up onto the stool. As soon as he let go Merrick tottered dangerously, his head swaying from side to side. Bytes rapped the stick.

'Give the call of the elephant,' he commanded.

Merrick hesitated, and Bytes banged the stick again. The audience quietened down, willing to be entertained, but the few quavering sounds that Merrick could manage soon had them grumbling their disappointment again.

'Louder,' demanded Bytes.

Merrick tried again but there was no improvement. A dozen jeering voices came from the audience. A dozen different languages exhorted him to make the noise of an elephant. He swayed on the stool and tried to save himself by stepping down, but it was too late. He had no strength left to do anything but collapse in a heap on the wagon floor. The crowd, no longer scared of this piteous helpless mass, burst into fury, screaming their disappointment and pelting the wagon with filthy objects.

Bytes, at first humiliated, swiftly became angry.

'Get up, you miserable bastard,' he screamed.

But the heap on the ground only moaned and wheezed, and seemed not to have heard him.

'*I said get up!*'

He jabbed Merrick a few times with the silver-tipped walking cane. The jeers of the crowd grew louder, and to them was joined a clap of thunder from overhead. Bytes spat his disgust.

'I'm beating a dead horse,' he said, half to himself.

He made nothing on that performance, and the very small profits from the two performances earlier that day were quickly expended on a bottle of cheap wine. He consumed it that night sitting over a small damp campfire and brooding on his wrongs. He felt hard-done by. Everything conspired against him.

The wine was making him quickly drunk. He was more used to gin, which he could drink in huge quantities with little ill-effect. Wine, being unfamiliar, got to him quickly. From the wagon behind him he could hear Tony urging Merrick to eat, almost pleading with him. Bytes growled. To his mind Tony was too soft with that creature. Once or twice recently he had seemed almost sorry for him.

Finally Bytes rose to his feet and stumbled clumsily over to the back of the wagon. He pulled aside the canvas.

'Another bleeding heart,' he mumbled.

Tony was crouched over Merrick, holding the plate out to him. The Elephant Man, to Bytes' fury, looked little better than a corpse. Bytes pointed a menacing finger at him.

'You sly bastard. You're doing this to spite me, aren't you?'

'Aw, Bytes,' said Tony, 'he's sick . . .'

'He's doing it to spite me, I tell you. And it's got to stop.'

'He's sick, Bytes.' More and more often now Tony dropped the "Mr". A rising contempt for Bytes was rapidly robbing him of his fear. 'He's going to die.'

'If he does it's his own fault,' said Bytes furiously. 'But I'm not burying that swollen bag of flesh.'

His arm shot into the wagon, grasped Merrick's arm and hauled him out, whimpering, on to the grass.

'What are you going to do?' said Tony, scrambling out after them.

'I'll show you! I'll show you.'

He dragged Merrick across to a small monkey wagon. The monkeys began to scream at his approach, and screamed louder when the door was opened and Merrick thrust viciously inside.

'Don't,' yelled Tony, in horror.

'Shut up,' Bytes told him.

He slammed the door and latched it, then wheeled back and started off for his own wagon. Tony tried to grab him.

'Bytes, please . . .' In another moment he was sprawling from a blow from the back of Bytes' hand. He lay on the ground, watching Bytes stagger back to the wagon and fumble about inside. After some muffled sounds Merrick's food bowl came flying out, followed by the stick, cloak and hood.

'Out,' Bytes' voice screamed from inside the wagon.

Tony picked himself up and turned to look at Merrick,

who was cowering into a corner, trying to keep away from the monkeys who shrieked at him. But the wagon was too small for him to get far away, and they were soon swarming over him like ants. Tony shuddered, and made his way back to the camp fire. As he neared it, he could hear Bytes muttering curses from inside the wagon. He wondered if Bytes would come out again, and stood, hesitant, ready to vanish if Bytes appeared. But nothing happened. The cursing sank to a rumble, and after a moment Tony sat by the campfire and pulled a blanket round him.

He felt uneasy with the darkness, uneasy with what he could see was happening to the Elephant Man, and uneasy about the eyes he knew were on him. They were the eyes of the freaks, who always seemed to be close when this kind of thing happened (and it happened more and more often these days). Tony looked up suddenly, and caught sight of Marcus standing nearby. But Marcus was not looking at him, he was relieved to notice. He was staring at the monkey wagon, and there was a frown on his face.

Merrick had pressed himself as far as possible into the corner of the cage, and for the moment the tumult seemed to have died down. But wherever he looked there were wizened monkey faces, eyes glinting at him out of the darkness, watching him, waiting . . .

Suddenly one of the monkeys darted forward with a scream, nipped him sharply on the arm and darted quickly away. Merrick yelped with pain and struggled to move further back, but there was nowhere to go. By now the other monkeys had got the idea. Following the lead of the brave one, they began to move warily towards Merrick, screeching all the while in a threatening way. Another one shot forward and clung to his shoulder, biting and scratching in furious glee at having a victim to attack, and, what was better, a victim that seemed incapable of fighting back. Merrick cried out, but his voice seemed to vanish into the darkness.

His heart was thundering violently in his breast, pumping so hard that he could feel the pain of it. He thought it would fail him – he hoped it would, for then he might die here and now and it would all be over. As he crouched there, cowering, he remembered incongruously, all the bright dreams that had come to him when he lived in the hospital. Dreams of a different life that had been held out to him, only to be snatched away. He wondered if it would have been better never to have known that life than to have known it and lost it, but he could not bring himself to believe that, not even now. Better anything than not to have known Treves, the friend he loved with his whole heart and whom he would never see again.

A whole contingent of monkeys seemed to descend on him, all restraint removed now by their recognition of his terror. They jumped onto him with savage screams, biting him on the head, neck and shoulders. He flailed his arms uselessly, but they came on and on without a break until at last he bent his head and covered it with his arms as best he could, and sobbed out his despair and terror into the stony night.

Exhausted at last the monkeys fell back and sat staring at him again. Merrick never moved, fearful that the slightest shift from him would bring on a renewed attack. He sat with his head resting on his knees, his arms covering it. Gradually the monkeys fell silent, but he kept his ears strained for their chatterings. There was nothing though, and as the camp slept the silence seemed to descend on him like a blanket.

He became aware at last that it was being broken by another sound, the sound of whispering. Slowly, nervously, he looked up, and found himself being regarded by an audience. Almost every freak in the circus had congregated outside his cage and was staring at him with sympathetic eyes. In the front stood Marcus.

Top, the female pinhead, reached into the cage and took Merrick's hand, which she patted gently. Top was a German who could speak no English, and on her visits to Merrick she had always held his hand and gone away again.

She took it now between her two hands and gave it a soft squeeze. Her eyes were full of tears.

Marcus came right up to the cage and stared upwards. From his tiny height it was a considerable distance.

'You all right?' he grunted.

'Y-yes.'

'Want to come out?'

Merrick did not answer this at first. In fact he hardly took the question in. Something else had impinged on his brain for the first time.

'You're English,' he said in surprise. Marcus's voice was not merely English, it was educated.

'Of course,' said Marcus, dismissing the matter with a shrug. 'Do you want to come out?'

'Yes.'

'Won't be a moment.'

He turned to the Lion-Faced Man and said something in rapid French. Lion-Face immediately lifted a hand and easily unlatched the cage door. Marcus began to speak to the others, using words that Merrick did not understand, but which were clearly instructions, for they began to assist him in his descent from the wagon. It was a slow business, and Merrick's heart thumped with fear lest any noise should wake Bytes. But over it all was the glow of kindness and friendship, given without question.

When he was safely on the ground Lion-Face turned and relatched the cage. Then he positioned himself on one side of Merrick, and the Armless Wonder came to the other side. Lion-Face pulled Merrick's right arm round his own shoulder, and Armless gave a jerk of the head, indicating that the left should be put round him. In this position Merrick could manage to stand. Marcus surveyed the little group with satisfaction.

'We've decided,' he said calmly. 'You've got to get away from here.'

He ignored Merrick's gasp of surprise at this cavalier attitude to the forces against them. He and another dwarf lit two lanterns and indicated that the other should follow them. Armless and Lion-Face began to move off, forcing Merrick to go with them, and the rest of the group fell into step behind. Slowly the little procession began to move out of the camp, its line of lanterns bobbing in the darkness.

Tony, dozing fitfully beside the camp fire, was jerked into wakefulness. He did not know what had wakened him; he was sure it wasn't a sound. After a moment he saw the lights receding into the distance. Then, as his eyes grew more used to the darkness, he noticed the group of three walking clumsily together, and realized who the man in the centre was.

Instinctively he opened his mouth to call for Bytes, but no sound left his lips. Something stronger than instinct held him silent, and slowly his mouth closed again. He rose and picked his way over the grass to where Merrick's things lay where Bytes had thrown them. He scooped up the stick, then the cloak and hood. Clutching them he began to run softly towards the slowly-moving procession.

At the sound of his coming, they stopped and eyed him warily. Merrick stiffened when he saw who it was, but Tony came on, walking straight up to him.

'Here—' he said in a quiet voice, holding the things out to him. 'You'll need these.'

He saw Merrick staring at him, saw the bewildered question in his eyes. But he returned his gaze levelly.

'Good of you,' said Marcus briefly, coming up behind them.

Tony never took his eyes from Merrick's face. 'Good luck,' he said.

'But – but—' Merrick hardly knew what he was trying to say, but Tony understood.

'I'll be all right,' he said, jerking his head in the direction of Bytes' wagon.

He began to back away, and at once the little band moved off, making slow but determined progress. Tony turned and wandered slowly back to the wagon. He moved indecisively, as though his feet would have taken him two ways at once.

At the wagon he stopped and stood looking at the poster of the Elephant Man. From inside he could hear the sound of Bytes snoring as though it would take an earthquake to wake him.

It took Tony only a moment to gather up a blanket and some belongings from round the fire. Then he turned and began to walk quickly away, taking the opposite direction to the procession of freaks. After a while he increased his speed to a run, and in a few seconds the darkness had swallowed him up.

CHAPTER EIGHTEEN

The darkness was a blessed friend, shielding them from the eyes of those who would have asked dangerous questions. The little group followed the lead of Marcus, the plume of his hat bobbing as he walked, his ark trailing incongruously behind him.

The journey was long, for Merrick was exhausted. And yet he walked further that night than he would have believed possible. Buoyed up by new hope and courage he felt strength flowing again into his limbs.

Once, when they stopped for a rest, Marcus said to him, 'If you can get back to England, have you somewhere to go?'

'Yes, I know where to go – if only I can get back . . .'

'It's not much further now.'

Their journey ended at a railway station just as it was getting light. Merrick was coming to the last of his strength when they stopped again, still in the shelter of the trees. The station could be seen up ahead, with a train standing in it.

'Just a little further,' said Marcus, looking him up and down. 'Once you're on the train to Ostend, you can get all the rest you like. You'd better put your cloak on now.'

The freaks helped him into his things. Top, who had carried his stick throughout the journey, handed it to him and squeezed his hand again. Merrick was weeping almost too much to speak, but he managed to say, 'Thank you, my friends.'

Marcus relayed this message back to everyone, and there was a small commotion as they all responded in their different languages.

'They say, "It has been a pleasure. People like us have to stick together," ' Marcus told him.

People like us: it was the first time Merrick had ever heard the comradely expression. He savoured it.

'I'll go in with you,' Marcus continued. 'You'll need a ticket.'

There was more jabbering in various languages, and as if with one movement the entire contingent began to riffle through their pockets to produce coins that they handed over to Marcus until a large pile lay in his hands. They beamed their goodwill on Merrick, but he could no longer see them. Tears of joy were running down his face behind the hood.

At the entrance to the station he turned and took a last look at his friends. They were smiling and waving at him, and he raised a hand and waved back.

Marcus bought the ticket, speaking in rapid fluent French, and escorted Merrick to the barrier where two ticket collectors were standing. There he said something else that Merrick did not understand, but it was sufficient to make the collector stand back and allow them both to pass.

'I told them that I was going to help my friend to board the train,' he said as they went down the platform.

He got Merrick down the platform as fast as he could, holding him tightly with one arm while the other hand never let go of the ark that trailed behind him. They headed for the far end where the third-class carriages were. As they passed the first class, Merrick caught a brief glimpse inside, just enough to register the ornate interior with its thick plush seats and glass lamps. In one carriage he saw a youngish handsome couple who looked as sleek and contented as a well-fed pair of seals. He wondered if they were as happy as he was at that moment, his spirits borne aloft by hope and friendship. He knew the difficulties that still faced him, but the simple, childlike religious faith instilled into him by Donner told him that if God had sent him this incredible means of escape, then God intended him to get home – to find Mr Treves.

Marcus searched in vain for an empty third-class compartment. At last he sighed and indicated the last one, which was crowded.

'This will have to do,' he said.

Merrick climbed laboriously aboard. At once the four other occupants edged as far away from him as was possible. Marcus sniffed in open contempt.

'I'm sorry I could only get you a third-class carriage,' he said. 'But it's all we could afford if you're to have enough for the rest of your journey. The money I've given you should be enough to take you to London, if you're careful. When you get to Ostend, go into the ticket office and just say "Dover". You won't need to say any more than that. They'll just assume that you're another Englishman who can't speak French. They're perfectly used to them. When you get to Dover, do the same thing again, and ask for "Liverpool Street".'

'Oh – my friend—' Merrick wept.

'Say hello to London for me,' Marcus went on, patting his hand which lay on the window-sill. 'I miss her.'

'Oh – yes.'

'You know. I saw you once there, in London. You're a great attraction.'

He gave a broad grin that transformed his ugly face. The whistle blew, the train jerked and began to move slowly away. Marcus began to walk down the platform, keeping pace and still talking to Merrick through the open window.

'Luck, my friend,' he shouted against the noise. 'Who needs it more than we?'

Merrick nodded and held out his hand, beyond speech. The train picked up speed. Marcus grabbed his hand and they shook. Then the train jerked ahead even faster and their hands were parted. Merrick leaned out as far as he dared to keep Marcus in his sights as long as possible. The dwarf was standing still now, waving violently, his plume nodding back and forth in the early morning sunlight. Then Merrick's eyes were blinded with tears and Marcus vanished from sight.

He followed the dwarf's instructions to the letter. At Ostend he said 'Dover' and received a ticket from a man who knew without question that he was dealing with a third-class passenger.

The boat was already in. Merrick waited till the last moment before boarding, the memories of his previous voyage swirling in his head. But no fear could be greater than his determination to get back to London, and Treves. Finally he stumped up the gang-plank and onto the deck. He searched for, and found, a dark corner beneath a stairway. There he sat crouched and prayed that no-one would disturb him. No-one did, and when a sharp lurch announced that the boat had cast off he felt a soaring sense of triumph. He was away. He had left Belgium. When he moved from this place it would be to step on English soil.

He slept the sleep of exhaustion. No storm came to trouble this voyage, and the gentle rocking of the boat soon lulled him off. He woke at the first touch of a few drops of rain, and scrambled up to find himself looking at the white cliffs of Dover.

In England the nervousness began again. In Ostend they had shrugged him off as a weird Englishman, but in England he could expect to attract more hostile attention. But again his luck held. The booking clerk was tired and hungry for his lunch, and in no mood to quibble. He just made out the words 'Liverpool Street' before he shoved forward a ticket, took the money and called 'Next'.

Merrick found another third-class carriage and climbed in. This time he got there first and that was a piece of luck, because after that no-one else would enter the carriage, and he made the journey to London in peace. Hope was rising in him. Not much further now . . .

The air was grey and smoky when he got out of the train at Liverpool Street. A high glass ceiling covered the station to let in as much light as possible, but already darkness could be seen beyond it. Merrick had no idea of the time, but he felt as if he had been travelling forever. Was it only this morning he had got on the train somewhere in Belgium?

Even in his state of nerves and excitement, the station was a wonderful place to him. He stood and regarded it, with its news-stands, sweet stalls and shoe-shiners calling their services. Passengers moved to and fro, carrying luggage, surveying noticeboards, seeking platforms. In one part of the station a row of benches stood for the benefit of passengers with a long time to wait. A woman in her early forties was seated at one of the benches, deep in conversation with another woman beside her. On her other side stood a large pile of baggage, atop of which was perched a boy of about twelve. He looked about to pass out from boredom, and his eyes roamed round the station in search of some diversion more interesting than his mother's conversation. Not finding it, he raised a pea-shooter to his mouth, aiming it at an elderly man and his wife who were passing. The woman beside him turned just in time and grabbed the weapon with the hand of maternal authority.

'Little beast,' she admonished him. 'I thought Mummy told you not to bring that horid thing. Can't you behave?'

The boy made a face, which she did not see, having resumed her conversation again immediately. He turned his attention back to the barrier at the end of the nearest platform, through which were streaming passengers from the newly arrived boat-train. There was one who caught his eye before he even reached the barrier, on account of his strange attire. He wore a long black cloak that enveloped him completely, and a grey flannel hood hung down obscuring his face. Even through this obliterating disguise the little boy could see that the creature's head must be vast. He began to tug on his mother's skirt.

'Mummy, Mummy! Look at that man! His head, it's huge! Mummy, why is his head so big? Mummy! Mummy!'

'Do be quiet, Tom,' she ordered. 'Can't you see Mummy is speaking?'

Merrick had passed the barrier now and stood uncertainly, trying to decide which way to go. His eyes, sweeping round the station, fell on Tom tugging at his mother's skirt and pointing at him. At once he turned away and began to walk in the opposite direction along a wall stacked with trunks and suitcases, trying to blend in and escape attention. His heart was filled with dread.

A few people gave him casual glances, but then looked away and passed on. But young Tom was not to be deterred. He had got down from his perch and was chasing after him, catching up.

'Hey, mister,' he called, 'why is your head so big?'

Merrick gave him a brief glance, then looked round for an escape. Across the station a large archway led out onto the street. He began to move towards it as quickly as he could.

'Mister,' Tom called after him, protestingly.

His voice attracted the attention of two other boys nearby. They moved over to join him, and the three of them watched the weird figure of Merrick escaping hastily across the station. As one, they ran after him, moving with the instinct that inspires a greyhound in pursuit of a mechanical rabbit. It moves: chase it.

'Mister – mister,' they called after him.

'Why don't you answer me?' wailed Tom.

One of them reached down and managed to seize the hem of the cloak. He lifted it, trying to catch a glimpse of the mysterious stranger. Merrick pulled away and tried frantically to go faster. Relishing the hunt now, the boys followed him, taunting him all the way. As they approached the arch Tom began to see where their quarry was going. Fearful that he would escape, the boy dashed in front and stood there, cutting him off.

'Now I'll see you,' he said.

His arm shot forward and grabbed the flannel hood before Merrick could back away. One yank and it was out of the cloak, another and Tom was able to lift the front and get a glimpse of what was beneath. At once he dropped it and staggered back, emitting a shrill scream of fear. Merrick turned wildly away, seeking another escape.

Tom's mother, deep in her conversation, heard the distant shriek that held the note of her son's voice. She looked up just in time to see Tom collapse to the floor, screaming, and the huge figure in the cloak, whirling round.

She began to cry out. 'My son, my son. Help!'

Her voice reached Merrick, who turned and tried to run in the opposite direction, towards another archway exit. He stumbled as he went. People stared, but did not try to stop him. In his panic he knocked down a little girl, but did not dare to stop. Behind him he heard her screams added to the bedlam that was growing. He saw the archway ahead of him filled with the solid figure of a blue-dressed policeman as Tom's mother, nearer now, cried, 'Stop that man! Stop that man!'

Merrick pulled himself up short to avoid the policeman, but it was too late. He had been seen by the law. The policeman, who wore a sergeant's stripes, made purposeful steps towards him. He changed course again, but now a group of men, alerted by the woman's screams, had closed in to cut off his path. They yelled at him and one of them darted forward and seized his hood. As Merrick turned frantically away, the hood came off and a roar went up from the crowd.

He had no way of escape now but to move back past Tom and his mother. As he did so, they screamed and shielded themselves from his approach. Another group had come up on his other side. He could only retreat.

He backed, and backed, and gradually he became aware that he was nearing the door of the urinal. He went through it, hoping for safety, but some of the men in the crowd followed him in. They were angry now, uttering deep braying noises that echoed fearfully inside the tiled walls. They hemmed him in, shouting with fear, blocking off all hope of escape.

Cornered at last, Merrick faced them, his head nakedly

exposed. He was breathing heavily with a strain and nervous exhaustion, but something was happening to him. A wave of feeling was growing inside, coming from a place deep down, so deep that he had never explored it or known of its existence. It was a feeling of anger that grew out of the self-confidence and knowledge of himself that Treves had striven so hard to give him. It was a realization that now if ever he must assert himself in the face of the world, or pass away without ever having really existed.

It seemed to give him strength, shaking his body uncontrollably as if it were a volcano about to erupt, and suddenly a cry burst from his lips, powerful and assured, such as he had never uttered before.

'*No!*' he screamed. '*I am not an elephant! I am not an animal! I am a human being! I – am – a – man. I AM A MAN!*'

He clutched the wall for support, feeling the last of his strength drain out of him. He saw the police-sergeant press forward to the front of the crowd before he collapsed on the floor. The last thing he was conscious of was the sergeant's face bending over him, shocked and kind.

When he regained consciousness a few moments later the crowd had gone. He was alone except for the sergeant, a large moustached individual who was supporting his head. He seemed not to have noticed that Merrick was any different from other men.

'My pocket,' Merrick said feebly. 'Left pocket.'

The policeman fumbled in the left-hand pocket of the cloak and came out with a small, very dirty visiting card. He looked at it for a moment, then rose and advanced on a young constable who was standing at the door of the urinal keeping intruders out.

'Jones,' said the sergeant in a low voice, 'I want you to take this card to the London Hospital and ask for Mr Frederick Treves. If he isn't there find out where he is, but whatever you do, don't come back without him.'

In less than an hour the constable returned with Treves, who came running into the urinal like a madman. The sergeant rose to meet him, but Treves passed on as though he hadn't seen him and went straight to the figure that was still collapsed on the floor by the wall. He pulled Merrick up and stood staring into his face. His eyes were brimming with tears.

'Mr Treves,' Merrick sobbed, 'Mr Treves.'

The sergeant coughed discreetly. 'You know this man, sir?'

'Yes,' said Treves through his tears. 'He's – my friend.'

CHAPTER NINETEEN

'I would not have believed such a change could come over any man in a mere two months,' said Carr-Gomm. 'But I suppose in his case . . .'

'Yes,' said Treves heavily.

They were sitting in the chairman's office. It was a fortnight since the London Hospital had been startled by the sight of a cab drawing up outside and Treves assisting the laborious figure of Merrick down onto the pavement; in the front door. Merrick had been weeping uncontrollably, clinging onto Treves as though terrified of being snatched away again. He had released him only when Mothershead's cry of 'John!' had reached him from the other end of the Receiving Room, and he had stumbled a few hasty steps forward to fall into her arms.

Within moments he had been whisked back to his old rooms that were still waiting for him, for Treves had refused to give up hope, and Mothershead had obstinately backed him in this. A message was despatched to Carr-Gomm, who turned out to have left for the night. Treves debated whether to send a note round to his house, but decided against it. Merrick heeded all his attention. He was suffering from exhaustion and malnutrition, besides being covered with small cuts. Worst of all, his head had grown noticeably larger, and he seemed to have aged twenty years.

Mothershead insisted on helping Treves minister to Merrick's needs, washing off layers of accumulated dirt, as she had done once before, and tending to the multitude of monkey bites. Merrick accepted her attentions easily now. His nervousness with her had quite disappeared, and Treves put this down to the new gentleness in Mothershead's manner.

Together they listened to the story Merrick had to tell.

251

They both blamed themselves for his failure to confide in them about Renshaw's visits, but Mothershead perhaps more so. She felt that she had failed as a woman and a nurse in not teaching Merrick to trust her. Her early irritation against him came back to torment her now. She became doubly kind, doubly sensitive to his needs, and had the reward of seeing him relax in her presence. She knew that in his own way he was offering her his tentative, wistful friendship. But she also knew, as did Treves, that it was too late.

Carr-Gomm came to see the Elephant Man on the morning after his return. Shocked by what he saw, he had gone away muttering about the benefits of rest and good food. Now, a fortnight later, two more visits had shown him that his hopes were in vain.

'It cannot be gone back on,' Treves said to him now. 'The ground he has lost this last two months will never be regained.'

'Does he know?'

'I don't believe so. I've said nothing about it. He's so happy, I don't want to spoil it for him. Now he's strong enough to get up, he spends all day working at his cathedral. Nurse Ireland got him a pile of fresh cardboard from somewhere, and since I don't permit any visitors he has nothing to do but work on it.'

'No visitors?' said Carr-Gomm with a faint smile.

'I had to make the two exceptions you know about. Anne flatly refused to be kept away. When I told her the glass on his mother's picture was smashed she brought him another frame and insisted on coming and giving it to him herself.'

'And Her Royal Highness, of course, also "flatly refused to be kept away",' Carr-Gomm mused.

Princess Alexandra had arrived the previous afternoon. At her own request she had been informed the moment the Elephant Man had been restored to the hospital, and as soon as she was assured he was well enough to see her she had come for a short, quiet visit. It had ended with her own signed photograph joining Merrick's mother and Mrs

Kendal, on the table, separate from the others on the mantelpiece.

'John cried over it when she'd gone,' said Treves. 'When he'd recovered he said he wanted to write and thank her. I've got the result here. I thought you might like to see it before it goes.'

He took out a sheet of paper and gave it to the chairman. Carr-Gomm regarded it with a frown.

'I know it's a little difficult to read,' said Treves apologetically. 'But he has to write with his left hand.'

'It isn't that,' said Carr-Gomm. 'It's just that I don't think Her Royal Highness is used to being addressed as "My Dear Princess". But in the circumstances I cannot believe she will object. And I am sure she'd prefer to receive Mr Merrick's own letter than some colourless official "version" edited by ourselves.'

'I agree, sir. I shall send it just as it is.'

Carr-Gomm leaned back in his chair. 'What do you plan to do in the future, Treves? I need hardly say that you will have my full support.'

'My only "plan", sir, is to make what is left of his life as happy as possible. Whatever he wants, I shall try to see to it that he has. He has a great longing to go to the theatre. I've written to Mrs Kendal asking what she advises. I received a letter back this morning saying that she will visit him this week to discuss the matter.'

'Another exception?' said Carr-Gomm pleasantly.

'When I said no visitors, I meant of the kind he had before. John's true friends will always be admitted.'

Mrs Kendal duly arrived and proved herself to have been hard at work. With an actress's flair for the right props and scenery she had arranged not merely that John should be taken to a performance at Drury Lane Theatre, but that he should do so against a background that fulfilled his dreams, and that the supporting cast should also be perfect. What ladies' man wanted to attend the theatre except in the company of elegantly dressed ladies?

'It's all arranged,' she told Treves as they walked along

the corridor towards Merrick's rooms. 'I'll send over some evening gowns for the nurses you select to accompany Mr Merrick. You'll be using the royal entrance and Princess Alexandra herself will be there to welcome him to her private box.'

'I'm very grateful to you, Mrs Kendal. This is just the thing to help him forget his ordeal. John will be very excited.'

'Does he know anything yet?'

'No. I've left it for you to tell him. He'll enjoy that more.'

She smiled. 'It's a miracle he ever got back. And I'm sure, Mr Treves, under your expert care, he'll have many happy years ahead.'

'I fear not, Mrs Kendal. Even in the short time he was gone, the side of his head has increased rapidly . . . as has his pain.'

She stopped walking. 'How awful for John.'

'And yet, not once have any of us heard him complain.'

She faced him. 'Is he – dying then?'

'Yes,' he said simply. 'There is nothing more frustrating, nothing that makes a physician feel more useless than standing by watching his patient deteriorate. And when that patient is a friend . . .' – with these last words he seemed to have been addressing himself almost more than her. Now he added abruptly, 'No, there's nothing I can do.'

He thought she was going to say something else, but she only walked on in silence until they had almost reached the door. Then she stopped again and spoke quietly, 'How much does John know?'

'I've told him nothing, and I honestly think he suspects nothing. How should he? He's grown stronger since he returned and he thinks he's recovering. He thinks he's going to spend a long, happy life here. I want him to go on believing that. I appreciate this will make it difficult for you to talk to him . . .'

'I'm an actress, Mr Treves. If you can keep the secret, I can.'

The choice of the two nurses to accompany him on his expedition to the theatre was left up to Merrick. As Treves had expected he asked for Nora at once. The other choice, Treves had half believed, would fall on Nurse Kathleen, who was a pretty girl and much easier in Merrick's presence these days. But to the doctor's pleasure, Merrick unhesitatingly picked Mothershead.

'She is my friend,' he said with shining eyes. 'And besides, Mrs Mothershead is always so busy – I don't suppose she ever gets an evening out.'

Since it hadn't even occurred to Treves to wonder if Mothershead ever got an evening out, this effectively silenced him.

With unerring instinct Mrs Kendal had selected the pantomime *Puss in Boots*. Intelligent as Merrick was, his uneducated emotions were frequently those of a child. Apart from the thinnest veneer, which his contact with society had given him, he lacked sophistication, and Treves felt entirely satisfied that the dazzling lights, bright colours and simple plot of the fairy tale were calculated to bring him the most pleasure.

Now no trouble was spared that might increase Merrick's enjoyment. He was to have his outing dressed in elegant evening clothes, provided out of hospital funds, specially authorized by Carr-Gomm. On the evening of the performance Treves went early to Merrick's rooms to help him with the finer points of dressing. He was himself clad in evening rig, and arrived just as Merrick was holding up a black bow tie, a puzzled look in his eyes.

'Let me fix that for you,' said Treves.

When he finished, he stood back to admire his handiwork.

'How do I look?' said Merrick.

The shapeless clothes, necessarily ill-fitting, hung ludicrously on him, seeming the more outlandish for their new, freshly tailored appearance. But Treves saw none of this. He had long ago forgotten how to look.

'You won't appear out of place, John,' he assured him, meaning it.

'Splendid. Shall we go?'

'We still have time yet. John . . .' Treves stopped. Several times since Merrick's return he had got as far as this and been unable to go on. This time he forced himself to. 'I can't tell you how sorry I am for what I allowed to happen to you. I had no idea. I was blind.'

'Please . . .' Merrick put out a timid hand to touch him. 'You must not blame yourself, my friend. How could you be expected to know? You have so much to think about here, so much responsibility, so many lives in your hands. I would be frightened to be you.'

'But, John . . .' Treves could not bear to be let off so lightly. He felt that every forgiving word that Merrick uttered was another load for himself to carry. But in a firm voice Merrick interrupted him, something he had almost never ventured to do before.

'No, Mr Treves. You must not worry about me. I *am* happy every hour of the day.' His eyes smiled as he repeated the words he had once uttered before, as though he would have taken Treves back to those happier times, and wiped out everything that had occurred since. 'My life is full, but if it had to end tomorrow I would have no regrets, because I know I am loved. I have gained myself . . . and I could not say that but for you.'

Treves was silent. He realized he must accept this, and endure the hardship of being judged far more generously than he felt he deserved. Except that he knew that judging him was far from Merrick's mind.

'Thank you, John,' he said at last. 'And you've done so much for me.'

He thought: You've rescued the human being who was in danger of being submerged in the doctor. But he could not say this. Merrick would not have understood.

To cover the moment's awkwardness Treves gave his own bow tie an extra tweak, wishing that there was a mirror to look in. When he spoke again, it was in a light-hearted voice.

'Well – I'll find Mrs Mothershead and Nora, and we'll be waiting for you.'

'Very good, my friend,' said Merrick.

As soon as Treves had left him, he turned to the row of photographs on his mantelpiece. The ladies seemed to smile back at him benignly. He straightened up. He was again the Mayfair dandy he had been on that night of Renshaw's invasion. His voice, as he addressed them, was grave and courteous.

'You women are such strange and wonderful creatures. Alas, it seems to be my fate to fall in love with each and every one of you. I especially wish you could all be with me tonight. I'm finally going to the theatre.'

He stood for a moment, reluctant to leave their company, but time was passing and his companions were waiting for him. How warm and friendly that sounded. He repeated the phrase to himself as he left the room.

His ladies were waiting for him by the front entrance: Nora in a deep red low-cut evening gown that provided a perfect background for her dark prettiness, Mothershead dressed more demurely. Nora's eyes were shining at the prospect of going to the theatre. For a few hours she could pretend that she was the actress beyond the footlights, as she might have been if only her father had been a little less adamant.

Mothershead had never been to the theatre in her entire life, but this fact was only partly responsible for the glow of pleasure that made her look ten years younger. Most of it was due to her gratification that John had chosen her as his friend, and her enjoyment of his happiness.

Treves helped Merrick up into the carriage, then stood back for the ladies to pass in. As soon as Nora was inside she deposited herself firmly on the seat next to Merrick and gave him her best beaming smile. Throughout the journey she kept up a stream of merry small talk directed at him. Treves regarded the two of them with satisfaction. They might have been any cheerful young couple out for a night's gaiety. Nora was playing her part to perfection.

They caught just a glimpse of the brilliantly lit front of the Drury Lane Theatre before the carriage swept round a corner to deposit them outside the royal entrance. The door was open and, standing just inside, Treves could see Mrs Kendal and the theatre manager. As the carriage stopped, Mrs Kendal swept forward to welcome them. Nora's eyes widened at the sight of the famous actress.

Merrick responded politely to Mrs Kendal's greeting, but he seemed in a daze. He only came out of it, when she said, 'Will you escort me into the theatre, Mr Merrick?'

Finding her standing on his left side Merrick at once offered her his arm, and they walked inside together. When they came to the stairs, Treves positioned himself discreetly behind Merrick, lest his help be needed. Merrick had always found stairs difficult, and now he was not as strong as he had been. But he climbed firmly, if a little slowly. Mrs Kendal slowed her pace to his, lingering now and then to point out a picture hanging on the wall, and so giving him a chance to pause and recover his strength unobtrusively. It was a masterly piece of tact that preserved Merrick's illusions and won Treves' admiration.

At the top of the stairs Mrs Kendal halted.

'There is the royal box just before us, Mr Merrick,' she said. 'Her Royal Highness is waiting to welcome you.'

'I am very glad to meet Her Royal Highness again,' he told her gravely. 'The last time we met we had such an enjoyable talk.'

In another moment a footman had pulled open the door, and Princess Alexandra was rising to her feet within, coming forward, holding out her left hand and saying,

'Mr Merrick, how nice to see you again. That was such a kind letter you sent me . . .'

Treves began to breathe more freely. The evening showed every sign of being a success – as long as Nora and

Mothershead didn't faint dead away at the Princess's feet. He spared an amused glance for Mothershead, who looked, for once, totally unsure of herself.

The seating of the box had been arranged with care. Nora and Mothershead were put to the front, to shield Merrick from curious eyes. The Elephant Man sat farther back, between Treves and the Princess. He seemed back in his daze again, his eyes wandering slowly round the ornate auditorium. It was impossible to tell how much he was taking in of the scene. A little below them an orchestra tuned up. In the stalls elegant, well-dressed people chattered like magpies, flirted, laughed. John sat silent amid it all, although outwardly he was paying courteous attention to the Princess, who was demonstrating to him the workings of a pair of opera glasses. Treves, watching him closely, felt that if Merrick was taking in his surroundings, it was not with his eyes or his ears, or with any one sense, but mysteriously through his whole being. As though by a process of osmosis he would absorb the theatre into himself and take it away with him to keep forever.

When the lights dimmed, Merrick gave a sharp intake of breath. Then he fell silent again, and carefully lifted the Princess's opera glasses to his eyes. After that he never moved.

When the overture had finished, brilliant light flooded the stage for the first scene – a lakeside setting, with Puss in Boots standing by the water, giving his master instructions. The scene proceeded at a fast pace, the young master pretended to be drowning, the King's carriage came by, the young master was rescued and passed himself off as the Marquis of Carrabus. The Princess fell in love with the Marquis at first sight, and Puss brought the curtain down by inviting the entire assembled company to dine at his master's castle. Princess Alexandra led the applause as the act finished.

Merrick replaced the opera glasses in his lap with a happy sigh.

'Puss in Boots is terribly clever,' he said.

A look of understanding dawned in Princess Alexandra's eyes. She did not need more than this to tell her that Merrick was not watching actors, but real people. He witnessed their antics with the unconstrained delight of a child, and he believed in their reality as totally as a child would have done.

Even Treves, who had half expected it to happen, was momentarily disconcerted by the extent to which Merrick took the performance seriously. After all, the Elephant Man had read the plays of Shakespeare, had acted a scene with Madge Kendal. Yet all that seemed to desert him now, and Treves realized that reading printed lines in his own room was a million years away from the lights and music and colour that now struck Merrick's consciousness with the force of a blow. Once again he marvelled at the way the different strands of Merrick's character lay together, how the man with the maturity to be generous to his persecutors interwove with the child whose eyes shone as he gazed at the stage, and who sometimes could not stop himself from leaning forward and panting in excitement.

Long years as a princess had made Alexandra a mistress of the art of meaningless talk. Having seen into Merrick's heart, she set herself to entertain him in the way that would please him most. Treves listened, diverted, as she launched into a discussion of the rest of the story, pretending not to know its outcome, and asking Merrick with apparent seriousness his opinion as to Puss's motives and the next stage of the plot. Merrick gave the matter his full attention, and the interval passed happily.

During the next act it began to occur to Treves that there might be disadvantages in Merrick's total involvement in what he saw. The plot was held up by a group of clowns who put on a slap-stick display, knocking each other flat with hefty blows and kicking each other around the stage. The audience howled with laughter, but Treves noticed that Merrick had quietly laid down the opera glasses as though he did not wish to see too much.

'They're not really hurting each other, John,' said Treves quietly. 'They're only pretending – to make us laugh.'

Merrick inclined his head politely but said nothing, and Treves prayed that the episode would be over soon. For he realized that the Elephant Man, who had suffered so many blows and kicks in his life, could not believe in pretended injury.

But the next moment Merrick had made a noise that might have been a laugh, and once again the glasses were at his eyes. Looking at the stage Treves saw that a large policeman had joined the clowns, who had all immediately turned their ferocity on him. The more they attacked him the more Merrick seemed to enjoy it. When the policeman's helmet was knocked off, Merrick uttered his little bark of pleasure again, and Treves realized that there must have been passages with policemen that had left the Elephant Man not sorry to see them get their come-uppance. It was somehow pleasant to know that Merrick, generous and forgiving as he was, was not above feeling the sweetness of a little human revenge.

The comedy was followed by a ballet sequence, which seemed to have little to do with the story, but filled the stage with pretty girls moving gracefully. Merrick watched entranced, and when the curtain descended he continued to sit in a happy dream. Treves moved further out to the side of the box, wanting to reassure himself that the Elephant Man was safely concealed where he sat. When he was easy in his mind, he continued to stand there, exchanging pleasant remarks with Nora and Mothershead who were also, in their different ways, in the seventh heaven of delight.

The audience below passed before his eyes like a huge tapestry. The royal box was on the lowest tier, just above the stalls, and from where he stood Treves could see individuals clearly. One in particular caught his eye. He was a young man, about the same age as Merrick, apparently about to expire from boredom. His slim, good-looking form was stretched negligently in his seat, and it seemed that only with the greatest difficulty was he prevailed upon to address a word or two to his companions. Now and then a yawn distorted his handsome face, as if he had not slept for nights, and all dissipation was the same to him.

Treves turned his gaze back towards Merrick who had come out of his happy reverie and was now engaged in an animated three-way conversation with the Princess and Mrs Kendal. Once he said something that Treves did not catch, but it made both ladies laugh immoderately, and Treves just heard the Princess say, 'That is an aspect that had never struck me before, Mr Merrick . . .'

At that moment Merrick lifted his head and caught Treves looking at him. A glance passed between them, and Treves thought that never in his life had he seen a man whose eyes glazed with happiness as Merrick's did. He wondered if it was better to be the man in the stalls, smiled on by fortune till his senses dulled and he cared for nothing, or a creature like Merrick, who felt every joy, every tiny pleasure, a thousand times over? At that moment he could not have said.

The pantomime resumed. Puss went to dine with the ogre who owned a nearby castle, tricked the ogre into turning himself into a mouse, and promptly seized him in his mouth. When he spat him out the ogre had changed into a frail old man and the stage set had been transformed into a dungeon. The old man was safely incarcerated in the dungeon and the way was clear for Puss to declare his master owner of the castle, and for the young master to marry the beautiful Princess. Puss came down to the footlights to address the audience directly. While the eyes of everyone in the box was fixed on him, Mrs Kendal rose and slipped out quietly.

Puss in Boots bowed elegantly and spoke with a flourish.
Now at last has come the joyous day,
For Clever Puss was all allowed to have his way.
And if I've had my way with you,
Then from your hands I claim my due.'

The audience responded and the air was loud with applause. The cast congregated to take their bows, there were curtseying, smiles and much delivering of bouquets to actresses who put up a good show of being surprised. Then, just as the applause was beginning to die down, everyone ranged along the front of the stage turned expectantly towards one of the wings, and in another moment Mrs Kendal had swept onto the stage. She waited a moment while the renewed clapping crashed over them, then raised her hand to gesture for the audience to quieten down.

'Thank you for your warm greeting,' she said when she had their complete attention. 'Ladies and gentlemen, tonight's performance was very special to me, because it was very special to someone else, a man who knows the theatre and loves the theatre, and yet tonight is the first time he's ever actually been here. I would like to dedicate – the whole company wishes to dedicate, from their hearts – tonight's performance to Mr John Merrick, my dear friend.'

As she finished she turned towards the royal box, but as very little could be seen in it the applause was modest at first. The crowd craned their necks to get a glimpse, and one or two who caught sight of him whispered hurriedly to their companions. A muted buzz began to run over the audience.

'Stand up, John,' said Treves. 'Let them see you.'

Merrick turned apprehensive eyes on him. 'Oh no – I couldn't.'

'It's for you, John. It's all for you. Go ahead, let them see you.'

He held out his hand and Merrick took it trustingly, allowing himself to be drawn forward to the front of the box. The ladies all drew back to allow him to pass, and when he had reached the edge of the box Princess Alexandra came and stood beside him, smiling at him. Her gesture left the audience in no doubt that he was under her

263

special protection, and their shock at the first sight of Merrick quickly passed into cheering.

Merrick stood rigid at the front of the box, overcome by what was happening to him, tears pouring down his face, his hand tightly grasping Treves' hand. When he spoke, it was almost to himself, and the words only just reached Treves standing beside him.

'I feel as if I've travelled my whole life just to stand here.'

Treves put Merrick to bed himself that night. It would have damaged the illusion if either Nora or Mothershead had helped. But both women saw him to his door and thanked him for their night out, before rustling away, their elegant taffeta gowns looking strangely fine in the severely prosaic hospital corridor.

Merrick spoke very little as Treves helped him on with his nightshirt, but the doctor could sense a difference in him, as though a light were shining outwards from within. He had wondered if Merrick would want to talk about the night, the new sights he had seen, his treatment as an honoured guest. But the Elephant Man seemed to want to hold it all within himself, as though it would all escape him and vanish if it were put into words.

'You'd better go straight to bed now,' Treves said. 'You've had a long night.'

Once Merrick would have taken this as a command to be obeyed, but now he sat down at the table where his new cardboard cathedral looked, to Treves' eyes, complete.

'No,' he said, 'I've just a little more I want to do here. I'd like to work a bit tonight.' He began to add minute dots with a pencil while Treves gathered up his things ready to go. 'I wonder if that poor man will ever get out of the dungeon.'

Treves was about to ask 'What man?' when he realized that Merrick was still pondering the fate of the "people" he had seen that night. To him the ogre was still confined in that dungeon.

He laid down his pencil and leaned forward to examine something more closely. The movement tilted his head forward heavily, and he had to jerk it back, struggling to control it. Even in the few weeks he had been back, his head had grown again. Treves watched him.

'Will the cathedral be finished soon, John?' he said quietly.

'Yes, very soon.'

'Splendid. It's truly a masterpiece. Well, I suppose I'll be on my way now. I hope you enjoyed yourself this evening.'

'Oh yes! It was a wonderful evening.'

'I'm glad, John. Goodnight.'

'Mr Treves . . .' Merrick's voice stopped him.

'Yes, John?' Treves returned to the table.

'Mr Treves, tell me . . . tell my truly. Is it all right? Did I make any mistakes that you can see?'

Treves bent and studied the cathedral. It was better than the last one, although no more perfect than would be expected from a man with only one good hand. But it had been made with care and love by someone who could only express his sense of beauty in this one way.

'No, John,' said Treves. 'No mistakes that I can see.'

'Then I shouldn't change anything?'

'No, no. I wouldn't change a thing.'

He met Merrick's silent gaze, hoping his own eyes did not betray him.

'I'll walk you to the door,' Merrick said at last. He rose and for the three yards to the door performed his duties as host admirably.

'Goodnight, John. Sleep well.'

'You too, my friend. Goodnight.'

He waited until Treves was half-way down the hall before he closed the door. He could still hear the sound of his friend's retreating footsteps as he went back to the table and studied his cathedral from different angles. He picked

265

up a fine brush and made a few final delicate strokes, then stood back to look.

'It is finished,' he said softly.

He had one final touch to add. With infinite care he used the brush to sign his name at the base of the spire.

'John – Merrick.' He repeated the words to himself incredulously. He had the oddest sensation that the man John Merrick had only come into being at this very moment, when he had completed one thing of perfect good and beauty. Out of the ugliness that covered him he had created something that was lovely.

'John Merrick—' he repeated, as though introducing himself to this man who had created such a little master-piece of detail and shading.

Now, tonight, he could savour fully the feeling that had been growing in him ever since he returned, and he knew it to be a feeling of triumph. As the anguish of those weeks in Belgium faded only one thing remained, and that was the realization that he had made a long journey, over land and sea – alone. True, he had started with the assistance of some of the best friends a man ever had. But for their courage, and their generosity, he could never have even begun the journey. But, having once begun it, he had completed it alone. Alone he had left the train at Ostend and bought his ticket for the boat, alone he had boarded and endured the journey, alone he had disembarked on the other side and found the right train for London. He had done all this, just as any other man would. He was a traveller, a man with experience of journeying on land and sea. He savoured the thought. It was sweet.

He sat down where he could look through the window and see the moonlight on the spire of St Philip's, and his mind ranged back over everything that had happened since his return, starting with Mothershead's heartfelt welcome, that had made him leave the safety of Treves' arms and fall into hers.

How different it had all been from his first arrival in the hospital. Then there had been suspicion, hostility, attempts

266

to drive him out. Now he was welcomed as a long-lost friend returned from a dangerous journey. Carr-Gomm had come to see him and rejoiced in his return, Anne Treves had visited him, Nora had arrived bearing a fresh pile of materials for his cathedral.

Treves and Mothershead had spent long hours with him. From them he had heard of Renshaw's dismissal. The story of how Mothershead had knocked him to the ground with a single blow would have made him laugh, if he had been able to.

His ladies were all waiting for him on the mantelpiece, their laughing eyes seeming to welcome him back. The picture of his mother was soon replaced in a new frame, brought by Anne Treves. It gazed on him now, and he inclined his head towards it.

The movement brought pain, and a renewed sense of how his pain had been growing recently. Mostly he managed to put it out of his mind. He tried to now, choosing instead to remember the day Mrs Kendal had come in and welcomed him home, bringing with her the incredible news that he was to go to the theatre. The scene slid easily into that very night – his first visit to the theatre – the kindness of the Princess – an evening of glittering colour for him who had known only drabness and squalor once.

There would be other visits, he knew that. Tonight was only the start of the new life that opened to him. He knew now that the difference between himself and others was not so very great. People had been frightened before, but they grew used to him. His skills were growing, he became more like other men every day.

The thought reminded him of the one thing in which he was still not like others. He still slept with his head forward on his knees, propped up by pillows. It had always been an uncomfortable posture, but more so now that pain shivered over his body and stretching his back was more difficult. Increasingly he turned his eyes towards the picture of the child sleeping that hung on his wall, and he yearned to be like that child.

He wondered how he had slept when he was little. He could no longer remember now. But surely, when he was a baby, he had lain backwards while his mother cradled him in her arms. He was sure that he had done so, for she had rocked him gently and sung to him. It seemed to him that the time could not be long before she returned for him, for surely now she must hear about tonight – and then she would know how hard he had tried to be a good son, and she would come back. If she could just manage this last hurdle . . .

Slowly he removed the pillows from the bed and began to lay them on the floor, taking care to place them neatly. The window was slightly open, and a breeze billowed the curtains inwards, causing them to touch his face gently. He wondered if her fingers would feel like that when she caressed his face for the first time.

He was ready now. He placed her picture where he could see it and eased himself into bed. As his head went down it lolled frighteningly, but he managed to catch it in his left hand and steady it until he was lying down. He was on his side now, his head resting on the single pillow that he had left. He thought he could have slept like this, but for the increased pain that came from the pressure on the growths on that side. He tried to relax, and to take his mind off his pain he began to repeat to himself the words of the poem he had read with Treves on that day when he had asked the doctor if he could be cured. He had returned to that poem a dozen times since, until now he could say it by heart.

'When will the stream be aweary of flowing under my eye,' he whispered. 'When will the wind be aweary of blowing over the sky?'

His eyes were fixed on his mother's picture. In the darkness he could just make out the faint smile on her lips.

'When will the clouds be aweary of fleeting?'

The pain was growing now. Any moment he knew he

268

must roll over onto his back, where he hoped it would be easier.

'*When will the heart be aweary of beating – and nature die?*'

He began to ease himself over onto his back. His head seemed to haul madly on his neck and he sucked frantically for breath. From this position he could no longer see his mother's picture, but somehow her face was still there, just before him, her eyes looking into his with a calm smile, and it was her voice that was saying to him, '*Never, oh never. Nothing will die . . .*'

The tightness was growing ominously in his throat, but he would not move and take his eyes off her. Her smile was telling him that all would be well.

'*The stream flows,*' she said in a voice that echoed in his head. '*The wind blows, the cloud fleets, the heart beats . . .*'

She was no longer in darkness, but surrounded now by a light that was so brilliant it blinded him. When he opened his eyes she was still there, smiling, reaching out her hand.

'*Nothing will die,*' she promised.

She had come for him at last.

EPILOGUE

John Merrick was found dead in his bed one morning in April 1890. Frederick Treves described the discovery in these words:

'He was lying on his back as if asleep, and had evidently died without a struggle, since not even the coverlet of the bed was disturbed.'

The exact cause of his death has never been entirely explained, but Treves was always convinced that Merrick had tried to lie down and sleep like other people, and so choked himself.

'The Elephant Man' was suffering from a disorder known as neurofibromatosis, about which almost nothing was known in his day. It is doubtful if Treves himself ever used the term, or even managed to make a complete diagnosis. The condition caused tumours to grow over almost every part of Merrick's body, around his nerves, under his skin and in his bones, until the whole body was dreadfully distorted.

Neurofibromatosis occurs in about one in three thousand people, but the degree of severity varies greatly, and there are very few other cases recorded where the disfigurement was anything like Merrick's.

After his death a post-mortem was conducted and plaster casts of his limbs were made, so that it is still possible to see how he must have looked. His skeleton, some of the bones horribly swollen and twisted, still stands in the Medical School attached to the London Hospital.

Treves himself received the fame he always longed for. In 1900 he was appointed Surgeon-Extraordinary to Queen Victoria. But his true moment of glory came in January 1902, when King Edward VII collapsed with appendicitis a few days before his coronation. Treves, as the leading authority on the illness, was called in and insisted on an immediate operation. A battle ensued between the man who was King of his country and the man who was king in his own sphere. Treves was not afraid to stand up to monarchs, and when Edward insisted that he must go through with his coronation, the doctor told him, 'In that case you will go to the Abbey as a corpse.'

Realizing he had met his match, Edward gave way and Treves performed an emergency operation. It was a success, and he was created a baronet.

By that time he already had a practice that was successful beyond his wildest dreams. The wealthy, the aristocratic – they all flocked to his consulting rooms in Wimpole Street until the house overflowed with them, and Anne declared that the bedroom was the only room she could call her own. But Sir Frederick Treves, who regularly commanded the highest prices and numbered royalty among his friends, would give up Sundays, his only free day, to return to the hospital to see the poor patients in the wards.

In 1908 he retired from active surgical practice and set off on his travels. He and Anne went to Palestine, Uganda, the West Indies and many other places, and it was now that he began his 'second career' as a writer of travel books. He was still writing in 1920 when failing health forced him to go to live quietly in Switzerland.

His last years were darkened by the tragedy of his younger daughter's death, ironically from an attack of appendicitis. He died in 1923, having lived just long enough to see his last book published to excellent reviews. It was called *The Elephant Man and other Reminiscences*.

The beginning of Treves' fame can be dated from his championship of the Elephant Man, and there were always voices raised to accuse him of exploitation. But those who knew Treves never doubted the sincerity of his affection for Merrick. If he gained much, he also gave much, and Merrick himself would have been overjoyed to know that his friend had benefited from their association.

To the end of his life Treves never forgot Merrick, and

in his very last book he tried to tell the world the truth about the good man he had discovered trapped inside the body of a monster.

'The spirit of Merrick,' he said, 'if it could be seen in the form of the living, would assume the figure of an upstanding and heroic man, smooth-browed and clean of limb, and with eyes that flashed undaunted courage.'

Of the Elephant Man's death he said this:

'His tortured journey had come to an end. All the way he, like another*, had borne on his back a burden almost too grievous to bear. He had been plunged into the Slough of Despond, but with manly steps had gained the farther shore. He had been made "a spectacle to all men" in the heartless streets of Vanity Fair. He had been ill-treated and reviled, and bespattered with the mud of Disdain. He had escaped the clutches of the Giant Despair, and at last had reached the "Place of Deliverance" where "his burden loosed from off his shoulders and fell from his back, so that he saw it no more".'

* Christian in *The Pilgrim's Progress* by John Bunyan.